The Piracy Crusade

A volume in the series

Science/Technology/Culture

Edited by
Carolyn de la Peña
Siva Vaidhyanathan

The Piracy Crusade

How the Music Industry's
War on Sharing Destroys Markets
and Erodes Civil Liberties

Aram Sinnreich

University of Massachusetts Press

AMHERST AND BOSTON

Printed in the United States of America

ISBN 978-1-62534-62534-052-8 (paper); 051-1 (hardcover)

Designed by Dennis Anderson
Set in Dante by House of Equations, Inc.
Printed and bound by IBT/Hamilton, Inc.

Library of Congress Cataloging-in-Publication Data

Sinnreich, Aram, author.
The piracy crusade : how the music industry's war on sharing destroys markets
and erodes civil liberties / Aram Sinnreich.
        pages cm. — (Science/technology/culture)
Includes bibliographical references and index.
ISBN 978-1-62534-052-8 (pbk. : alk. paper) —
ISBN 978-1-62534-051-1 (hardcover : alk. paper)
1. Copyright—Music.   2. Piracy (Copyright)—Prevention.
3. Music trade—Law and legislation.   4. Music and the Internet.
5. Sound recordings—Pirated editions.   6. Civil rights.   I. Title.
K1450.S56 2013
346.04'82—dc23
                                        2013040189

British Library Cataloguing-in-Publication Data
A catalogue record for this book is available from the British Library.

This one goes out to Dunia.

The world of grownups is so corrupt!
Can it be, can it be, can it be stopped?
Ari Up

The most important thing is to realize
that you *can* accomplish something.
Aaron Swartz

CONTENTS

ACKNOWLEDGMENTS

LIKE ALL creative work, this book resulted from the contributions of a great many people and institutions. Although the genesis of my research on digital music and "piracy" dates back to my work at Jupiter Research at the turn of the century, my interest was rekindled when I served as an expert witness for the defense in *Arista Records v. Lime Group* in 2010–11. Several attorneys for the defendants, including John Oller, Joseph Baio, Tariq Mundiya, Todd Cosenza, and Chris Miritello, served as sounding boards for my expert report in the case, which is a distant ancestor to the book you are now reading.

As I wrote the book manuscript itself, I received copious help from several sources. I thank Kathleen Fitzpatrick and her colleagues at MediaCommons Press for graciously allowing me to post my draft chapters for open review on their website. Seeing each section in "print" as soon as I had completed it, and knowing it was instantly available to the public sphere, gave me the fortitude to continue working on a project that would have been far more difficult to finish had I been consigned to the book author's standard vacuum. I am also thankful to my colleagues at Rutgers University's School of Communication and Information, and especially those within the Department of Journalism and Media Studies, for consistently supporting my work and affording me the resources to complete it.

A great many people read and commented on my draft manuscript, via both personal interactions and the MediaCommons website. The feedback was overwhelmingly positive and constructive, but I appreciated every comment, even those that were neither. Although some commenters have opted to stay anonymous, I can explicitly thank Jesse Lifshitz, Samantha Kretmar, Frank Bridges, Vicki Simon, Peter Axelrad, Billy Pidgeon, Richard M. Stallman, Mark Mulligan, John McCartney, Cory Doctorow, Vivien Goldman, Norman Savage, Marissa Gluck, Nicole Lewis, Eric Steuer, Ray Beckerman, Fred von Lohmann, Lucas Gonze, Joost Smiers, Bryce Renninger, Judah Phillips, Josh Chasin, Evan Korth, Joly MacFie, Tom Hughes, Mark Oltarsh, David Ritz,

Michael Carrier, Mark Latonero, Kathryn Tasker, Parker Higgins, Karl Fogel, Alissa Quart, Peter Maass, Mike Brown, Camille Reyes, Daniel Timianko, Ben Kallos, Robert Schultz, Todd Nocera, danah boyd, Jesse Gilbert, Larry Gross, Barbara Reed, Susan Keith, Nancy Zager, Masha Zager, Jonathan Sinnreich, and the late Tom Barger for their feedback and encouragement.

I also owe a great debt to those more instrumentally involved in the development of this book, including all of my interviewees and primary sources, my extremely thorough and supportive no-longer-anonymous peer reviewers, Nancy Baym and Patricia Aufderheide, my patient and overtasked friend Nathan Graham, who whipped the manuscript into submission shape, the brilliant Josh Neufeld, who graciously agreed to create cover art on a tight budget and an open license, and the folks at University of Massachusetts Press, specifically my series editors, Siva Vaidhyanathan and Carolyn de la Peña, as well as Bruce Wilcox and Clark Dougan, who have been willing to go out on more than a few limbs on my behalf.

Finally, I thank four generations of my family for continuing love and support, especially my wife, muse, and bandleader Dunia Best Sinnreich, without whose unwavering faith and patience I could never have written a word of this book.

Each of you is reflected in these pages. I hope you like what you see.

Introduction

Piracy Crusades Old and New

The fight by creative industries against digital piracy is an economic necessity, not a moral crusade.
International Federation of the Phonographic Industry (IFPI), *Digital Music Report 2011*

A business model built on infringement is not only morally wrong but legally wrong.
Hilary Rosen, CEO, Recording Industry Association of America (RIAA), 2001.

I'm on a little crusade, and I do have personal interaction with these students. . . . I think these young kids are going to understand that it is not only morally wrong, they're stealing.
Jack Valenti, president and CEO, Motion Picture Association of America (MPAA), 2003

We remain the national leader in the crusade against illegal copying and distribution of software and content online. . . . In 2010, we intend to be even more vigilant in our pursuit of software and content piracy.
Software & Information Industry Association, *Anti-Piracy Year-In-Review 2009*

In 1390, an army of crusaders set out to wage war on piracy, with disastrous consequences for the soldiers themselves, their nations, and the entire Western world.

The story begins in Genoa, a coastal city located at the western "hip" of Italy's boot, which was emerging as one of Europe's wealthiest and most influential seats of power. Like its chief competitor, Venice (located at the boot's eastern hip), the city had developed its wealth by dominating the trade of commodities with the Syrian and Egyptian "infidels" across the Mediterranean sea, despite a prohibition against such commerce handed down by the Pope.

Genoa had one problem that Venice lacked: in order to gain access to the eastern end of the Mediterranean, its sailors had to pass through the Strait of Sicily, a relatively narrow aperture separating Europe from the jutting shores of North Africa. For centuries, Tunisian privateers had policed these waters, and for centuries Genoese ships had done battle with them, raiding one another in countless skirmishes and a few full-scale assaults. Yet the Tunisian pirates were becoming bolder, thanks to the encouragement of the reigning sultan, Ahmad II ibn-Muhammad, who had begun to shift his European political allegiances from Italy to Catalonia.[1]

Back in Italy, the canny prince Antoniotto Adorno, doge of Genoa, was having problems of his own. He was facing fierce political opposition for what was supposed to be a lifelong elected position, and would soon be forced out of office (for the second time). So Adorno developed a plan that he hoped would solve his domestic, Venetian, and Tunisian problems in one fell swoop: he would launch "a secular enterprise to suppress the pirates" in the form of an assault on their stronghold in the Tunisian city of Mahdia, and dress it in "the aura of a crusade."[2] With any luck, this would simultaneously boost the business sector and provide him with a heroic platform to prove his worth to the city.

The only hitch in Adorno's plan is that Genoa didn't have the military strength to launch such a siege. Fortunately, someone else did; France, which had recently called a truce in what would come to be known as the Hundred Years War with England, was chock full of knights who had "nothing to do," and "would be glad to join in the warfare." The plan appealed to France's young King Charles VI, who was facing his own challenges at home and could use a "ready-made adventure with no need of . . . serious political maneuvering" to bolster his political and religious credentials.[3]

On July 1, an armada set forth from Genoa bound for Mahdia. The Mahdians, who had received advance word of the attack, secured the sturdy walls of their city and stocked it full of provisions, determined to wait out the European invaders rather than attempting to repel them with military force. Shortly after the "crusaders" arrived, the Tunisians sent out emissaries to negotiate. They asked the French what their purpose was in joining the assault, given that "they had troubled only the Genoese, which was natural among neighbors, for it had been customary 'to seize mutually all we can from each other.'" The French replied that they had joined the crusade as a matter of religious duty, for the Mahdians were Muslim "unbelievers . . . which made them enemies, and also to retaliate upon their forefathers 'for having crucified and put to death the son of God called Jesus Christ.'" At this, the Mahdians simply laughed, reminded the French that the Jews were more apt scapegoats, and returned to their walled city, where they prepared for the onslaught.[4]

The Genoans had promised the French a swift and easy victory, but the assault took months. During this time, not only did Europeans and Africans alike die in various skirmishes, but the crusaders suffered and perished from thirst, hunger, fevers, parasitic infections, and swarms of insects. Additionally, their attempts to take the city were stymied by the fact that they had failed to bring any battering rams, and what siege equipment they did have was "hopelessly inadequate."[5] Once it became clear that military victory was impossible, the Europeans cobbled together a face-saving diplomatic one, exacting promises of reduced piracy (to which the Tunisians fleetingly adhered) plus a substantial monetary tribute (which was apparently never paid).

All in all, the crusaders had lost 20 percent of their forces in the failed assault, and more died of disease when they returned home, but these costs were nothing next to the invasion's long-term fallout. Under political pressure to show something for their efforts and expenses, Charles and Adorno trumpeted the crusade as an unmitigated success for Christendom and for European commercial interests, and this, in turn, began a cascade of defeats that would soon reduce Europe to a shadow of its former glory.

Despite the Mahdian debacle, "the enthusiasm of the returning nobles helped recruit the major crusade directed at Nicopolis" in Bulgaria six years later, which would prove to be Europe's last such adventure.[6] Because the French had learned "absolutely nothing" from their failure, and "still believed themselves supreme in war,"[7] their ill-conceived assault on Nicopolis would not only cost a great many lives, it would ultimately cost European control over the Bosporus, which was the continent's primary conduit of trade and communication with the East and the crux of its economic and political power. As a result, the Ottoman Empire would soon rise and come to dominate large swaths of Central Europe, North Africa, and the Middle East. Only after centuries of colonization and global naval exploration would Europe regain its wealth and influence.

In short, we can understand the Mahdian Crusade as a vital factor (albeit one of many) leading to Europe's downfall in the late Middle Ages, like the proverbial butterfly whose flapping wings cause a tsunami halfway around the world. Or as Sigismund, the king of Hungary (and future Holy Roman emperor) said when the battle of Nicopolis was over, "We lost the day by the pride and vanity of these French."[8]

Over six hundred years later, we are in the midst of another, very different crusade, which nonetheless shares many similarities with Mahdia and may threaten to wreak just as much havoc and destruction over the long term. In this instance, it is Hollywood, rather than Genoa, playing the role of the righteous crusader, with the US government as its military ally, and digital technology innovators and their millions of online users cast in the role of the "pirates." While a variety of industries, including film and software, have participated in this modern piracy crusade, the recording industry is its emblematic leader and continues to be its most vocal advocate.

I'm certainly not the first to make this comparison; a Google search for the terms *music industry piracy crusade* currently yields over 4.3 million results, and the metaphor is routinely applied in press coverage, including articles by the *Hollywood Reporter*,[9] the *New York Times*,[10] and *MTV News*.[11] It seems that nearly everyone but the recording industry and its anti-piracy allies considers their efforts to be a "crusade" (and, as this chapter's epigraphs demonstrate, even they have wavered in their aversion to the term). As for the piracy side of the metaphor, it is the crusaders themselves who have devoted hundreds of millions of dollars and considerable political influence to framing activities such as peer-to-peer (P2P) file sharing and unlicensed streaming in these terms, and these initiatives have been so successful that content-sharing websites such as The Pirate Bay and pro-sharing political movements like the Pirate Party have willingly wrapped themselves in the Jolly Roger, in a form of rhetorical one-upmanship.

The similarities between today's piracy crusade and its fourteenth-century predecessor are more than superficial, and more extensive than a cursory comparison might suggest. To begin with, the two crusades began under similar auspices. In both cases, it was an established commercial interest that promoted the engagement, in an effort to stem the rising economic power of a competitive upstart that threatened to usurp access to its goods and markets. In both cases, this commercial interest courted assistance from a stronger ally, by framing its economic motives in moral terms and painting the crusade itself as a matter of duty. In both cases, the stronger ally agreed to participate in part because it seemed like an easy political victory supported by a clear mandate. And in both cases, the enemy was dehumanized and delegitimized by being branded with the mark of piracy (even in the case of the Mahdians, who actually did intercept and plunder ships rather than merely clicking buttons, the so-called pirates perceived themselves as the Genoese's "neighbors" involved in an ongoing "mutual seizure" of goods, rather than as malicious and unilateral aggressors).

There are also similarities in the circumstances of the crusade itself, although the Genoese and the French were fighting for control over the Mediterranean, while today's crusaders seek control over the Internet. Like the Genoese, Hollywood and its allies have used excessive force in place of actual strategy, and yet found their methods "hopelessly inadequate" as P2P networks and other "digital pirates" have strengthened their electronic garrisons in response to the siege. Like the French, the US government was initially promised that its participation would be brief and effective, only to find itself engaged in a classic quagmire. As the major film studios pledged in a 2000 court filing, the strict new copyright law for which they and the music industry had just fought and won (the Digital Millennium Copyright Act of 1998) would suffice to "stop infringement, to stop digital piracy, before copying becomes truly ubiquitous."[12] Since then, dozens of newer, stricter laws and treaties have been proposed, and many of them have been enacted, under similar promises; yet unlicensed copying and distribution have only continued to increase,[13] as the stalemate between crusaders and "pirates" has expanded to encompass the globe and the collateral damages have continued to mount. Finally, like the Mahdians, the targets of today's crusade are often surprised and dismayed to find themselves under assault, and typically view their own activities as ethically valid, even if they do not conform to the (ever-expanding) letter of the law.

The "pride and vanity" of the French has its analog in the attitudes of today's crusaders, who invariably treat each newly enacted law and treaty, and each newly concluded litigation, as a decisive turning point for their cause. To cite a few such examples, the Recording Industry Association of America (RIAA) called a 2000 settlement against MP3.com a "victory for the creative community and the legitimate marketplace,"[14] a 2001 court ruling against Napster a "victory for copyright holders,"[15] a 2005 Supreme Court decision against Grokster "the dawn of a new day,"[16] and a 2010 court ruling against LimeWire "an extraordinary victory for the entire creative community."[17] The industry also frequently follows these legislative and litigious successes by promoting research showing that online "piracy" has been diminished as a direct result of their actions. The fact that these claims are often debunked by independent third-party researchers,[18] and that online sharing in the aggregate continues to climb with every passing year, is conveniently forgotten by the crusaders, and the press that cover them, until the next legal campaign is mounted.

The most important, and troubling, similarities between the medieval and modern piracy crusades can be seen in their devastating social aftermath. Just as overconfidence, bred by a false sense of victory in the Mahdian Crusade, led directly to the Europeans' rout at the hands of the Turks in Nicopolis, the hype and false promises attending today's piracy crusade have undermined the viability of the marketplace and the strength of our democratic institutions, and obscure the fact that these efforts have done nothing to protect the long-term interests of either the crusaders themselves or the government institutions they rely upon as allies.

Had the Genoese approached their Tunisian neighbors as partners rather than waging holy war upon these supposed infidels, perhaps the Ottomans would never have succeeding in dominating Mediterranean Europe and North Africa in the centuries that followed. By the same token, today's piracy crusaders have thus far squandered their opportunity to develop constructive partnerships with the legions of online innovators who have radically reimagined our social and cultural universe in recent decades. This has prevented powerful new ideas and technologies from being fully exploited by either the legacy media industries or new and emerging ones, and has impeded their adoption and use by the general public. Even worse, the laws and policies that have been promoted as cures for the ostensible piracy epidemic have only succeeded in strengthening the hands of those who oppose free speech, privacy, and open discourse as well as the "trolls" and criminals who use such laws to extort and defraud billions of dollars from legitimate businesses and blameless individuals.

Ultimately, what's at stake in today's piracy crusade vastly exceeds the consequences of Mahdia. Losing the ability to travel freely on the Mediterranean cost the Europeans dearly, and it took centuries before colonization, industrialization, and the cultural effects of the Renaissance would provide the continent with new sources of wealth and innovation, and new avenues of exchange with the rest of the world.[19] In the meantime, Europeans' losses amounted to gains for the Ottomans, who provided their own contributions to both European and global society and culture.[20] But losing the ability to share information freely on the Internet and other digital networks will have negative repercussions for billions of people around the globe, and will benefit only a minute handful of narrowly defined commercial and political interests. Today, these networks are already foundational elements of our lives, from our most intimate relationships[21] to our most public dealings and debates.[22] Online communications have brought together millions of couples, fueled the dreams of visionary entrepreneurs, and fomented major political revolutions. In the years to come, networked digital technologies will most likely play an even deeper role in our lives, becoming cognitive prosthetics and cultural platforms to aid and augment human processes from birth to death, and perhaps beyond. We can't afford to give that up in the name of fighting our own shadows. This time, the pirate menace isn't merely our neighbor across the sea—it's us.

THIS BOOK is not a traditional work of academic scholarship. To be sure, I draw upon scholarly sources in a variety of fields, including law and policy, critical theory, musicology, economics, anthropology, history, international relations, neurobiology, and science and technology studies. But my aim here is to develop a line of inquiry and a resulting argument rather than to advance the theoretical foundations of a given discipline.

This focus on practical consequences rather than "pure" theory owes much to the fact that my personal interest in music as a subject of analysis predates my academic career by a few decades. First of all, I have been a songwriter and a musical performer since adolescence, and in the years since then, I have published dozens of recordings and taken part in hundreds of performances with a wide variety of musical ensembles. Though my ASCAP checks and gig money have never sufficed to pay the rent, it would be accurate to say I am invested professionally in the music economy as an artist.

Second, I have spent over fifteen years as a commercial researcher, consultant, and business analyst focused on the intersection of digital technologies and music economies, as an Internet analyst at Jupiter Research during the dot-com years (1997–2002), and then as a principal at Radar Research, a consultancy I cofounded with a former Jupiter colleague soon thereafter. In this capacity, my primary role has been to advance the interests of both media and technology companies (my clients have included major labels and film studios as well as tech titans such as Google and Microsoft), by delivering tactical research and strategic advice regarding the distribution of music and other "content" via digital channels for profit. I have also played the role of expert witness in several court cases related to music, technology, and intellectual property—

perhaps most notably as a witness for the defense in *MGM v. Grokster,* the peer-to-peer file sharing suit decided by the US Supreme Court in 2005.[23] Finally, I have written previously about the business, aesthetics, and culture of music for a range of publications including the *New York Times* and *Billboard* and in my first book, *Mashed Up.*

I recite my personal history here not with the aim of establishing my credentials but rather to illustrate that I can hardly claim to approach this book with clinical disinterest. To the contrary, I could not be more interested, or personally invested, in the continuing coevolution of music, communication technology, and society. Yet my interest encompasses multiple vantage points; I understand the conflicting needs and perspectives of musicians, listeners, policymakers, record labels, broadcasters, and technology firms because I have stood in their shoes, so to speak. My aim in this book is to ask questions and answer them in a way that acknowledges this diversity of viewpoints and yet makes a strong case for a specific course of action. Ultimately, I believe that everyone benefits when free speech, civil liberties, and cultural innovation are privileged over the narrowly defined interests of a handful of stakeholders; as history shows, those most resistant to change often come to embrace its effects most ardently.

Yet, although I am hardly dispassionate, and though my explicit aim is to debunk the dominant narrative informing the laws and policies that govern the sharing of music via the Internet, I stake my position firmly on the research rather than advocacy side of the fence. My primary concern here is to erase ideology not to supplant it, thereby to bring a saner and more clear-eyed perspective to the public debate over the role that intellectual property plays in regulating the operations of the public sphere and the marketplace.

In this respect, if *The Piracy Crusade* has a theoretical home within the academic landscape, it belongs to the emerging field of critical information studies (CIS), a term first proposed by my colleague (and Science/Technology/Culture series editor) Siva Vaidhyanathan in 2006 to describe the multidisciplinary confluence of work that focuses on "the ways in which culture and information are regulated by their relationship to commerce, creativity and other human affairs."[24] This orientation allows CIS researchers to put laws and policies in dialogue with cultural and economic forces, rather than to treat each sphere as a discrete, and unrelated, field of inquiry. Several of the scholars whose work I cite in this book, such as Lawrence Lessig, Michael Carrier, Peter Drahos, John Braithwaite, Jessica Litman, Joe Karaganis, Gabriella Coleman, Jonathan

Sterne, Nancy Baym, and Adrian Johns, have produced work that belongs to this field, even if they themselves do not always make the connection explicit.

This book also shares some of its DNA with research and advocacy groups that exist primarily outside of the academy (although with many points of scholarly contact). While there is not yet a single conceptual tent to house these disparate interests, the free culture movement, the free software movement, the access to knowledge movement, the transparency movement, the Internet freedom movement, and the open access movement all share an interest in reprioritizing communication policy to privilege free speech, privacy, and innovation over the private interests of market oligopolists.

Both as a mark of intellectual kinship with these movements and as a practical method of honing my work by exposing it to scrutiny and critique, I opted to publish the draft of this book online as I wrote it and to promote newly published pieces of it via Twitter, Facebook, and several industry associations and online forums in which I regularly participate. MediaCommons Press, an open scholarship platform, graciously offered to host the book-in-progress,[25] and in the five months from its launch to the time of writing this final manuscript, the site has seen thousands of page views and has garnered both public and private comments from music industry executives, industry analysts, attorneys, and academic researchers in addition to friends, family, and other interested parties (the final manuscript has been considerably improved by this ongoing feedback). Additionally, both the online book draft and this "finished" version are available under the Creative Commons 3.0 Attribution-NonCommercial-ShareAlike license, which grants noncommercial actors the freedom to read, reconfigure and redistribute it as long as I am credited for the work.[26]

Finally, before I discuss the specific contents of this book, I believe a word of clarification is required. I frequently use terms such as "music industry," "recording industry," and "music cartels" to discuss the subjects of my research and analysis. Although such terms are, by virtue of their brevity, imprecise, I do not use them interchangeably, and my aim is to be as accurate as possible in my nomenclature. To be clear: when I use the term "music industry," I am discussing the broad constellation of individuals and institutions that collectively exploit musical expression for profit. At other times, I discuss a subset of this larger group, using terms such as "the broadcasting sector," "the major labels," and so forth, to pinpoint a specific group of actors whose interests are distinct from those of the industry at large. When I speak of "cartels," I refer specifically to the oligarchic corporations that exert disproportionate influence on the economies and practices of the industry, through economic cooperation and, at times, collusion. Throughout the text, I bear in mind John Williamson and Martin Cloonan's argument that "the notion of a single music industry is an inappropriate model for understanding and analyzing the economics and politics surrounding music. Instead it is necessary to use the term 'music industries.'"[27] And I draw inspiration from (and, I believe, give credence to) Patrik Wikström's assertion that "the contemporary music industry is best understood as a copyright industry."[28]

THE PIRACY CRUSADE has nine chapters in addition to this one, which fall into three sections. The first section is about the legal and economic foundations of the music industry and about the complex relationship that the industry has historically had with innovative technologies.

Chapter 1 charts a brief social history of the music industry, from its origins at the dawn of print publishing through the development of electronic recording and broadcasting in the twentieth century. The chapter aims to show that our current ideas about music as a form of property, and as a variety of entertainment, are neither natural nor inevitable, and are instead the contingencies of specific social, economic, and technological forces and events over the past two hundred and fifty years. Similarly, the chapter examines the origins of copyright as a regulatory framework for the distribution of music in industrial society and as an instrument of leverage and control for established commercial interests.

Chapter 2 examines the music industry's ambivalent relationship to new technologies during the twentieth century. It begins by looking at the progression of dominant recording formats, from the wax cylinder to the MP3, and at the industry's wary reliance on the "format replacement cycle" as a continuing engine of new revenues and business models on the one hand and a continuing threat to cartelized distribution on the other. The chapter also charts the complex constellation of forces that led to the broadcasting industry's rejection of the higher-quality FM format for nearly half a century before it achieved market dominance in the 1980s. Finally, it reviews the role of innovative music production technologies in creating and maintaining an aesthetic "pro/am gap" to distinguish between commercial and amateur recordings over the decades, as well as the social and economic implications of widely accessible recording and production tools in the digital age.

Chapter 3 reviews recent innovations in digital music technology, and examines how the industry's resistance to these technologies (and the market's embrace of them) diverge from the pattern established over the prior century, undermining the industry's economic and political power. The chapter uses Elisabeth Kübler-Ross's well-known "five stages of grief"[29] as an explanatory framework for these developments, arguing that the industry's paralysis in the face of digital innovation was the result of a kind of industrial psychological crisis, stemming from an organizational inability to adapt to the changes wrought by digital dematerialization.

The second section of the book directly challenges the dominant narrative surrounding the economic and structural changes the music industry has undergone in the digital age. The crusaders and the press have largely painted the recording industry's measurable losses as a direct result of online "piracy," but this claim doesn't stand up to available evidence. Rather, the industry itself deserves the burden of the blame for any misfortunes it may be suffering, stemming from its inability to address digitization proactively and its problematic relations with artists, consumers, and even its own business partners.

Chapter 4 takes a close look at the piracy crusade's bête noir, peer-to-peer file sharing. While there are certainly many other forms of online music sharing that have emerged in recent years, P2P has remained the best-known and most vilified among them, and its user base continues to grow. The chapter summarizes a number of recent research studies on the economic consequences of P2P, which fail to reach any consensus on whether its net effect is positive, negative, or neutral. It also reviews the many economic benefits of P2P for both artists and music industry organizations, from concrete revenue opportunities to defrayed costs to reputational enhancement. Finally, the chapter contrasts traditional music economics with P2P, arguing that musicians have more to gain from P2P's potential strengths than they have to lose from the obsolescence of a system that has historically exploited their work.

Chapter 5 directly challenges the piracy crusaders' claim that "online piracy" is responsible for most, or all, of the drop in music retail revenue since the turn of the century. Using the recording industry's own published sales data as a foundation, I review the many other factors that contributed to the "perfect bubble" in music sales from 1985 to 2000, as well as those that led to the "perfect storm" beginning in 2000. I conclude the chapter by examining some of the industry's claims of significant losses in jobs and productivity attributed to piracy. I show that these claims are not only baseless, but are given the veneer of legitimacy through repetition by reputable sources, and are then used as justification for stricter anti-piracy laws and policies.

Chapter 6 investigates the role that the recording industry's own actions have played in undermining its goodwill, and therefore its market value and commercial earning power. The chapter begins by examining the industry's historical dealings with artists, consumers, and business partners, showing that, in each case, the major labels have relied upon their oligopolistic market dominance to exact concessions that have generated a simmering reservoir of bad will against the industry. The chapter then looks at the labels' more recent "public education" and mass litigation campaigns, exploring the ways in which they have further undermined public trust and respect. Finally, the chapter concludes by reviewing some of the other major public relations fiascos the industry has faced in recent years, from corruption scandals to massive computer hacking charges.

The third and final section of the book focuses on the "collateral damage" of the piracy crusade, measured in terms of delayed innovation, failed enterprises, and, most important, threats to free speech and civil liberties. The book concludes by arguing that the costs will only continue to mount as we come to rely on networked communications increasingly in our personal lives, public affairs and social institutions.

Chapter 7 uses interviews with music industry executives and visionary digital music entrepreneurs to present case studies for five failed digital music initiatives over the past fifteen years. Although these initiatives are differentiated by the years and circumstances in which they arose, each faced a similar fate: because the major record labels refused to grant them viable licenses, they were unable to spread their innovations to musicians and audiences, impoverishing both the marketplace and the musical public sphere. Ultimately, my industry sources explain, these initiatives were starved to death or sued out of existence not because they lacked market viability, but precisely because they possessed it; factions within the major labels, afraid of competition and unwilling to take risks, opted to control a diminished marketplace rather than to share a growing one.

Chapter 8 examines the most devastating consequences of the piracy crusade: namely, the increasingly draconian laws and policies that have governed the use of intellectual property since the dawn of the web. The chapter aims to show that, far from isolated responses to discrete legal threats, these laws and policies represent a coherent and consistent "anti-piracy agenda" that sacrifices constitutional rights, civil liberties, and international relations in the name of protecting the outmoded business models of a few multinational corporations. The chapter also traces the origin of these policies to billions of dollars in lobbying and campaign finance spent by these companies and their trade associations. Finally, the chapter explores the very real social and political consequences of the anti-piracy agenda, from organized crime to political repression to the loss of millions of lives.

Chapter 9 concludes the book by looking at the potential long-term costs of the piracy crusade. What will the world look like in a generation or two, if the anti-piracy agenda continues to progress, while networked communication technologies continue to advance and proliferate? How can interpersonal relationships, creative communities, and democratic political processes survive in an environment in which every song, every e-mail, and every debate is subject to potential surveillance, censorship, and misappropriation by powerful and unaccountable commercial and government institutions? In addition to asking these questions, I also review several alternatives to the piracy crusade promoted by both legislators and independent scholars.

Finally, I close by suggesting that the very notion of "copyright" itself is based on an industrial metaphor whose expiration date has long since passed. In an era such as ours, in which our lives are so thoroughly mediated by communication technologies, the line separating copying from expression can't even be defined, much less policed. Ultimately, I am hopeful that we can develop new methods of encouraging cultural and technological innovation while providing economic benefits to those who contribute creatively and financially to the process, in a way that safeguards free speech and civil liberties now and for the foreseeable future. But before we can get there, we'll need to end the crusade.

PART I

Lock and Key: Music as a Scarce Resource

As RHETORICIANS and communication scholars have long known, the way in which a debate is "framed" is at least as important as the manner in which it is argued. To accept a set of terms and definitions at the outset of a conversation is to accept the worldview that gave rise to those terms and therefore to preclude alternate interpretations of a given object or situation.

My aim in the first part of this book is to reframe the debate surrounding music, technology, copyright, and "piracy" by examining the historical circumstances that gave rise to our current understanding of their meanings and relationships. This is a necessary precondition if we are to have a more nuanced understanding of the complex changes currently taking place within our musical cultures and industries, as well as our legal systems, as digital networked technologies continue to grow in power and scope.

To reduce the staggering diversity of innovative digital music technologies and practices that have emerged over the past fifteen years to a simple permission/theft binary is not only to miss the point of these innovations completely but to ensure that they can never be effectively integrated into our cultural, legal, and commercial systems. Instead, we must take a "first principles" approach to understanding the role that music plays in society, the methods by which it has been commercially exploited and legally categorized, and the reasons for which these decisions were made.

In the chapters that follow, I examine the coevolution of music, technology, law, and industry, from the dawn of movable type, through the era of recording and broadcasting, and, finally, to the emergence of the networked age. Seen from this vantage point, we can understand what is currently referred to as "digital music piracy" as merely one in a long line of innovative disruptions, rather than the death knell of a static and unchanging industry.

CHAPTER 1

Stacking the Deck

The Monopolization of Music

THE EARLY years of the twenty-first century have been a tumultuous time within the music industry and musical culture at large. Many people working throughout the recording, publishing, and broadcasting sectors are legitimately concerned that they may lose their jobs, or even their careers. The new digital communications tools that have changed the way we work, play, and express ourselves have also altered our relationship to music. On the one hand, they have whetted our appetite for making, hearing, and sharing it in greater volume and variety than ever before. On the other, they have underscored the limitations of twentieth-century music technologies, and in so doing have undermined their viability in the marketplace.

To many within the music industry, the problem appears very clear. Enabled by illegal technologies, millions of consumers have turned to "piracy" because the lure of free music is too great to pass up. This renders traditional commerce impossible. Why would anyone pay for something when it's just sitting there, waiting to be taken? The only possible way forward is to use copyright laws, security technologies, and consumer education to contain the threat and mitigate the damage.

To many outside the industry, the situation seems equally simple, but the blame is reversed. Instead of supporting or embracing exciting new platforms that allow people to enjoy music to the fullest extent possible, the industry has attempted to squelch innovation at every turn, using copyright laws, security technologies, and propaganda as their weapons. The only possible way forward is to move deeper and deeper underground, using cutting-edge technologies that the industry hasn't yet learned about or figured out how to kill.

Both arguments appear to have merit, but they originate from such irreconcilable vantage points that they can never generate a meaningful dialogue, let alone come to a satisfying accord. What both viewpoints lack is a degree of historical perspective. Where did this cat-and-mouse game begin? How did the recording industry come to possess the powers it wields? When did music sharers become "pirates"? In this chapter, I argue that music began as a "public good" and trace the course of its gradual propertization, as well as the development of the legal framework that enabled this process. I also examine the history of "music piracy" and discuss some of the ways in which our uses of the term today diverge from those of the past.

Although my own vantage point is largely critical of the music industry's most powerful organizations, I also sympathize with those who feel threatened by the changes at hand. It is my hope that, by providing a broader context for today's conflicts both in this chapter and throughout the book, I can help to navigate a better path forward than the stonewalling, violence, and recrimination that have characterized industry-consumer relations thus far.

Music of the People, by the People, for the People

What is music?

For those of us who came of age in late twentieth- or early twenty-first-century America, the answer may seem obvious. It's a form of entertainment, a packaged product, and a powerful (if sometimes infuriating) industry dedicated to the manufacture and exploitation of that product. Music is what wins Grammys, it's what the "M" in MTV used to stand for, it's the stuff that Super Bowl halftime shows are made of. And musical artists—"real" artists, the kind with major label deals and professional-quality videos—are a type of brand. Like our choices in clothing, movies, and computers, the music we buy, watch, and listen to says something about who we are, what groups we belong to, and what kind of values we have.

Theoretically speaking, if I were to amend my Facebook profile tomorrow to delete musicians like Thievery Corporation, Fela Kuti, and Ornette Coleman and replace them with popular acts like Toby Keith, Kelly Clarkson, and Drake, my closest friends and family would think I had gone crazy, was pulling a lame prank, or had entered a desperate phase of midlife crisis (and they'd probably be right). It's an entirely reasonable assumption that I might enjoy the music recorded by these artists, but as a forty-year-old, northeastern American musician/professor/ retired hipster, it would be completely uncharacteristic for me to define myself publicly by affiliating with them.

Music means many things to many people, and it continues to play an important role in churches, parties, and politics. But our primary use for it as a society is arguably as a form of "cultural capital,"[1] a marker of identity acquired through the acts of public consumption and affiliation. Music's intrinsic power to bond groups and communicate affinities has been adapted to the logic of late capitalism and harnessed to serve its dictates. And the control of this power has been restricted to a dwindling handful of very large corporations with an ever-growing scope of legal authorization to decide what the rest of us do with music. The more normal and inevitable this relationship between music and the market seems, the less likely we are to question the underlying premises of our social and economic systems. Yet, as I discuss in my book *Mashed Up*,[2] the long-standing association between modern musical codes and social institutions may be nearing its end, or at least approaching a radical re-formulation; our market-based assumptions about music no longer make sense when we look at the increasingly diverse ways in which we use it in our daily lives.

Music and the marketplace haven't always been so deeply intertwined; in the scope of human history, it's a relatively new development. In recent years, scholars in a variety of social and biological sciences have begun to converge on the question of why human beings seem uniquely adapted to make and respond to music, and their answers, though still tenta-tive, offer some fascinating clues about its enduring sway over our lives and societies. The neurobiologist Mark Changizi, for instance, makes a compelling argument that music is, neurologically speaking, a kind of sonic code for human motion that hacks into our nervous systems and redirects our interests and energies. Without music, Changizi argues, humans could never have evolved beyond our "wet biology" to become the socially organized, self-aware, culturally immured creatures we are today.[3] Similarly, scholars such as Oliver Sacks[4] and Daniel Levitin[5] have argued that music is one of the most complex and comprehensive aspects of human consciousness, and that music not only was central to human evolution but remains vital to our cognitive and social processes from infant development to the treatment of age-related dementia. In short, music isn't just something we manufacture, like cars and shoes; it's some-thing that shaped us as a species, and continues to shape each of us as individuals throughout our lives.

Of course, we don't need to invoke prehistory or biology to find musical traditions and applications that fall outside the confines of the marketplace. As a great many cultural historians and ethnomusicologists have demonstrated, music's current role as a commodity is the exception, rather than the rule. In most societies, for most of the past five thousand years, music has served other functions, and other masters. For nonindustrialized societies such as the Mbuti of Zaire,[6] the Venda of South Africa,[7] and the Kaluli of Papua New Guinea,[8] music's central role (often in the company of dance) has been to bind together communities and reaffirm the values and philosophies that united them. In feudal and dynastic societies, music served as a kind of public news medium, as well as a vector of oral history; jongleurs, griots, bards, minstrels, skalds, and udgatars, though specialized conveyors of musical information, were hardly its "owners" or monopolists. Even within postindustrial societies, a great many uses of music still fall beyond the market's expanding footprint; from "traditional" music styles such as blues and bluegrass to quotidian musical events like birthday parties and religious ceremonies, music is still sometimes produced without claims to ownership or the promise of remuneration.

Consequently, as many economists and legal scholars have observed,[9] music outside of its commodity context can be understood as a kind of "public good"—a universally accessible, ubiquitous resource that all members of a society may draw upon to fulfill their individual and collective needs. Similarly, to use a term introduced by the media theorist James Carey, music can be understood as a quintessential form of "ritual communication"—in his words, communication "directed not toward the extension of messages in space but toward the maintenance of society in time; not the act of imparting information but the representation of shared beliefs."[10] In other words, music today may be a product, an industry, and a talisman of consumer culture, but it has always been, and continues to be, a constituent element of human consciousness and collective social action as well. And in an age marked by the increasing corporate ownership of culture as well as a rapidly evolving person-to-person networked communications infrastructure, these two functions of music have come into an ever greater degree of conflict.

Music and the Marketplace

At what point did music cease to be merely an aspect of human life akin to speaking, dancing and dreaming, and become something that can be bought and sold, shared and stolen, stockpiled and monopolized? When, and how, did music become a commodity?

Despite its historical status as a public good, music has never been completely free. Powerful social institutions have always played a role in regulating musical aesthetics, practices and technologies. From dynastic Egypt and China to present-day America, music's capacity to influence people's behavior, opinion, and collective action has always been recognized as a vital tool—and a dangerous weapon—by those holding the reins of power.[11] Yet throughout most of history, this power has been exercised politically, militarily, religiously, and ideologically; only with the dawn of modern capitalism did music enter the marketplace and thereby become regulated through economic measures as well.

The French economist Jacques Attali has argued persuasively that, in the Western world, this shift began in the fourteenth century, at the birth of the Renaissance. At this time, he writes, the age of minstrels and jongleurs began to wane, and musicians "became professionals bound to a single master, *domestics,* producers of spectacles exclusively reserved for a minority."[12] This was part of a broader trend; throughout the Renaissance, all of the cultural behaviors we now consider "fine arts" were professionalized and separated from more common, craft-oriented, and unmarketable ones, and professional artists were distinguished from mere amateurs and audiences.[13] In that cultural moment, the music industry was born.

It is no coincidence that, at the very time when control over music and the arts shifted from religious to market mechanisms, the political power of the church was diminishing and that of the bourgeoisie was rising. Not only did the professionalization of music turn musicians themselves into commodities, requiring that people pay for access to something which had hitherto been free, but the new musical modes of production actually served to validate the underlying logic of the market system itself. If access to music could be bought and sold, then what other aspect of the human experience could legitimately be excluded from the marketplace?

Over time, the new focus on professionalization within music crystallized into an emerging set of aesthetics that didn't just reward professional skills, but demanded them. By the turn of the nineteenth century, the shift was complete; as the music historian Joel Sachs argues, the "modern" music of the time emphasized virtuosity as a way to exclude both amateur musicians and uneducated audiences.[14] These new aesthetics, in turn, paved the way for an even greater set of social transformations, centered around industrialization and massification. As the musicologist Christopher Small writes, the professionalization of music, and the resulting "exclusion of the consumer" from the musical process, can be linked directly to the "homogenization of human relationships brought about by the industrial society of today."[15]

Even as musicians were becoming a commodity through the process of professionalization, musical expression itself was undergoing a simultaneous and parallel transformation. Although systems of musical notation have existed for millennia, it was only with the dawn of movable type in the fifteenth century that the concept of an intrinsically valuable musical *score* began to take hold. Unlike mere notation, scores can be understood as something logistically prior to, and of equivalent commercial value to, musical performance. In other words, they stand on their own as independent musical commodities, whether they're used by amateurs or professionals, or merely sit gathering dust on a bookshelf. Also with the increasing capacity for large-scale print reproduction came the standardization of notation, which in the sixteenth century crystallized into the five-line staff system we know today. With standardized notation and cost-effective mechanical reproduction came the growth of an international music community, and a marketplace for the scores that bound that community together. In time, this marketplace led to the development of a printing industry and a professional publishing field. And for centuries, this field has been organized around the mechanism of copyright.

The Origins of Copyright

Countless authors have documented the boggling array of meanings, forms, and functions represented by the word "copyright" from age to age and nation to nation. Put simply, it is a set of property laws establishing who has the right to communicate (or prevent the communication of) ideas, to whom, via what media, and under which circumstances. To say more than that is to enter into a hotly contested theoretical arena, in which virtually any assertion or interpretation tends to be viewed as an ideological declaration. Although it is not my aim here to present a comprehensive history of copyright, or even to stake out a particularly partisan perspective on the subject, my argument can't proceed without a brief review of its history and some of its basic functions.

Most historians of copyright trace its origins to 1557, when a group of English book publishers received a royal charter to become the Company of Stationers of London. This charter gave the company the power to grant a "stationer's copyright" to a given publisher, conferring exclusive privileges to reproduce a given work. As the legal scholar Lyman Ray Patterson describes it, "the primary purpose of the stationer's copyright was to provide order within the . . . book trade,"[16] essentially stabilizing market rates and practices, and minimizing the risk of outside competition or internal strife. Yet, from the very beginning, this proto-copyright law had a secondary function: state control over the content of the public sphere, and by extension, a monarchical check on the rising power of the bourgeoisie. In Patterson's words, "censorship was a major policy of the English government." The stationers' charter, therefore, granted the company "large powers . . . in order to have them serve as policemen of the press."[17] Given the central role that political pamphleteers and publishers would play in the Glorious Revolution of 1668 and the American Revolution a century later, the British crown's concern was clearly well warranted.

Ironically, one of the unintended early consequences of copyright was to accelerate the consolidation of the publishing industry. By raising the barriers to entry for newcomers, creating exclusive rights to exploit popular works, and thus spurring new economies of scale, copyright laws helped to ensure that publishing would become a field dominated by a few large firms. This, in turn, eventually helped to undermine the unilateral power of the monarchies themselves, as the concentrated capital and political influence of the biggest publishing houses would make them increasingly autonomous.

It was only in the eighteenth century, after these political and economic changes were well under way, that copyright became something conferred on British authors by statute rather than on publishers via membership in the company, and similar laws were enacted elsewhere in Europe as well. In the United States, which came into being just as this shift was taking place, the question of whether to have copyright laws at all was hotly debated by the "founding fathers"; while Thomas Jefferson abhorred such laws as a form of monopoly, James Madison considered them a necessary evil as "encouragements to literary works and ingenious discoveries."[18] Ultimately, the US Constitution would provide the foundation for all copyright laws that have followed, by giving Congress the power "To promote the Progress of Science and useful Arts, by securing for limited Times to Authors and Inventors the exclusive Right to their respective Writings and Discoveries."

In the two and a half centuries since this clause was penned, the founding fathers' debate has continued to reverberate through American legal scholarship and the creative industries. Why do we have copyright? What are its costs, and its benefits? The Madisonian view that it provides an incentive for skilled individuals to produce and share innovative concepts, thus contributing to what John Stuart Mill called the "marketplace of ideas" and enriching our cultural environment, still reigns as the primary rationale.[19] A more economically oriented, "neoclassical" view holds that copyright enables culture to enter the marketplace because that's where the true "value" of a work is established, and this valuation guides future investment in similar work.[20] A regulatory understanding of copyright views it as an instrument of policy, setting the terms for competition between rival media and communications firms.[21] A more critical approach would hold that the propertization of culture makes authors and composers beholden to the dictates of the marketplace (undermining their independence and resistant capacity) and masks the inherently collective nature of cultural production by ascribing ownership over ideas to discrete individuals.[22] These are not mutually exclusive viewpoints, and either way, the effect of this function has been the same: namely, providing a legal basis for the professionalization of music and the commodification of musical expression. In other words, copyright is the glue that binds music to the marketplace.[23]

Growing Industry, Expanding Copyright

From the music industry's inception through the beginning of the twentieth century, printed scores were the primary commercial music product, and throughout this period, music publishers were the industry's dominant, and growing, economic power. In the United States, most sheet music was imported from Europe during the colonial era, but around the time of the Revolution, a homegrown music publishing industry emerged, initially dedicated to printing sacred anthologies. Many early American publishers, such as Benjamin Carr of Philadelphia, were composers as well, seeking a commercial outlet for their own work.[24] With relatively small catalogs and limited reach, their businesses were in many ways more akin to today's "DIY" music producers than to the large, established publishing houses that account for most of the compositions we hear on contemporary radio and television programs.

By the turn of the nineteenth century, as the young American republic started to establish a coherent sense of its cultural identity, a popular music industry, dedicated to the printing of more secular and socially oriented scores, began to form. Within the first quarter of the century, these new publishers had released nearly ten thousand secular titles in a broad range of genres and themes,[25] many of them tailored to suit the needs of the country's growing bourgeoisie, an increasing number of whom boasted pianos and other instruments in their homes.

Although it may seem surprising, given the emphasis we place on intellectual property as an incentive for musical creation and distribution, American law did not provide copyright for printed scores at this time. Composers and publishers in Europe had the ability to copyright music in the late eighteenth century, but only with the Copyright Act of 1831 were musical scores considered eligible in the United States.[26] Ironically, as the music historian Richard Crawford suggests, the introduction of copyright may have undermined the domestic market for American composers in the nineteenth century because it created an incentive for profit-oriented publishers to distribute European works (for which they didn't owe a royalty) rather than domestic ones (for which they did). As he writes, "the American appetite for European music owed much to the notion that Old World culture was superior. But the dollars-and-cents advantage to publishers also promoted the circulation of foreign music."[27] This is an early, and notable, example of how the financial interests of the music industry, enforced through the mechanism of copyright, can often come into direct conflict with the cultural and economic interests of musicians and audiences.

The American publishing industry continued to grow sharply throughout the nineteenth century, in conjunction with the rise of minstrelsy, expanding national borders and accelerating technological change. By the middle of the century, five thousand titles were being published each year. By the turn of the twentieth century, this number had grown to twenty-five thousand songs per year, and a single hit song from commercial songwriting capital Tin Pan Alley, such as "After the Ball" by Charles Harris (1892), could sell millions of copies. Throughout this era of rapid expansion, the largest music publishers worked to reinforce their industry dominance and economic power on legal fronts, by lobbying to expand the scope and duration of copyright, and strategically, by using "song pluggers," trade associations, and other forms of market leverage to promote their songs among performers, music sellers, and potential purchasers.

As the music industry expanded, so did the scope of copyright law. In the span of a few generations, American copyright developed from zero statutory protection for music in 1830 to the coverage of scores (1831), public performances (1897), and "mechanical reproduction" (e.g., piano rolls and phonograph records, 1909), while the term of copyright doubled from fourteen years (renewable for another fourteen) to twenty-eight years (renewable for another twenty-eight) and statutory penalties for copyright violation expanded from pennies per page to imprisonment.[28]

These changes were brought about, at least in part, by an increasing degree of organization, collaboration, and even collusion among the nation's largest music publishers. In 1855, the first music industry trade association, dubbed the Board of Music Trade, was founded, with the explicit aim of stemming price-cutting. By 1880, this association had grown to encompass every major publisher, renamed itself the Music Publishers' Association (MPA), and clarified that its purpose was "the regulation of the music trade by fixing and sustaining a uniform and standard price for all music publishers."[29] From this point to the present day, music industry trade organizations have played an active role both in the process of regulating industry practices and pricing (sometimes in violation of antitrust law, as I discuss in chapter 6), and in lobbying for continual copyright expansion. As early as 1909, for instance, the MPA was actively lobbying for a copyright term of the composer's life plus fifty years[30] (this ambition would finally be realized in 1976, and surpassed in 1998).

The same economic, legal, and technological expansion that helped the music publishers to grow in power throughout the nineteenth century would contribute to their relative decline in the twentieth. After World War I, the rapidly evolving capabilities of audio recording and broadcasting technology gave rise to two new powers in the music industry—the record labels and radio networks. These sectors exploded in size and power, and before long, they had outstripped music publishing both economically and politically. Following in the footsteps of music publishers, the larger labels and broadcasters consolidated their market share, founded influential trade organizations, and played a central role in the continuing expansion of copyright, placing an ever-greater range of musical practices and products into private (primarily corporate) hands, and eliminating them from the freely shared cultural "commons" for a functional eternity.

As the music industry and the legal apparatus that binds it both ballooned in the wake of technological advancement, its economic and institutional foundations crystallized around the idiosyncrasies of these particular technologies. Much as molten glass will harden in the form of any mold into which it's poured, the twentieth-century music industry slowly ossified in the form of its own enabling technologies, such as the vinyl record and AM/FM radio. In turn, these newly fixed industrial practices were reinforced by further legal and technological development, in a self-perpetuating cycle.

By the second half of the century, the industry had fully congealed around the broadcasting/label dichotomy, with the former sector based on advertising-supported, over-the-air programming, and the latter based on consumer-supported, over-the-counter retail distribution. Although they both solved essentially the same "problem"—that is, capitalizing on consumer demand for access to recorded music—the two sectors consisted of entirely different firms operating according to separate laws and licenses, using totally distinct technologies, and deriving income from two entirely separate sources. There was a great degree of symbiosis between these sectors (radio "promoted" the sales of recordings, while recordings provided programming for broadcasters), but there was also friction; for instance, the decades-long debate over whether broadcasters should pay labels a royalty for public performance of their recordings or whether the promotional value of airtime obviated such a need.[31]

Despite such tensions, this arrangement persisted for the better part of a century, weathering continuing technological innovation and shifting political tides. As 78 rpm records gave way to 45 rpm singles, LPs, cassettes, 8-tracks, and CDs and as stereo FM supplanted mono AM as the dominant broadcast format, radio conglomerates ruled their roost and record labels ruled theirs, while the once-powerful music publishers stood by as largely silent partners to each. As I argue throughout this book, part of the reason that twenty-first-century digital communications technologies have proven so disruptive to the music industry is precisely because they undermine the theoretical distinction between broadcasting and retail, thereby upsetting the elaborate ecosystem that has emerged around this distinction, bringing former market allies into greater competition and conflict with one another and muddying the legal and economic waters.

At the end of the twentieth century, on the cusp of this change, the American music industry had reached the apex of its concentrated political and economic power. In 1999, the field was dominated by five major record labels (soon to be three), four large publishers (all of them affiliated with major labels), four major radio groups, and a single music television titan (Viacom), wielding copyright powers that had been extended significantly by two radically expansive pieces of legislation in the previous year,[32] and consolidating rapidly in the wake of recent media deregulation.[33] Collectively, this handful of highly litigious corporations, and their trade associations, controlled more than just the music market-place; they regulated global musical culture to a degree that is arguably unparalleled in history. In practice, this meant everything from the broadly general (e.g., promoting and censoring different styles, genres, and artists; shaping and constraining the development of music record-ing and playback technology) to the minutely specific (e.g., threatening to sue Girl Scout camps for allowing campers to sing Woody Guthrie songs;[34] micromanaging and tracking consumers' music listening habits through the use of "digital rights management" technology).

In short, the music industry as it existed immediately before the in-troduction of the pioneering file sharing service Napster was hardly a timeless, or even a particularly stable, institution. Its economic and legal foundations had accreted around the idiosyncrasies of an outmoded tech-nological system, and its unprecedented cultural power was the result of two centuries of sustained concentration of ownership and successful lobbying for ever-greater degrees of copyright protection over a broad-ening field of musical practices and products. What had once been a pub-lic good and a native form of "ritual communication" for our species had been successfully commodified, and then monopolized by a multibillion-dollar cartel, but the very rationale for this cartel's existence was already being called into question.

Music as "Entertainment"

The portrait I've just painted is somewhat at odds with the popular nar-rative of the music industry's formation. Most histories, biographies, and documentaries tend to focus on stylistic disruptions (e.g., how rock 'n' roll fomented youth rebellion in the 1950s and '60s), or the larger-than-life personalities of celebrated music industry executives (e.g., how Walter Yetnikoff of CBS Records waged war on Steve Ross of Warner Communications, while injecting untold millions of dollars into superstar contracts and mob-related promotion companies).[35] To the extent that corporate strategy and copyright law are invoked at all, they tend to be treated as peripheral to the story—executive gambits and the rules of the game, respectively. And though few dimensions of the music industry typically escape the scrutiny of critics and historians, one thing that's often taken for granted is the industry's raison d'etre; namely, the premise that music is an untapped resource just waiting to be mined by entrepreneurial spirits capitalizing on the demand for entertainment.

As should be clear from my discussion in the previous section, the characterization of music as a natural resource was a necessary conceit for the process of commodification; only by metaphorically invoking industrial models of production could this universal public good be successfully privatized. Yet, in order to make this economic sleight of hand both believable and palatable, a second conceit was necessary as well. If music-as-resource satisfies the supply side of the industrial metaphor, then music-as-entertainment satisfies the demand side of the equation.

Obviously, music has always been entertaining. Whether we are participating in the process of making it, or just bearing witness to a ritual or performance, we generally find music pleasurable, emotionally gratifying, and at times even transporting. And, at least since the earliest days of minstrelsy, music has been an attraction specifically sought out by those looking to experience such things. But the concept of music as a discrete product of a larger "entertainment industry," categorically similar to movies, books, and games, is a relatively new idea.

Many cultural historians agree that the premise of entertainment as we now think of it—as a commercial diversion from the demands and cares of our daily lives—emerged with the dawn of "consumer culture" in the late nineteenth century. However, theorists differ on the reason for this shift. Within a Marxian analytical framework, especially among the Frankfurt School, the entertainment industry serves the purpose of rationalizing and ameliorating the "alienation of labor" during industrialization; workers, deprived of the opportunity to take pleasure in their work, must purchase that pleasure in the form of commodities, thereby perpetuating the capitalist logic at the heart of their alienation.[36] Others have argued that consumer culture was deliberately manufactured by the ruling elites as an instrument of control over the growing ranks of recent immigrants and the working class.[37] Still others view it as a less coercive and more negotiated process: either the result of dialectical tensions between "top-down" and "bottom-up" social forces,[38] or the inevitable result of the increasing complexity of postindustrial capitalist society and the expanding role of the marketplace in daily life.[39]

Regardless of the power dynamics that heralded its arrival, the era of consumer culture has been marked by the relegation of music to the category of entertainment and the gradual obfuscation of its other, older functions. The premise that music is a commercial product, developed as a natural resource and packaged to serve consumer demand, seems obvious to the point of transparency. Many analyses of contemporary music culture and industry treat this point as axiomatic, never taking care to ask whether or why music should be exploited in this way, but only who should be doing the exploiting, and under what conditions. This dynamic occurs both within and outside the academy, and among both those who sympathize with the commercial music industry and those who challenge it. It is unsurprising, if rather telling, that the recording industry's own publications refer to the selling of music as "creative product exploitation,"[40] but a bit more problematic when a nonprofit organization offering "education, research and advocacy for musicians" produces events and publications titled "The Band as Business."[41] There seem to be few advocates for music or musicianship outside of a commercial context, and little recognition of music's role outside of entertainment. The fact that skilled and venerated musicians such as Elvis Presley and Michael Jackson, both of whom died relatively young as a result of sustained self-abuse, have been publicly quoted claiming that "our job is to entertain,"[42] suggests some of the human costs of this paradigm, and Kurt Cobain's Generation X rallying cry, "Here we are now, entertain us," perfectly encapsulates the ambivalence felt by both musicians and audiences confronted by such market reductionism.

I am not simply making an "art-for-art's-sake" argument here, or suggesting that creative expression is some pure and delicate substance corrupted by the nefarious influence of capitalism. Nor am I suggesting that musicians shouldn't take advantage of the opportunities the marketplace offers, and equip themselves with the same degree of leverage and expertise as any other labor force negotiating with an industry that exploits its work. My aim is simply to point out that the economic privatization of music has required us to adopt a framework of analysis whose totalizing effect is to reduce our expectations of music's social application to the limitations of "entertainment" as a field,[43] thereby undermining alternative measures of value and systems of reward and incentive. And despite the measurable success of music as a commercial product, and the thousands of willing laborers within its industrial economy, this compromise still sits uneasily with us as a society, and weighs on none more heavily than the musicians who "succeed" the most in market terms.

Music and "Piracy"

The name of this book is *The Piracy Crusade*, and I would be remiss if I didn't spend some time in this introductory chapter discussing the concept of piracy as well. Usually, when a child dresses up as a pirate for Halloween, the outfit might include a false peg leg, an eye patch, and even a plush parrot doll for good measure. The child will swagger around with plastic cutlass in hand, uttering phrases like "Arrrghh" and "Shiver me timbers!" and generally making things difficult for younger siblings and house pets. Adults occasionally like to play pirate as well, and each year on September 19, hundreds of thousands around the world celebrate "International Talk Like A Pirate Day" by adopting this garb and garbled speech to one degree or another. At the time of writing, people have paid over $3.7 billion in box office ticket sales just to see Johnny Depp swashbuckling across the screen as Captain Jack Sparrow in the Walt Disney Company's massively successful Pirates of the Caribbean movie franchise.[44] For most of us, he is the dictionary definition of a pirate.

The International Federation of the Phonographic Industry (IFPI; the global trade association for record labels) has a very different definition. On their website, a page titled "What is piracy?"[45] mentions nothing about ships, parrots, or cutlasses. Instead, they use the term to mean "the deliberate infringement of copyright on a commercial scale," and identify four types relevant to their industry: "physical music piracy," "counterfeits," "bootlegs," and "Internet piracy." In this fourth category, the IFPI acknowledges that even its own definition of piracy doesn't really apply. Internet piracy, they argue, is "not necessarily due to the motivation of the perpetrator." So much for "deliberate." They also claim that the term refers "more generally to any use of creative content on the Internet that violates copyright." So much for "commercial scale." Given the fact that since the enactment of the 1976 Copyright Act every piece of text, audio, video, and imagery ever created is automatically subject to copyright, anyone who e-mails, blogs, or shares any document, song, video clip, or image he or she did not personally create from scratch is, according to the IFPI, a pirate. So much for Johnny Depp.

How can this one word mean two such different things? Is the distinction between Blackbeard and BoingBoing merely one of scale and means, or are they truly as different as they seem? What possible similarity can exist between blasting a ship to smithereens and making off with its bullion, and posting a mashup to Facebook? In order to address these questions, we need to look briefly at the history of the concept of piracy itself, and trace its evolution from antiquity to the present day. Fortunately, other researchers have done a lot of this work already, so I will try my best to give credit where it is due, lest I be branded a pirate myself.

As it turns out, the definition of piracy has been continually revised and debated since its earliest appearance. Cicero, writing two thousand years ago, was the first to outline a comprehensive definition and theory of piracy, arguing that pirates are those who, by virtue of being "the common enemy of all," have forfeited all rights, including those to fair dealing. "For example," he wrote, "if an agreement is made with pirates in return for your life, and you do not pay the price, there is no deceit, not even if you swore to do so and did not."

Daniel Heller-Roazen, a professor of literature who uses Cicero's words to title his excellent social history *The Enemy of All: Piracy and the Law of Nations,* argues that the exceptionalism inherent in Cicero's definition is the thread that ties together all subsequent concepts of piracy. He identifies four distinguishing features of this paradigm: first, piracy must take place outside of traditional legal regions (e.g., on the high seas); second, piracy is committed by an agent of "universal" antagonism; third, piracy collapses the categorical distinction between the criminal and the political; fourth, and consequent to the first three features, piracy requires a redefinition of "war." From the beginning, then, piracy has operated as a kind of negative category—a placeholder for malicious actors and activities that fall outside obvious social and political categorization. What it *hasn't* always meant is the theft of property; this property/theft dialectic, so central to our contemporary understanding of piracy, is a relatively recent affair, likely dating to the dawn of modern nation-states and international commerce. As Heller-Roazen observes, even plunder on the high seas was considered a legitimate economic model and political tactic for most of history, until international accords in the mid-nineteenth century abolished privateering, and in so doing, relegated the plunderers that remained to the negative category of pirates.[46]

The application of the term "piracy" to what we now call intellectual property is of relatively recent vintage, as well. As the professor of history Adrian Johns demonstrates, this use of the term can be traced directly to the dawn of the modern publishing industry in late seventeenth-century England, from whence it spread to other Western European nations. Like Heller-Roazen, Johns emphasizes that the definition of piracy has always been fluid, "a matter of place—of territory and geopolitics." In this case, the territory was the modern European nation-state, and the geopolitics involved the international trade in mass-produced printed goods. And although the IFPI's definition hinges on the "infringement of copyright," Johns makes it clear that the term was not only adopted prior to the development of copyright, it was actually a constituent element of the original argument in favor of legal protection for publishers. In Johns's words, "the invention of copyright itself was largely a response to a piracy feud overflowing with national resentments" between publishers in London and Scotland.[47]

Unlike textual piracy, the concept of music piracy does not seem to have existed before copyright. Although the concept of musical plagiarism had begun to emerge along with eighteenth-century notions of authorship, it wasn't until the turn of the twentieth century that the music industry identified piracy as a systematic problem. According to Johns, the problem arose from the confluence of two factors, one on the supply side (photolithography, which offered rapid, inexpensive reproduction) and the other on the demand side (the boom in piano ownership). Earlier in this chapter, I described the process by which the music industry successfully lobbied for an ever greater scope of legal control over the works they published. Arguably, this gradual encroachment on what had previously been a musical "commons" constituted a third factor in the growth of music piracy. As Johns acknowledges, the industry's monopolistic practices at the end of the nineteenth century contributed to a "widespread . . . sense of resentment at the traditional music publishing companies" on the part of consumers, which in turn conferred a degree of social legitimacy on "pirate" publishers.[48]

Even throughout most of the twentieth century, the concept of "music piracy" referred primarily to unlicensed publishers and manufacturers undercutting the market for legitimate commercial goods. It wasn't until the 1970s that an entirely new paradigm emerged: "home piracy." Two factors contributed to this change. First, the development of the phonorecord copyright in 1972 (which covers the sound of a recording, rather than the composition that has been recorded, and confers "master use rights" on the owner) gave the record labels a greater incentive and stronger set of tools to police and punish unlicensed reproductionists. Second, the development of home electronics based on magnetic tape (especially the microcassette format) gave musicians and listeners far greater power to reproduce, alter, and redistribute musical recordings.

Because these behaviors were even more difficult to control than "traditional" music piracy, the extension of the term "piracy" to cover non-commercial reproduction was largely rhetorical in nature. In fact, it had no legal basis in the United States; Congress explicitly declined to prohibit home taping in its 1972 law, and subsequent to its passage, "judges . . . acted as though an exemption for home taping existed."[49] Even some official and semi-official organs of the music industry had a hard time accepting that home taping constituted a piratical act; as late as 1979, *Billboard* magazine was still referring to it as "so-called 'home piracy.'"[50]

Figure 1. Logo for the anti-taping campaign launched by the British Phonographic Industry in the 1980s.

In 1984, the US Supreme Court ruled in the landmark "Betamax case"[51] that home taping of television for personal reasons was "fair use" (a legal concept limiting the powers of copyright holders in the interest of preserving cultural innovation and free speech). This decision was widely held to apply to a variety of "time shifting" and "librarying" behaviors, including home music taping. Left without legal recourse to prevent such behaviors, the music industry doubled down on its rhetorical efforts to brand them as piracy. Beginning in the early 1980s, for instance, the British Phonographic Industry (BPI) initiated its now-iconic "Home Taping Is Killing Music" campaign, which featured a skull-like image of a microcassette tape above a pair of crossbones (fig. 1), even though it publicly acknowledged that the UK had the lowest "piracy rate" in the world.[52]

By some measures, these rhetorical efforts paid off over the long term. Although librarying and time shifting have successfully jumped from analog to digital media and have likely become far more widespread than they were in the "home taping" years, the legal status of noncommercial duplication has gotten grayer and grayer, and protection for fair use has waned and withered.[53]

A major blow came in the form of the Digital Millennium Copyright Act (DMCA), a 1998 law that acknowledged fair use but made it a felony for businesses or consumers to bypass technological copy protection, even if it was the only way to exercise fair use rights (such as "ripping" a song onto a hard drive). Another blow came with the February 2001 federal appeals court decision in *A&M Records v. Napster, Inc.,*[54] which found that the popular file sharing service (which operated on a noncommercial basis) did not enjoy the same fair use protections as Betamax, because the network's centralized architecture gave its operators the power to identify and prevent copyright infringement. A third blow was struck by the 2005 Supreme Court decision in *MGM Studios, Inc. v. Grokster, Ltd,*[55] which found that even technology providers who had no knowledge or power over the use of their products for copyright infringement, and who did not benefit financially from such infringement, could still be found liable for "inducement."

Mitch Bainwol, the head of the Recording Industry Association of America (RIAA), celebrated the ruling against Grokster for its role in "contain[ing] piracy" and for providing *"moral* and legal clarity."[56] Many legal scholars and public advocates disagreed. As Fred von Lohmann of the Electronic Frontier Foundation (EFF) argued at the time, the broad and vague applicability of this new precedent gave rise to a "new era of legal uncertainty,"[57] in which nearly any media technology could be construed as a vehicle for piracy.

This is, of course, exactly the outcome devoutly pursued by the music industry (and its entertainment industry partners). As the law professor Lawrence Lessig has astutely observed, every new medium is pioneered by "pirates," who use the contents of older media to populate their new platforms and test their technologies. This was true of the recording industry (once dubbed pirates by music publishers), the radio industry (once dubbed pirates by record labels), and also the film and cable television industries.[58] In other words, yesterday's pirates have become today's establishment, and their aim is to stay put by keeping the cycle from repeating. If the price is fair use, free speech, and cultural and technological innovation, then so be it.

BOTH MUSICAL culture and the music industry are in a state of flux, and the rapid changes we have witnessed since the turn of the twenty-first century clearly have something to do with the explosion of networked digital technologies such as PCs, smartphones, portable media devices, and the Internet, which binds the rest together. On this much, nearly everyone can agree.

Where this book differs from the bulk of the commentary and coverage of these changes is in how these disruptions are *framed*. The recording industry, which has been highly successful in setting the terms of the public debate thus far, paints a bleak portrait: a venerable industrial sector, bolstered by centuries of copyright law and responsible for billions of dollars in economic value, has been ransacked by digital pirates intent on destruction and the ignorant masses who have fallen under their sway. We see this story told all the time, in news articles, business reports, and legal decisions. The only problem is, it's not the whole story.

As I have argued in this chapter, music is a fundamental aspect of human consciousness, akin to language or gesture, and the privatization of musical expression is a relatively new development in the scope of social history, motivated primarily by profit seeking and social regulation rather than cultural innovation and the public interest. And ever since its inception, the music industry has been in a state of constant flux, seeking to exploit new technologies, expand its legal scope of powers, and otherwise "stack the deck" in its own self-interest, with the aim of naturalizing its unnatural monopoly.

Copyright laws are not handed down by God on stone tablets; they are written by legislators, who respond to lobbying by corporations and trade organizations (more on that in chapter 8). In order to justify the creation and continued expansion of copyright, the music industry has had to identify a problem that the laws are intended to solve. From the beginning, this problem has been framed in terms of "piracy," although the exact nature of the purported piratical threat has evolved along with the technological and legal environment, from the importation of foreign scores to the reproduction of domestic ones to the use of popular compositions on radio and recordings to the redistribution of popular recordings, and finally to "home taping" and online peer-to-peer sharing.

If a pirate in Cicero's day was the "enemy of all," a malevolent agent exploiting the vulnerabilities of the weak and the outer boundaries of sovereignty in the interest of personal profit, consider who best fits that description today. Is it one of the tens of thousands of Americans who have been prosecuted for sharing songs with one another via LimeWire or BitTorrent? Is it one of the billions of people around the world who share music, videos, text, and images via YouTube, Twitter, and Facebook? Or is it one of a tiny handful of commercial enterprises that jealously protect their financial interests in our shared culture by maligning, surveilling, bankrupting, and imprisoning those who are too obstinate to acquiesce, too poor to fight back, or too weak to resist?

CHAPTER 2

Riding the Tiger

Why the Music Industry Loves (and Hates) Technology

THE MUSIC industry as we know it today began more or less by accident. When Thomas Edison first developed the technology for sound recording, it was an unintentional by-product of his attempts to improve the telephone. Of course, the canny entrepreneur rapidly moved to publicize the invention. In an 1878 article for the North American Review, he enumerated ten possible uses for his new discovery, with letter dictation at the top of the list (typical of his business-oriented market strategy). "Reproduction of music" came in only fourth, after "the teaching of elocution."[1] Today, all ten of his uses, from audiobooks to voicemail, are staples of our technological and cultural landscape. But without question, the definitive use of sound recording has been in the field of music and entertainment. Of the first three major American record labels (all launched in the 1900s), two of them (Victor and Columbia) still exist as elements of Sony Music Entertainment, the second-largest of today's three major labels. The other, Edison's own company, went out of business in 1929.

Similarly, when "wireless telephony," or radio sound transmission, was first developed by Nicola Tesla, Guglielmo Marconi, and others around the turn of the twentieth century, the medium was initially considered appropriate for person-to-person communications. In the decade before World War I, hundreds of thousands of independent radio enthusiasts took to the airwaves, using their often self-assembled sets to share news, gossip, and advice on everything from homework to dating. None of these enthusiasts were merely "transmitters" or "receivers"; they were each participants in a rapidly growing, technologically enabled community spanning thousands of miles. After the US government temporarily banned amateur radio during the war, the medium grew into something very different. During the 1920s, the government established the Federal Radio Commission (later to be supplanted by the Federal Communications Commission), equipment manufacturers started shipping a significant number of radio receivers (for listening only), major broadcast networks like NBC and CBS emerged, and hundreds of stations across the country took advantage of federally licensed "clear channels," free of amateur clutter, to broadcast news and music to millions of listeners across the country. By 1930, the radio industry looked, and sounded, much as it would at the end of the century, with a handful of major networks broadcasting music, news, and entertainment to a massive but largely passive audience.

In short, neither of the technologies that came to define and dominate the music industry in the twentieth century was initially invented or conceived for this purpose. Nor was the existing music industry, in the form of the publisher titans of the nineteenth century, necessarily keen on these technological innovations. To the contrary, as I alluded to at the end of the previous chapter, these new distribution channels were initially considered "pirates" by the industry's vested interests, for their disruptive economic potential. Nor were recording and broadcast technologies especially well suited to music distribution, at least in their initial forms. The high level of noise and single-channel audio provided by wax cylinders and early AM radio offered a listening experience that today's musicians and music fans would have little use or patience for. Yet, despite all of these challenges, records and radio grew rapidly in popularity, performance, and power, generating billions of dollars in market value and contributing to radical changes in our musical cultures and practices.

As I discuss in this chapter, these developments were neither necessary nor inevitable. Rather, the development of the modern music industry reflects a complex, long-standing love/hate dynamic between the industry's most powerful institutions and the technologies that enable and constrain them. In science and technology studies (STS), this process is called the "social shaping of technology"[2]—a dialectical process of push-and-pull between social dynamics and technological innovation, in a perpetual circuit with neither beginning nor end. Such a dynamic has been integral to music industry evolution. On the one hand, new technologies have allowed labels, publishers, broadcasters, and musicians continually to reinvent themselves and their products and to refine their economic and aesthetic models. On the other hand, each new technological innovation complicates and challenges established economies and aesthetics, putting powerful institutions at risk and providing an opportunity for upstarts to gain leverage. Consequently, the industry has often treated technological innovation like the tiger in the Chinese proverb: dangerous to ride, but more dangerous still to dismount.

Higher Fidelity, Longer Plays: A Brief History of Recording Formats

"Have you heard The EDISON PHONOGRAPH play an Amberol Record?" So screams the headline of a full-page ad in a 1909 edition of *Harper's Magazine Advertiser*. The rest of the ad copy, short and punchy for those prolix times, goes on to list the many superior qualities of these two products, and challenges readers to experience them directly:

> You can do this at the store of any Edison dealer. When you go, note the longer playing time of Amberol Records (playing twice as long as the standard Edison Records), note the Amberol selections, not found on any other record of any kind; note also the reproducing point of the Edison Phonograph that never wears out and never needs changing; the motor, that runs as silently and as evenly as an electric device, and the special horn, so shaped that it gathers every note or spoken word and brings it out with startling fidelity.

At the bottom of the advertisement, two drawings are juxtaposed. On the left, three young women gather around a phonograph's horn, clearly enraptured by the music they are hearing. On the right, his back to the three ladies, a pianist in formal attire sits at a piano. His right hand is on his knee, his left hand rests idly on the keys, and he gazes away from the sheet music, mouth set in a stoic line, eyes fixed on some distant or imaginary object; he looks like a man considering a new career. Beneath the drawings is the legend, "The Rivals" (fig. 2).

This advertisement, quaint and dated as it may seem, contains almost every element that would come to characterize the music industry's continuing drive to develop and market new recording formats and playback technologies during the ensuing century. The Amberol is touted for its longer playing time, and contrasted with earlier formats used by *the same record label,* demonstrating a willingness on the part of Edison to cannibalize its existing products in the interest of driving consumers to its newer ones. The use of format-exclusive content ("not found on any other record of any kind") provides further incentive for consumers to upgrade. The playback equipment is celebrated for its durability and its "startling fidelity." The visual tableaux at the bottom suggest that the sound fidelity is so great that it rivals the experience of live music (similar to Victor's

Have you heard

The EDISON PHONOGRAPH

Thomas A. Edison

play an Amberol Record?

YOU can do this at the store of any Edison dealer. When you go, note the Amberol music, not found on any other record of any kind; note also the reproducing point of the Edison Phonograph that never wears out and never needs changing; the motor, that runs as silently and as evenly as an electric device, and the special horn, so shaped that it gathers every note or spoken word and brings it out with startling fidelity. It is these exclusive features, vital to perfect work, that should claim your attention.

Edison Phonographs are sold at the same prices everywhere in the United States, $12.50 to $125.00.

Amberol Records, 50c.; regular Edison Records, 35c.; Grand Opera Records, 75c.

One of the greatest pleasures which the Edison Phonograph affords is making Records at home. This can be done only with the Edison.

Ask your dealer or write to us for catalogues of Edison Phonographs and Records.

NATIONAL PHONOGRAPH COMPANY, 20 Lakeside Avenue, Orange, N. J.
New York, 10 Fifth Ave.; London, Victoria Road, Willesden; Sydney, N. S.W., 340 Kent St.; Mexico City, 4a Tacuba 35; Buenos Aires, Viamonte 515; Berlin, Sud Ufer, 24-25; Paris, 42 Rue de Paradis.
The Edison Business Phonograph enables the stenographer to get out twice as many letters.

"The Rivals"

125

Figure 2. Print advertisement for Edison Amberol Records, 1909.

contemporary "His Master's Voice" trademark, and the "Is it live or is it Memorex?" campaign of the 1970s and 1980s). There is also a whiff of cyborgian sexual innuendo, as the young ladies shun the impotent virtuoso for their "special horn." Finally, there is what advertisers refer to as the "call to action," offering consumers the ability to preview the technology in a controlled, in-store environment. Each of these factors remains a vital element in the marketing of music technology to this day.

Even many casual music fans are aware of the progression of dominant recording formats during the twentieth century.[3] Edison's wax cylinders gave way to shellac 78 rpm (rotations per minute) records in the early 1900s, which were replaced by 45 rpm "singles" and 33-1/3 rpm "long-play" or "LP" vinyl records in the middle of the century. These, in turn, were supplanted by electromagnetic cassette tapes in the 1980s and then compact discs in the 1990s. After music fans began using the digital MP3 format to back up and share their music collections around the turn of the twenty-first century, the recording industry began selling "digital singles" in a variety of downloadable formats, which became the dominant sales medium around 2011.

Although this well-worn narrative is technically accurate, the full story is far more complicated, and interesting. First of all, this teleological tale of upward progression ignores a great many failed formats that have fallen by the wayside. From Pathé discs to 8-track cartridges to DVD-Audio discs, the entire history of the recorded music industry is littered with dozens of once-promising technologies that died without achieving market dominance (or, in many cases, prevalence or even recognition). Far from a carefully orchestrated progression from one stable platform to another, the evolution of recording technology has been a full-scale battle royal with far more casualties than victors.

Another complicating factor is that neither successful nor failed media formats ever completely disappear. In the words of the historian Jonathan Coopersmith, "old technologies never die, they just don't get updated."[4] At the time of writing, both vinyl records[5] and cassette tapes[6] have seen significant recent growth in market popularity, and all three of the failed formats I mentioned above can still be found for purchase online (a single eBay search for "8-track" returns over 25,000 results—not bad for a second-tier commercial format that hasn't been sold at retail for three decades).

Another related twist in the format progression story is the question of what "dominant" and "popular" mean in the context of the broader music marketplace and musical culture. When recording industry research data show cassettes outstripping vinyl in 1983 or CDs achieving market dominance in 1992, they refer to a very specific kind of market success: namely, the *retail purchase* of *new, pre-recorded, popular music at major retailers*. These data don't claim to offer a comprehensive snapshot of all of the ways in which musicians and fans use recording technology but merely all of the uses that generate income for the handful of labels who dominate the industry and subsidize market data collection.

From the vantage point of musicians, fans, and independent music sellers, the uses of these technologies are far more varied and persistent. The official narrative doesn't include the use of prerecorded media created by independent artists and sold directly to consumers in performance venues or via artists' websites. Nor does it include the used music retail market. Nor does it include the significant volume of recording and "librarying" that takes place within consumers' own homes. Long after prerecorded cassettes waned as an over-the-counter retail product, they remained a vital element of mixtape and automotive cultures, partly because millions of people still carried around Walkmans and drove cars with cassette decks. I still remember the day in 2002 (a decade after the CD ascended to market dominance) that I somewhat reluctantly dropped a cardboard box full of old cassette tapes on the curb outside my Brooklyn apartment. Within ten minutes, some enterprising music fan or street vendor had made off with the whole lot. Even today, I still have a box of cassettes I didn't get rid of, consisting of non-fungible recordings such as my own bands' rehearsals and live recordings, and bootlegs from my favorite performing artists. I never listen to them, but one of these days, I tell myself, I'll digitize it all and add it to my personal "cloud."

There are many reasons why some recording formats succeed in the marketplace while others fall by the wayside. Higher fidelity, higher storage capacity, and other factors noted in the marketing materials for Edison and his modern descendants certainly account for part of a given technology's ascendance. But there are other factors that come into play as well. One of the challenges to format replacement is coordinating the adoption of the new technology across all major content providers and manufacturers of media and electronics. Consumers will feel confident buying a new format only if they're assured of its longevity and breadth of adoption, and such confidence can be achieved only if there is significant support throughout the industry. Oftentimes, format wars (such as the battle between Super-Audio CDs and DVD-Audio at the turn of the twenty-first century) or other socioeconomic factors (such as the tariffs levied on manufacturers of digital audio tape [DAT] in the 1990s) will slow industry development, and consumers, unsure of which horse to bet on, will simply walk away from the racetrack.

This paralysis is damaging to the music industry, which has historically relied on the "format replacement cycle" as an engine of economic growth. There is a classic scene in the 1997 film *Men in Black* in which Tommy Lee Jones's character, a veteran agent at a top-secret government agency, shows the younger agent, played by Will Smith, all of the revolutionary new technologies the agency has access to. At one point, he picks up a disc the size of a quarter and says, "This is gonna replace CDs soon; guess I'll have to buy 'The White Album' again." The scene is funny, and widely quoted, because it reflects an economic reality immediately familiar to music buyers; whenever a new format successfully replaces an older one, a significant number of purchases during its first decade in the market consists of people replacing the titles they already own, rather than investing in new music.

The challenges to technological innovation I have discussed thus far fall on the *supply* side of the recorded music economy; but in addition to the internecine battles between labels, electronics manufacturers, and other industry sectors, there are also challenges on the *demand* side. While music fans are certainly receptive to promises of higher fidelity, enhanced storage capacity, and other benefits such as portability, there are additional considerations influencing their adoption of new recording formats as well. Most important, there is a vital question regarding what kinds of social music activities are permitted—and proscribed—by the technology in question.

From the music industry's perspective, the ideal consumer would learn about a new artist or song, purchase a recording, eventually lose interest in it, and move on to the next purchase. Periodically, a new format would require that consumers repurchase their existing collections, and repeat the cycle. Selling the record is the last step of the "value chain," and the sole focus of the recording industry's business model. But to music fans, buying a record is only the starting point of a much richer and more involved social process. For one thing, we don't tend to listen to our music singly, and in solitude. One of the main reasons we buy music is to listen to it with our friends, to share our tastes, and to enliven our cultural environments. We amass libraries, in part, to exercise our creative faculties as curators of our personal collections. Sometimes, we even use the recordings as the basis for more involved acts of creativity, which I refer to as "production-adjacent" cultural practices in my book *Mashed Up,* such as assembling mixtapes or composing sample-based music. To the music industry, these behaviors are not merely threats to their ability to sell new recordings but also criminal violations of their copyrights. To music fans, these behaviors are what make records appealing in the first place. And the more that technologies allow us to collect, share, curate, and reinterpret our music, the more excited we become as consumers, and the more likely we are to embrace a new format.

Consequently, there has been a consistent tension within the industry between the desire to promote formats that have adequate consumer appeal and the desire to promote formats that will limit consumers' range of freedom in the name of protecting the bottom line. In the era of "vertical integration" (a term referring to a single parent company owning many complementary business units), this tension can even result in conflict within a given corporation. For instance, Sony Electronics, which pioneered the portable music market with its Walkman product in the 1980s, began selling portable digital music players in 1999, two years before Apple introduced the market-transforming iPod. With its unrivaled branding power, engineering expertise, and knowledge of the consumer electronics marketplace, Sony should have dominated this emerging product category long before Apple could make its entry. Yet, in what has now become a classic cautionary tale taught in business schools around the world, the company shot itself in the foot. Because Sony also owned a major record label (worth a small fraction of the electronics business), the company chose not to allow its digital music player to support MP3s, for fear that the open format would encourage "piracy." Sadly, the device would only play songs encoded in Sony's proprietary, copy-protected digital format, which could only be obtained from Sony's music store or created using Sony's specialized software.[7] Naturally, music fans showed little interest in the device, and the path for Apple's eventual victory with the MP3-compliant iPod was cleared. Like the dog in the classic Aesop fable, Sony dropped its prize in its haste to have another.

To summarize, we can understand the progression of dominant recording formats over the past century as a kind of moving scrimmage line in a sustained contest between consumers and the record industry, with consumer electronics manufacturers acting as (not entirely objective) referees. Some formats (such as LPs and CDs) offered higher quality audio in exchange for limited convenience, while others (such as cassette tapes and MP3s) sacrificed fidelity for greater portability and writability. Many of the formats rejected by consumers, such as cassette singles,

MiniDisc, and slotMusic, are those that failed to provide adequate leaps in quality to compensate for their diminished utility or vice versa.

Today, we are still in the midst of this process. The rise of MP3 ripping and CD burning at the turn of the century disrupted the traditional format replacement cycle, in large part because the industry hadn't prepared adequately for digital business models (a subject I explore in greater depth in chapter 3). Initially, the industry tried, and failed, to introduce new formats (such as secure CDs and encrypted digital files) that sacrificed utility without improving quality. It also attempted to sell higher-quality audio discs, such as Super Audio CD and DVD-Audio, but was hamstrung by the format war I mentioned earlier as well as the fact that, given the CD's claim to "perfect" digital fidelity in its 1980s market debut, most music buyers who weren't audiophiles failed to recognize any difference in sound quality.[8]

Very recently, the industry has put significant weight behind digital subscription and "cloud" services, which offer listeners a high degree of utility and access to an extensive library of music at relatively low cost, while retaining far more centralized surveillance and control over music than any previous format. Later in this book, I hazard some observations about the potential for these models to succeed in the marketplace and about their significance for musical culture and social practices. For now, I want simply to observe that, innovative as these platforms may be, they are still subject to the same drivers and constraints as past music distribution technologies and represent the continuing evolution, rather than the demise, of the format replacement cycle.

Music in the Air: Radio and the Record Industry

In some ways, the development of radio closely paralleled the evolution of recording formats during the twentieth century: there was a general trend toward greater sound fidelity and utility but also a significant amount of conflict, compromise, and confusion along the way. The two industries are deeply interdependent, which furthered the connection in their development. Radio is a promotional vehicle for recordings, so format innovations such as stereo sound, higher fidelity, and longer playing time could only be adequately marketed if radio standards and practices were adapted accordingly. At the same time, radio has always threatened to cannibalize music purchasing; one of the reasons consumers continued to buy records over the years is because broadcast technology did not allow them to listen to their choice of music on demand. Radio developed as what media analysts call a "lean back" technology for passive consumption, while records were a "lean forward" technology for active engagement—and this arrangement was not so much an accident of technology as the outcome of the "social shaping" of these platforms, laws, and industries by the various interested parties over the decades.[9]

As close as they are, the two industries also differ in a few important respects. First, while the recording industry developed with very little government oversight, as a classic "free market," the evolution of the radio industry was guided heavily by the FCC and other federal agencies, and radio was therefore more constrained both in its ability to innovate and in its capacity for self-destruction.

Second, the record industry is organized around a single economic transaction, the retail sale of a song or album. Once the music is sold, labels have little concern with consumers' use of their products (as long as they don't "pirate" it!). By contrast, the radio industry earns its revenues from advertising, which are tied directly to the measurable audience for any given station at any given time. Hence there is an immediate correlation between consumers' listening habits and the economic success or failure of the broadcasters. This difference has contributed to some interesting divergences and tensions between the two industries. For instance, while record labels have historically limited the content of albums to two or three "radio hits," supplemented with an ample amount of "filler" (like fast-food burgers), radio playlists (with the exception of specialty formats, such as "Album-Oriented Rock") consist almost entirely of hits. Similarly, while for half a century long-playing vinyl records and their descendants have enabled popular recording artists to experiment with more extended compositional and improvisational musical styles, popular music broadcasters typically remain focused on songs of three minutes or less, in order to retain audience attention and keep listeners from turning the dial or, even worse, switching off the radio.

Just as the recording format replacement cycle on examination reveals the complex interplay of forces and stakeholders behind the market progression from vinyl to cassette to CD and beyond, the evolution of radio as a platform has not been quite as tidy a process as it may appear on the surface. Although the medium has been evolving for more than a century, perhaps the greatest development of the pre-digital age was the shift from AM (amplitude modulation) to FM (frequency modulation) as the dominant broadcast standard. At first glance, this change appears to be an obvious case of the better technology winning out; after all, FM has a clearer signal, and the ability to carry stereo (or even quadrophonic) sound. While it's true that AM signals can travel farther at lower expense, a strong enough FM transmitter can easily blanket an urban market of millions, and has the added feature of passing through thick walls and nasty weather. Yet, as was the case with recording format evolution, the change from AM to FM had at least as much to do with social and political factors as with technological ones.

It took half a century after FM was first patented by Edwin Armstrong in 1933 for its share of the radio market finally to eclipse AM's, in the early 1980s. What accounted for this delay, if the technological benefits of the newer standard were so obvious? It certainly wasn't for lack of knowledge or interest within the general public or the industry; as early as 1944, *Billboard Magazine* (then titled *The Billboard*) dedicated significant coverage to the emergence of FM and "to the opportunity FM presents," and anticipated a boom in what it presciently (or optimistically) referred to as "post-war FM." At the time, the new technology was viewed by labor organizations and other marginalized voices as a valuable opportunity to provide more mass media representation for groups and interests that had been structurally excluded from AM radio. In the same issue, however, there were signs of trouble brewing for the new format. Specifically, the American Federation of Musicians (AFM) decided not to allow existing radio networks to repurpose musical programming licensed to their AM stations for their new FM affiliates. According to the article, this decision could be "interpreted virtually as an FM nix," due in part to the perception that there was "no financial gain to the networks in feeding programs to FM."[10]

Despite the buzz around this new technology, FM radio failed to materialize for decades after World War II. An oft-repeated version of the story suggests that the large AM networks, content with their business model and focused on developing television rather than improving radio, stalled the new format's progress by manipulating the FCC into redistributing the broadcast spectrum at a crucial moment of adoption and by undermining support among consumer electronics manufacturers. Armstrong's suicide in 1954, after years of patent disputes and disappointments, provided poignant support for his reputation as a lone innovator at odds with big business.

While this narrative certainly appears to have some basis in truth, the media historian Hugh Slotten has shown that the full story of the delay in FM's adoption involves the "complex nature of regulatory decision making, the defining role of different institutions and individuals, the contingencies of historical context, and the essential role of nontechnocratic strategies in shaping technological development" and can't be reduced to the "inherent 'technical superiority' of such inventions as FM radio [or] grand conspiracies."[11] As the *Billboard* article about the AFM suggests, for instance, some stakeholders legitimately questioned FM's financial value as a music distribution channel, and full-scale acceptance of the format could only take place once its risk-to-reward ratio could be adequately agreed on across the entire industry.

When FM finally did begin to gain some market traction, in the 1970s, the factors driving it were just as complex as those impeding it earlier in the century. For decades, the FM band had been seen widely as a kind of highbrow wasteland, the province of classical music and didactic talk programming, earning jibes from cultural critics such as Woody Allen, who jokingly laments that he "sound[s] just like FM radio" in the 1977 film *Annie Hall*. Yet, a decade later, by the time Allen's nostalgic *Radio Days* was released in 1987, the industry had so completely adopted the new format that AM music radio seemed like a relic of the past.

Part of the slow-to-arrive, suddenly transformative success of FM was due to recent changes in America's socioeconomic organization and marketing landscape. With the success of the civil rights and women's rights movements in the 1960s, advertisers grew interested in developing relationships with the burgeoning ranks of the black and the female consumer bases. While many AM stations were ossified around old-fashioned formats that segmented audiences on the basis of traditional demographics, FM stations had the freedom to experiment with newer lifestyle and genre-driven formats, such as "Urban," that aimed for bigger audiences by combining black and white, male and female, and even members of different generations.

Another important (and related) factor was stylistic change. The radio entrepreneur and historian B. Eric Rhoads argues that "the death of AM came in 1978 when record promoter Robert Stigwood released the musical film *Saturday Night Fever*." Rhoads observes that disco's sudden explosion into the mainstream that year drove a record number of music listeners to new FM stations such as New York's WKTU, which "rose from nowhere to become New York's No. 1 station overnight," purely on the basis of its disco playlist. By the time the dance music sensation imploded a year or two later, he argues, the damage had been done; listeners had discovered the FM dial, and many would not return to AM.[12]

Perhaps the most important factor in the ascendancy of FM was a larger shift in popular music aesthetics across a range of different styles, all of them coevolving with innovations in recording technology. The development of cheap magnetic tape in the wake of World War II contributed to new multitrack studio techniques such as overdubbing and phasing, which were first introduced to popular music by experimenters like Les Paul in the 1950s, exploited fully for psychedelic effect by producers such as George Martin and Brian Wilson in the 1960s, and became standard practice in many genres by the 1970s. The most significant aesthetic consequence of multitrack studio techniques was, of course, multichannel sound (mostly stereo) and resulting innovations in both panning (e.g., location of instruments and voices in the sound field) and reverberation. However, the improvements in recording quality also contributed to a renewed emphasis on musical aspects such as dynamics (the loudness or softness of a given sound) and timbre (the unique "voice" of a given instrument or part). These new aesthetic trends made FM's ability to carry multichannel sound with less noise and richer bass stand out in stark contrast to AM's tinny mono signal. And as a new generation of adolescents and young adults, exposed to these innovative aesthetics via their local FM college radio stations, reached maturity, advertisers increasingly recognized the need to migrate with them to commercial FM stations that could adequately accommodate their stylistic tastes.

As with recording formats, then, radio broadcast technology has been shaped less by a teleological march toward sonic perfection than by a complex array of competing interests, technological innovations, and regulatory interventions. The recording industry both loves radio (for its promotional power) and hates it (for its cannibalizing potential), and has both impeded and assisted its technological development at different stages and in different ways over the years. And just as in the case of recording technologies, concerns about granting too much power to listeners (sometimes framed as "piracy") have been a significant factor throughout the development of this industry. If anything, these concerns have only increased since the ascendancy of FM, with newer broadcast platforms such as satellite radio, Internet radio, and digital radio offering new capacities—and with them, new perceived threats ranging from "stream-ripping," or the unpermitted download of online broadcasts, to the inclusion of DVR-style personal storage functionality in satellite radio receivers. As I discuss in chapter 1, "home taping" of FM radio failed to kill the music industry as promised (to the contrary, it inaugurated the greatest rise in music retail sales in history), but that hasn't stopped the recording industry from using both law and leverage to limit radio's functionality across both analog and digital platforms in the years since then. More on that later in the book.

Studio Wizardry and the Pro-Am Gap

Thus far I have discussed the music industry's love/hate relationship with technology in terms of distribution platforms. Innovations in broadcast and storage formats are both welcomed and feared for their disruptive potential, and both processes are driven in part by the push-pull dialectic between industry and consumer power. But there is another important field in which similar dynamics apply: namely, the ever-evolving world of music production technology.

As I argue in this book and elsewhere, the entire edifice of the recording industry is built on the premise that its value resides in delving into the muck of our shared culture, discovering sonic diamonds in the rough, then polishing them up and bringing them to market. This questionable premise is reinforced through television shows like *American Idol* and *The X Factor,* through countless boilerplate rags-to-rock puff pieces in the music press, and through a never-ending stream of self-congratulatory public relations events and communiqués, culminating in the annual Grammy awards, watched each year by approximately forty million simultaneous viewers. But the most powerful symbol of the music industry's assumed superiority to the broader musical culture resides within the music itself—specifically, in the persistent audible gap between the aesthetics of professional and amateur music production.

In the early years of the industry, the very fact of a sound recording's existence was enough to establish professional provenance. Unlike radio, which was fueled in its infancy by so-called amateur users, early recording equipment was expensive and complex enough that only a handful of professional institutions possessed the resources to generate a salable volume of recordings. And from the beginning, the circumstances of studio recording began to alter the aesthetics of popular music, as performers, composers, and producers adapted their arts to the music industry's technosocial requirements, and as the industry self-consciously privileged and celebrated aesthetic innovations that would emphasize the superiority of a professionally recorded performance. For example, the music theorist Mark Katz has extensively chronicled the ways in which innovative musical aesthetics ranging from classical violin vibrato to Ellingtonian jazz instrumentation to the "crooning" style of Frank Sinatra and Bing Crosby can be understood as "phonographic effects," or the product of the complex relationship of recording technologies, economics, and cultural forces.[13]

Over time, as the cost of recording equipment fell, an increasing number of independent and "home" studios appeared across the country, undermining the exceptional role of the major record companies. While they solidified their economic positions by cartelizing distribution channels to retail stores, they also needed to revamp their aesthetic styles in order to emphasize the difference in quality between their own products and independently produced music. Thus, a kind of cat-and-mouse game developed, whereby first, innovations in studio technology would emerge, often from outside the industry; second, the industry would adopt and refine these innovations, spending the capital to mainstream a "polished" version of the sound; then the cost for independent record producers to adopt a given innovation would drop to accessible levels, and it would become ubiquitous; whereby the cycle would repeat itself.

There are countless examples of this process in action, and an entire book could be written (and should be written) on this subject alone. For now, a few paragraphs will have to suffice. An interesting case, to which I've already alluded, is overdubbing. Before World War II and the introduction of magnetic tape in the United States, overdubbing was so difficult and expensive as to be something of a novelty technique. The multi-instrumentalist Sidney Bechet used overdubbing on a few recordings in 1941, playing six interlocking parts on songs such as "The Sheik of Araby" (which took three months to record and edit). The technique was sufficiently new that *Time* magazine called it a "unique stunt" in its review later that year.[14] It was also instantly perceived as a threat to working musicians—after all, Bechet hired no sidemen for the recording. Consequently, the AFM (the same group that would nix FM stereo a few years later) called for a ban on the technique and imposed a fine on Bechet's record label for what it perceived as exploitative labor relations. As he relates in his autobiography, "the newspaper men . . . raised so much hell that the union made the company pay me for seven men, and it was forbidden to do it again!"[15]

By the end of the decade, the war was over and magnetic tape was widely available. Experimentalists such as Les Paul in the United States and Pierre Schaeffer in France began to adapt the technology specifically for the purposes of multilayered sound composition. Although there were some early market successes (such as Paul's "Lover (When You're Near Me)"), it wasn't until the 1960s that major labels adopted it as a standard element in studio recordings. Throughout the next two decades, stereo multilayered sound became the hallmark of professional recording; it was one of the sonic factors that would immediately distinguish an independently produced "demo" from commercial products. By the end of the 1970s, producers like Donald Fagen and Walter Becker of Steely Dan had carried the technique to its logical extreme, crafting meticulously constructed recordings featuring opulently overdubbed instrumentation and vocalization (such as Michael McDonald's virtuosic background vocals on "Peg").

Many musicians and fans at the time balked against this newly elevated aesthetic standard, complaining that Steely Dan and similar bands were, as many have described them, "too perfect."[16] Resistant aesthetic movements such as punk music emerged at exactly this moment as well, championing a sound that was exuberantly and adamantly imperfect. Yet many independent musicians still aspired to commercial success, and to the aesthetics of the major labels. It was to serve these musicians that consumer electronics manufacturer TASCAM released the Portastudio, the first low-cost, cassette-based 4-track recording tool, in 1979. Using a device such as this, musicians without access to professional recording studios could overdub, multitrack, and emulate the sound of the industry. Naturally, this democratization of the technology undermined its value as a marker of superiority, and the industry moved quickly on to other studio technologies to maintain its dominance in this sonic arms race, using even newer tools such as digital fidelity, sample-based drum machines, and music sequencers in the 1980s.

This process has repeated, and accelerated, over the years. A recent example is pitch correction technology such as Auto-Tune, a digital software tool enabling producers to change the pitch of a recording, and primarily used to "fix" out-of-tune vocal tracks. When Auto-Tune was first released in 1997, it was essentially a trade secret, employed like airbrushing (or Photoshop) to cover the sonic blemishes of popular singers. Soon thereafter, the technology became incorporated more directly into popular music aesthetics, with inhuman, mechanical leaps between "perfect" pitches emerging in a range of popular musical styles, from Cher's 1998 dance music hit "Believe" to T-Pain's self-produced 2007 R&B hit "I'm Sprung." Over the course of the 2000s, the technology appeared in an increasing number of independently produced recordings, and then reached ubiquity in 2009 with the debut of YouTube viral video sensation *Auto-Tune the News,* quickly followed by the release (and market success) of a mobile application called "I Am T-Pain," which enabled any smartphone owner to auto-tune her own voice in real time, with a price tag of three dollars.

Predictably, with the democratization of pitch correction came its devaluation within the industry, and its waning as a mark of professional distinction. In 2009 the simmering resistance against its cyborgian aesthetic exploded into a full-scale backlash, led by some of the music industry's leading lights. Jay-Z's single "D.O.A. (Death of Auto-Tune),", released in the same year, perfectly captured this reactionary sentiment with lyrics such as "This ain't for iTunes / this ain't for sing-alongs / This is Sinatra at the opera." In other words, Jay-Z laments the role of pitch correction in the development of an aesthetic that privileges accessibility and collaboration (e.g., sing-alongs) and aligns himself with the music of elitism, virtuosity, and professionalism (e.g., Sinatra, opera).

Although pitch correction continues to be used on many if not most commercial tracks (including some by Jay-Z!), the backlash continues—especially against independent musicians who employ the software. For instance, in 2011 a thirteen-year-old girl named Rebecca Black became the subject of worldwide ridicule and vitriol (and became measurably the most-hated performer on YouTube) for the crime of releasing an amateur song and music video called "Friday" that used pitch correction technology in a noticeable but un-ironic fashion. One of her most voluble critics was Miley Cyrus, the teen pop star whose music is probably indistinguishable from Black's by the majority of Americans over the age of thirty. Although Cyrus later retracted her critique, the sentiment remains central to public discussions of the "Friday" phenomenon: amateurs who violate the aesthetic boundaries demarcating "real" musicians from wannabees will be punished and held up for public scorn as examples to the rest of us.

Paradoxically, one of the unintended consequences of the studio technology arms race has been the gradual weakening of the music industry's claims to aesthetic exceptionalism. As the onus to produce distinguishably commercial music has shifted farther and farther from musicians to music producers to technology manufacturers, claims the industry could once have made no longer ring true. For recording artists, for instance, a strong singing voice is not as important as it was in the jazz or rock eras. While it's true that Mary J. Blige and Adele have rich, well trained, powerful voices, the same claim cannot be made for equally successful singers like Rihanna or Jennifer Lopez, or indeed the majority of vocalists on the pop charts. Similarly, while A&R (artists & repertoire) executives at major labels once staked their reputations on their "golden ears," or their ability to hear a diamond in the rough, that work is increasingly shifting onto computerized music analysis services such as Polyphonic

HMI and Platinum Blue, which use predictive algorithms to "pick hits" on behalf of the labels. Research services then cross-index those findings with analyses of online consumer sentiment, leaving little room for surprise, intuition, or aesthetic innovation. In short, by allowing itself to become increasingly dependent on studio technology to set itself apart, the music industry has lost track of its primary source of legitimacy, undermining its already tenuous foundations.

CRITIQUES OF music industry anti-piracy campaigns are often framed in terms of the industry "hating technology" or being "resistant to innovation." Yet history shows that technological change has always been a central facet of the industry's evolution.

From the beginning, the music industry has viewed emerging technology as a double-edged sword, offering the promise of greater power and the threat of obsolescence in equal measure. The industry has often branded itself as a champion of both cultural and technological innovation, and has invested heavily in a narrative of perfectible fidelity and sonic quality in order to migrate consumers to new platforms that either increase industry power or boost sales and advertising revenues. Yet there is some truth in critics' accusations of music industry Luddism or obstructionism; innovative technologies like FM stereo have taken half a century to take root, while other promising developments have withered on the vine, because of political and economic factors rather than quality or potential market demand.

In addition to the record companies and broadcasters, several other stakeholders have played a role in the development of music technology; these include other music industry sectors such as publishers and musicians, as well as electronics and software manufacturers, government regulators, and consumers themselves. This last group has perhaps added the greatest amount of complexity to the process; production, distribution, and broadcast platforms can all be understood as battlefields on which the competing interests of music buyers and sellers vie for superiority, and this dialectical tension continues to steer technological development in unexpected directions.

We cannot understand the industry's reaction to recent innovative technologies such as peer-to-peer file sharing, the MP3, and the iPod without taking these historical processes into account. Just as "digital music piracy" is a concept that obfuscates the transient and ephemeral nature of the legal codes and economic systems it ostensibly threatens, the premise of "pirate technology" suggests a stable and unchanging technological system compromised by a rogue element. As I have argued in this chapter, nothing could be further from the case. The invention and adoption of these technologies are part of the same constellation of competing and collaborating forces that have shaped the evolution of music industry technology since the days of movable type. As I discuss in the next chapter, the industry's combative stance in the face of these innovations was a conscious choice among several possible strategies, rather than the only logical response to an inevitable threat.

CHAPTER 3

"We've Been Talking about This for Years"

The Music Industry's Five Stages of Grief

ONE OF THE most enduring myths about the "digital music revolution"[1] concerns the level of technological cluelessness and absence of foresight within the music industry at the close of the twentieth century. Whether you see them as victims or villains, canaries in the coal mine or endangered dinosaurs, you probably believe that the major record labels were taken unawares by the new century's innovations, and that the unforeseeable consequences of digital sharing are at the root of any problems the industry faces today.

If so, you're in good company. Most journalists, academics, and other chroniclers of the Internet age have repeated this myth so frequently over the past fifteen years that it's considered common knowledge. The industry was "unprepared"[2] and "surprised"[3] by MP3 and peer-to-peer file sharing technology, even "blindsided"[4] by it (a term I myself have invoked in a previous publication).[5] This myth functions primarily to generate sympathy and support for the decisions the major labels and other institutions have made in the wake of these innovations; after all, we may reason, they did the best they could on short notice under difficult and unprecedented circumstances. Had they seen the potentially transformative effects of digital technologies on the horizon, they could have made adequate preparations, and spared themselves and us a lot of trouble.

The problem is, this myth has very little basis in fact. In reality, the record industry knew better than anyone what the potential effects of digital and networked technologies would be, and still failed to act in a proactive and responsible manner. RIAA head Hilary Rosen acknowledged this much as early as 1999, a few months after the launch of Napster and subsequent to the record labels' defeat in a suit against the MP3 device manufacturer Diamond Multimedia. In Rosen's words, "It's not like MP3s caught us by surprise or anything. We've been talking about this for more than 10 years."[6] Even in retrospect, record industry executives have conceded that they suffered not from a lack of foresight but rather from a lack of vision. As Doug Morris, then the CEO of Universal Music Group, told *Wired* magazine in 2007, there's "a misconception writers make all the time, that the record industry missed this. They didn't. They just didn't know what to do."[7]

Yet, if Morris's account is descriptively accurate, it doesn't provide much in the way of analytical self-reflection. Why did the industry fail to act proactively on its market intelligence? Was is simply, as Morris suggested in his *Wired* interview, that "there's no one in the record company that's a technologist" and "we didn't know who to hire"?[8] This seems unlikely. First of all, as I argue in chapter 2, technological innovation was hardly an unfamiliar force within the music industry; to the contrary, it is a constitutive element of the business, and music distribution technology has always been in flux. Second, it is a matter of public record (and a fact to which I can personally attest, having known them) that the major labels employed a number of celebrated technologists and tech strategists during this period, including inventors and innovators such as Albhy Galuten, Ted Cohen, and Larry Kenswil.

If we rule out ignorance and inexperience, then, a far more likely explanation of the music industry's failure to meet the challenges of digital media head on can be found in its institutional culture and practices, or what we might metaphorically understand as the "psychology" of the companies involved. The law professor Michael Carrier insightfully describes these challenges in terms of an "innovator's dilemma," in which legacy industries have little short-term incentive or ability to innovate, even if the long-term circumstances demand it.[9] In public discussions of these matters, I've often made a similar argument using the framework of Elisabeth Kübler-Ross's famous "five stages of grief,"[10] which describes the process whereby grieving individuals deal with death and other forms of radical change. This is not a flippant comparison; having advised, researched, and reported on the music industry as an analyst, journalist, and academic between 1997 and the present day, I believe that it was precisely the sheer scope of potential market transformation implied by digital and networked technologies that provoked the music industry's strategic paralysis.[11]

Denial and Isolation: CD's "Original Sin" and the Rise of MP3

According to Kübler-Ross, the first stage of grief is denial, which can be followed or accompanied by an increasing sense of isolation from one's peers or surroundings. One could argue that the recording industry was in denial about the potentially transformative capacity of digital technologies from the very moment it introduced the compact disc as a new commercial music distribution format in 1982. This format, which was thoroughly vetted by all of the major labels and successfully won out over several competing digital prototypes,[12] was endowed with a kind of technological "original sin"—namely, that its digital information was unsecured by encryption or other means and therefore available to be copied freely by anyone using a computer equipped with an optical media drive, then copied and redistributed ad infinitum without any loss of quality.

Although we may think of CD "ripping" and "burning" as a uniquely twenty-first-century development, the plans to use compact discs for data storage and transmission were already in the works when music CDs were first introduced into the marketplace, and the first CD-ROM drives were available to consumers as early as 1985. Both music CDs and CD-ROMs reached market maturity in the 1990s, and by the time the CD had ascended as the dominant music format, pioneering CD-ROM publishers such as the Voyager Company were shipping millions of titles per year. Thus, while not every record label executive in the early 1980s necessarily had the expertise and the foresight to realize that the CD format betokened the end of their cartel's control over music distribution, it was hardly beyond consideration for their in-house technologists even in the earliest years, and would have been increasingly obvious to all interested parties well before the market transition from cassette to CD was complete. So why wasn't this new format aborted before it achieved ubiquity? Because, as I discuss further in chapter 5, CDs also yielded an unprecedented amount of revenue for the music industry and inaugurated the longest and steepest rise in total market value in the industry's century-long history. With an upside that large, why worry about the downside?

The industry exhibited a similar degree of willful blindness when it came to the potential market impact of digital distribution formats and the Internet. As the music industry journalist Steve Knopper relates in his excellent book *Appetite for Self-Destruction,* Fraunhofer, the developer of MP3 technology, "tried to warn the industry in the early 1990s" of the potentially volatile combination of unsecured CDs and its new encoding format, "but didn't get anywhere. 'There was not that much interest at the time,'" Knopper writes, quoting a Fraunhofer employee.[13]

As the 1990s wore on, CD-ROM drives became ubiquitous, and MP3 became an increasingly popular format on the Internet. Yet the industry appeared ever more isolated from its own artists and customers, continuing to operate its still-thriving CD business as though nothing much had changed. By the end of the decade, many industry analysts including me were clamoring publicly for the industry to embrace new technologies and distribution models, and proactively to release music in online digital formats before control over distribution eluded its grasp completely. Even the popular and trade press caught on and took the record labels to task for their inaction. As the *PC Magazine* columnist John C. Dvorak lamented in 1997, "While the music industry moans and groans, it obviously isn't doing the job needed. . . . This concept is not going to disappear, and the record companies should look at this as a new form of distribution."[14]

To be fair, many in the music industry paid lip service to what was then known as "digital distribution" in the mid-to-late 1990s. At virtually every meeting or conference I attended in the presence of record executives from 1997 to 1999, I was assured that a decisive digital music strategy was right around the corner, and that the industry was excited about the possibilities presented by new technologies. As Cary Sherman, then a senior executive vice president at the RIAA, told *Business Week* magazine in 1998, "We think digital distribution and the Net provide great opportunities, and we love that."[15] Yet very little in the way of actual digital music distribution materialized, and for online music fans, "pirate" tracks distributed on MP3-hosting websites were the only downloadable source of commercial music during these years.

The hemming and hawing, promises and procrastinations continued until the sudden rise of Napster in the summer of 1999, when the online explosion of MP3 content fueled by peer-to-peer file sharing would force the major labels to acknowledge that digital distribution had arrived without them. Yet even this sudden confrontation with reality would not be enough to bring the industry to its senses and encourage it to embrace a viable digital distribution strategy.

Anger: Lawsuits, Threats, and Propaganda

According to Kübler-Ross, the second stage of grief is characterized by anger, which in the case of medical patients can be "displaced in all directions and projected onto the environment at times almost at random."[16] This has been true in the case of the music industry as well, which responded to the popular emergence of digital music with a wide array of threats, accusations, and lawsuits aimed at virtually everyone involved in any way. Of course, neither threats nor lawsuits are new to the music business; in a way, they are the industry's lingua franca and modus operandi. But both the volume and the range of targets significantly expanded in the digital era, especially in contrast to the period of relative peace and plenty during the previous two decades.

The first digital music lawsuits took place in June 1997, when the RIAA and its constituents sued three noncommercial "Internet music archive sites," which allegedly hosted MP3s of music controlled by the major labels, available for free download. Even though all three websites were shut down by their publishers once legal action was taken, and the degree of market harm and potential amount of damages to be recovered were insignificant, the plaintiffs in the case acknowledged that the point was, as RIAA chief Hilary Rosen told a reporter at the time, to obtain a court "decision affirming the rights of copyright owners."[17] In other words, the aim was to set a precedent, and to send a warning.

This was the first drop in what would soon become a deluge of litigation against any Internet sites and services hosting or facilitating access to major label content, including high-profile lawsuits against innovators like Napster, the music locker service MP3.com, and the Internet radio pioneer LAUNCH Media, as well as countless other, less celebrated, defendants. In the meantime, a 1998 revision to copyright law called the Digital Millennium Copyright Act (DMCA) gave record labels and music publishers the power to issue "takedown notices" to any site or service they believed were violating their copyrights. As the law scholars Jennifer Urban and Laura Quilter have demonstrated, these takedown notices, which require no evidence or judicial oversight and entail a difficult appeals process, are routinely abused by copyright holders "to create leverage in a competitive marketplace, to protect rights not given by copyright . . . and to stifle criticism," while failing to adequately protect copyright in many legitimate cases.[18]

Wielding the DMCA in one hand and the threat of costly litigation in the other, the music industry effectively shut down hundreds or perhaps thousands[19] of independent web publishers, software developers, and service providers in the early years of the new century. There is little question that many of these sites and services were providing their users with major label music, or the means to access it, without a license. But they were also doing the socially and economically valuable work of exploring the capacities of emerging technologies, pioneering new business models, and developing the rudiments of twenty-first-century musical culture. A great many of them even sought licenses from the labels and publishers but were either rebuffed or offered rates that quickly would have put them out of business (more on this in chapter 7). To contemporary observers, the music industry's strategy was clear. As the *Los Angeles Times* (normally a great sympathizer with the content industry's perspective) described the scenario in a 2001 article, the "barrage of lawsuits by record labels" had "hampered the Web-based companies' innovation and growth."[20]

The music industry's legal assault wasn't limited to online sites and services; it also attempted to shut down or intimidate consumer electronics manufacturers and consumers themselves. As I mentioned above, the industry attempted to stem digital music usage by suing the manufacturer of the first portable MP3 player, Diamond Multimedia. But unlike most of the industry's claims against content and service companies, this lawsuit was unsuccessful, and the decision established a legal precedent that copying music from a hard drive to a portable device constituted a "personal use," and was not a right the music industry had the power to grant or withhold.[21] Notwithstanding this ruling (or perhaps in response to it), the Disney Corporation's CEO Michael Eisner testified before Congress in 2002, arguing that the "Rip. Mix. Burn." advertising campaign behind Apple's first-generation iPod was tantamount to telling consumers "that they can create a theft if they buy this computer."[22] Eisner's aim in this case was to convince Congress to pass new legislation undermining the Diamond precedent, requiring all consumer electronics and computer manufacturers to integrate copy protection into their devices, thereby preventing any unsanctioned uses of any music or video whatsoever (including, presumably, legally established "fair uses" such as backing up music collections or making mixtapes for personal consumption). Although the industry was unsuccessful in this particular campaign, its fantasy of total control over the distribution and use of all content has persisted over the past decade and has led to some highly problematic developments, as I discuss throughout this book.

Of course, the music industry hasn't limited the targets of its litigation to other businesses. In a 1999 interview, Hilary Rosen pledged not to sue individual music downloaders, arguing that "it doesn't seem practical. It's virtually impossible to do. . . . Besides, I have very strong views about privacy, so I'm not going to start doing it."[23] Despite these very good reasons, the RIAA began suing alleged music downloaders less than four years later, shortly after Rosen stepped down and ceded the reins to the veteran political operative Mitch Bainwol. The lawsuits, which targeted at least thirty-five thousand Americans, including a significant number of children, elderly, disabled, and deceased people, continued at least until the end of 2008, when the RIAA announced it would discontinue the strategy (although there is evidence that it continued the practice at least through 2010).[24]

These lawsuits alone suggest that the music industry views its customer base with a degree of suspicion bordering on contempt. Yet when viewed in combination with industry rhetoric claiming its own mission as analogous to the civil rights movement[25] and comparing unlicensed digital music users to shoplifters,[26] drug dealers, and terrorists[27] (no mere idle rhetoric, considering that the film industry and the FBI invoked the Patriot Act to pursue a fan of the TV show *Stargate SG-1* for allegedly infringing copyrights on his website),[28] a larger narrative emerges. The music industry, in its anger, has apparently cast itself as the hero in a tragedy of epic proportions. Like Michael Caine in the film *Zulu,* the industry believes itself to be the last bastion of civilization, outnumbered in a wilderness redoubt by a malevolent horde and firing endless volleys into the throng in a last-ditch effort to preserve itself. Of course, like the actual Zulu warriors of the nineteenth century, many of us cast in the role of "savages" are more likely to see ourselves as the protagonists, defending our ancestral homeland and our culture from our would-be colonial overlords.

Bargaining: The Myth of "Secure" Distribution

The third stage of grief, according to Kübler-Ross, is bargaining, which, she argues, is "really an attempt to postpone" the inevitable.[29] Following its long period of denial and its initial outburst of litigious anger, the music industry plunged headlong into the process of trying to negotiate a halt, or at least a deceleration, of the changes brought about by digital music technologies. It pursued this goal on a number of fronts, including bargaining with consumers about what they could and couldn't do with their music using digital rights management (DRM) technology, and bargaining with music sellers to reaffirm the dominance of the traditional wholesale / retail economic model. While these tactics did little to halt the advance of new digital music behaviors and technologies, they certainly slowed down the economic development of digital music as an industry and, by extension, undermined the financial well-being of the traditional music industry during a pivotal moment of transition.

Digital rights management, a technology that creates a kind of digital padlock around a file such as a song, movie, or game, seemed to many rights holders like a promising technology in the web's early years. As I myself proposed in a syndicated report I wrote as an analyst for Jupiter Research in 1999, "DRM is absolutely integral to protecting copyrights online. . . . The only way to track and prevent misuse of online intellectual property is through a proactive solution that includes both watermarking and secure distribution technology."[30] Although I tempered this message with the cautionary addendum that such a strategy would only work if the technology were also used to improve the consumer experience and develop new business models that moved beyond retail transactions, the overall vision was flawed. This is because it was based on the erroneous belief that control over online content distribution was still a viable option for the media industry.

The same month in which my DRM report was published, a college student named Shawn Fanning launched a new peer-to-peer (P2P) file sharing service called Napster, and within weeks it had spread like wildfire. By the end of the year, millions of people were swapping their entire MP3 libraries, making hundreds of millions of files available to one another. Previous industry estimates had placed the total number of MP3s on the web at somewhere near half a million, so this was an explosion in the range of three orders of magnitude. I quickly realized that my vision had been wrong and started to advocate for "post-Napster product formats"[31] that acknowledged the inevitability of free distribution and attempted to improve upon, rather than control, the P2P experience. Unfortunately, my clientele in the recording industry were more receptive to the earlier vision, and spent most of the next decade using DRM and other forms of "secure" distribution technology on virtually every song, album, and video they released, to disastrous effect.

The primary problem with DRM, of course, is that it doesn't work. Even if a million copies of a song are all locked down, preventing unlicensed users from listening to or sharing it, a single unfettered copy (such as one ripped from a CD) can be reproduced ad infinitum online. But its strategic problems run even deeper than this. For one thing, the restraints on fair use presented by DRM undermine consumer trust and patience—to say nothing of musical culture—and make unlicensed music from P2P networks or elsewhere seem even better by comparison. For another thing, DRM is prone to technical malfunction and tends to be used heavy-handedly, with content owners erring on the side of overprotection; even ostensibly permitted uses are often difficult for consumers to accomplish, and there is a frustrating propensity for "server error" messages.

In practice, DRM also presented many unforeseen strategic difficulties for retailers and forced them to violate their customers' trust even further. For instance, when high-profile digital music sellers such as Yahoo! and MSN decided to shut down their stores for financial reasons, they were forced to choose between maintaining their DRM servers indefinitely and at significant cost (which would allow consumers to continue listening to the songs they'd purchased), and shutting them down (which would cause all the music they'd sold over the years to become nonfunctional). In both cases, the companies chose the latter course, and consumers and artists lost out, with a significant blow to goodwill for both the retailers and the record labels. The opening sentence of a 2008 *Wired* article on the Yahoo! shutdown put it succinctly: "If you bought DRMed, copy-protected music, you are an idiot."[32]

As a final indignity, DRM actually ended up undermining the market power of the labels that used it, by increasing the leverage enjoyed by Apple, which used the technology to erect a "walled garden" around its iPod hardware, its iTunes software, and its digital music retail business, excluding third party retailers and manufacturers from the process and creating a near-monopoly. The industry, as it turns out, was stuck within a walled garden of its own. Once it had committed to DRM, it became increasingly difficult to disentangle its business model from the technology.

This was exacerbated by another, related form of bargaining on the part of the labels. If DRM functioned as a cybernetic straitjacket to lock consumers into an obsolete, pre-digital mode of consumption, it also helped to bolster the industry's obsolete, pre-digital economic models. Since the days of Edison's wax cylinders, record labels had made their money as a wholesale business, shipping products to retailers, who then marked them up and sold them to consumers. According to classical economics, this model is premised on a scarce, physically distributed commodity; each individual "unit" that is shipped and sold has a price determined by the intersection of supply and demand, and profitability is based on the ability of each party to eke out a margin on a per-unit basis.

Clearly, in the case of digital goods, which can be reproduced infinitely at any stage in the value chain at little or no incremental cost, the markup pricing model makes no sense for buyers, sellers, or content providers. Record labels can forego expensive manufacturing and distribution costs and focus their energies on developing and marketing music, while retailers, flush with an unlimited supply of product, can experiment with a wide range of price points and product formats, finding "sweet spots" that bring in the greatest consumer expenditures at the lowest cost of goods. Together, they can share in the benefits that accrue, while consumers can gain access to a higher volume and broader range of music at the same level of expenditure. It's a potential win-win-win situation. Yet, for a variety of reasons ranging from cautious skepticism to willful ignorance to entrenched power relations, the music industry failed to embrace this new set of opportunities, opting instead to artificially prolong the life of the traditional music wholesale model by using copyright (in lieu of physical control over distribution) as a mode of enforcement.

Nearly every digital music store (including some operated by the major labels themselves) crashed and burned under this model, hampering the growth of the digital music industry and undermining sales overall. While it's true that the exception, Apple, sold billions of dollars' worth of digital "singles," it is also widely acknowledged that the company has done so by selling music at zero profit margin, recognizing its upside from the sale of iPods and other high-cost devices whose value to consumers is increased by the availability of the digital music in the iTunes store. This, in turn, has exerted downward pressure on the ability of rival music sellers to sell at a higher rate, reducing the overall value of the industry and undermining competition across the board.

In 2007 (as the major labels began to discontinue the use of DRM for digital downloads) Edgar Bronfman Jr., then CEO of Warner Music Group, conceded during a speech at a business conference that the industry's attempts to stall digital music through these methods of bargaining had failed, and even backfired. In his own words:

> We used to fool ourselves. . . . We used to think our content was perfect just exactly as it was. We expected our business would remain blissfully unaffected even as the world of interactivity, constant connection and file sharing was exploding. And of course we were wrong. How were we wrong? By standing still or moving at a glacial pace, we inadvertently went to war with consumers by denying them what they wanted and could otherwise find and as a result of course, consumers won.[33]

Depression and Acceptance: Moving beyond the CD

The final stages of grief, Kübler-Ross tells us, are depression and acceptance. During the first decade of the twenty-first century, the music industry faced depression in both senses of the word. Economically, the traditional music retail market imploded; global music sales plummeted from roughly $44 billion in 2000 to $28 billion in 2011.[34] Although this is certainly a precipitous drop, the economic impact wasn't quite as dire as it may appear at first glance. As I discuss in greater detail in chapter 5, the losses were, to an extent, both foreseeable and preventable, and they were also offset by a number of economic gains not reflected in these figures. Yet there is little question that the market data reveal a profound transition in music industry economics, with fundamentally destabilizing effects that worked to the benefit of some and to the detriment of others.

Emotionally and culturally, it was a decade of depression as well. There was a growing sense of unease and frustration among many throughout the industry, from recording artists to executives to support staff. For some, it was merely a sense of impending doom associated with the bad market data and waves of layoffs. Yet there was also a pervasive sense, especially among some of the most successful artists and highly placed executives, that the music industry was either hopelessly obstinate or otherwise incapable of adapting to the new reality of empowered consumers and digital distribution networks. In public, most hewed to the RIAA narrative, excoriating digital upstarts and their user bases for destroying a venerable industry. But privately, many expressed bafflement or outrage at the slow pace of change within their own organizations and among their partners. Anyone who worked in or around the music industry during these years can attest to this.

I can't share the sources or contents of my private communications with executives and artists critical of their own organizations (beyond the interviews in chapter 7), but the corollary of these opinions can be seen in the exodus of some of the industry's most visionary thinkers and most powerful businesspeople from the major labels. The list is far too long to publish in full, but some notable examples include executives such as Michael Nash (former head of digital strategy for Warner Music Group), Cory Ondrejka (former head of digital strategy for EMI; he returned to his tech origins by working for Facebook), Larry Kenswil (former head of digital strategy for Universal Music Group, now an attorney), and Strauss Zelnick (former CEO of BMG Entertainment; he left the music industry to run Take-Two, a video game publisher), as well as recording artists such as Radiohead, Prince, Nine Inch Nails,[35] Ok Go, and Madonna,[36] all of whom abandoned their major label contracts in the midst of thriving careers.

When I first started using Kübler-Ross's framework as an explanatory metaphor for the music industry's self-immolation in 2006, there was scant evidence of the fifth phase, acceptance. At the time, I cited a promising (if poorly named) initiative called SpiralFrog, the first digital music service to offer licensed major label downloads for free in an advertising-supported environment,[37] as well as highly publicized plans for Warner Music Group to launch an "e-label" for online-only music distribution, granting artists control over their own copyrights.[38] Although the major labels were still primarily dependent on the CD format and deep in the grip of DRM, it appeared they were at least willing to consider a way forward.

In the years since then, the music industry has taken major strides to move beyond its twentieth-century business models and technologies. Depression has abated somewhat and acceptance has been on the rise. Starting in 2007, the major labels allowed iTunes and other retailers to begin selling digital downloads without DRM. The recording industry appears largely to have stopped suing customers in 2008. Labels and publishers have granted licenses to some high-profile digital music sellers employing novel, twenty-first-century business models, including "cloud" music services such as Apple's iCloud and "freemium" mobile subscription providers like Spotify. And there have even been some mea culpas from senior music industry executives, like Edgar Bronfman Jr.'s quoted above and the acknowledgment by Geoff Taylor (CEO of the British collection society BPI) that "I, for one, regret that we weren't faster in figuring out how to create a sustainable model for music on the internet."[39] The music economy seems to be responding to these changes; in 2011, the RIAA reported that music retail sales revenue had climbed for the first time in seven years, driven primarily by digital music.[40]

Yet for all the indications that the music industry is beginning to work through its challenges and biases, in many ways it is still mired in the legal, economic, and ideological detritus of the past. Rather than ceding copyright to creators, the labels have been fighting tooth and nail to prevent their artists from regaining control over their own work per the "reversion" clause of the 1976 Copyright Act,[41] while insisting that newly signed artists agree to "360 deals" that grant labels a much broader ownership stake over an artist's work and life than traditional contracts did.[42] And despite their refreshing willingness to grant licenses to innovators like Spotify, the labels are still essentially requiring that licensees pay them on a "per use" basis, rather than collecting a share of revenues, a condition that structurally excludes smaller and more innovative companies from competing with the well-funded Apples and Googles of the world, and makes it difficult for any music seller, no matter how large, to recognize a profit.

Underpinning all of these decisions is the recording industry's continuing commitment to a narrative in which it plays the role of victim and the Internet's billions of users are painted as aggressors or, at best, suspects. In the name of this narrative, which routinely invokes Napster as the ground zero in this imagined assault, the industry has pushed, and continues to push, for the enactment of laws and treaties that would effectively subject people around the world to a degree of digital surveillance and censorship that has no precedent in free society.

PART II

Who Really Killed the Music Industry?

In Agatha Christie's classic detective novel *The Murder of Roger Ackroyd,* the titular character is killed, and nearly everyone he knew immediately becomes a suspect, from the obligatory butler to members of the victim's own family. At the end of the book, it turns out (spoiler alert) that the narrator himself, who is assisting detective Hercule Poirot in his investigations, is to blame for the heinous deed. In his "Apologia," the murderer even confesses to being "rather pleased with myself as a writer," for having told the story in a way that obscured his own guilt, thereby shifting the readers' focus to the other, innocent suspects.

In the narrative of the music industry's decline since the turn of the century, a very similar dynamic is at work. This narrative, which has been constructed and promoted aggressively by the music industry itself, positions the steep drop in music retail sales revenue as a kind of industrial murder, and fingers nearly everyone for the blame, from digital music startups to major companies like Google and Apple to the hundreds of millions of people who use their products. P2P file sharing even plays the role of the butler, as the inevitable primary suspect. In truth (spoiler alert), it is the music industry itself that deserves the bulk of the blame for its own misfortunes, a fact it has tried its best to obscure by carefully curating the narrative to emphasize some details while obscuring others.

My aim in this section is to debunk the music industry's version of events and offer a more thorough counter-narrative that fully explores the industry's own role in the process, while exonerating those parties who have been wrongfully accused. I begin with the "butler," examining the pros and cons of P2P and showing that it can't reasonably be blamed for the majority of the music market contraction. I then move on to examine the many economic factors that contributed to the boom in music sales revenue during the 1990s and the bust in the following decade, and describe the music industry's decisions that contributed to both boom and bust. Finally, I review some of the ways in which the industry's own methods of doing business with partners, musicians, and consumers has eroded its goodwill, further undermining its market value and revenue potential.

CHAPTER 4

Dissecting the Bogeyman

How Bad Is P2P, Anyway?

So-called digital music piracy comes in many flavors. The music industry's earliest online targets for litigation, in the mid to late 1990s, were MP3-sharing websites, simple platforms that enabled user X to upload a song to a web server, and user Y to download it. As Internet technology has exploded over the past decade and a half, fueled by at least three waves of investment frenzy, surging global demand, and the unrelenting pace of Moore's law,[1] enterprising developers have conceived of countless new variations on this theme.

Why is music sharing such a popular application for computer programmers to develop? Since the first MP3 was posted to the web, the challenge of sharing and obtaining digital music has been, as coders would say, "trivial." Yet it remains one of the most popular functions of new programs by independent developers, startups, and big software firms alike. The universal popularity of music itself is partially responsible for this trend. As I discuss in chapter 1, music is an integral element of human culture and consciousness, and therefore it should not be surprising that we seek it out in every medium we develop. Music's ubiquity and universality also make it an ideal test case for software developers to try out new ideas. It's easy to find content, easy to build a user base, easy to manipulate relatively small files like MP3s, and easy to find existing code libraries, APIs (application programming interfaces), SDKs (software development kits), and other building blocks for new software projects.

Yet the allure of music sharing applications can likely be attributed to more than the appeal of the content or the ease of production. Just as computer hackers are engaged in what the infamous hacker-consultant Kevin Mitnick calls a "constant cat-and-mouse game"[2] with their intended targets and cybersecurity forces, music software developers and their users are always looking for ways around the legal, technological, and social roadblocks that the music industry erects in cyberspace. Whether it's creating a method of sharing that falls on the legal side of the latest court decision or a method of decryption that cracks the latest form of DRM, the fundamental psychosocial pull of music, combined with the unique thrill of resisting the imposition of authority, has helped to generate a hothouse environment in which music software innovation has flourished. In other words, the industry's own efforts at cracking down on unlicensed music distribution have been a crucial element in driving both software developers and music fans to explore newer and more esoteric methods of sharing.

This activity hasn't stopped the music industry from trying, however, nor discouraged it from branding an ever-wider range of activities and technologies as "piracy." Yet the poster child for the industry's economic and strategic woes continues to be its bête noire, peer-to-peer file sharing. Even in 2012, more than a decade after the service was shut down and then sold to Bertelsmann, which at the time owned the major label BMG, RIAA chief Cary Sherman published a blistering op-ed in the *New York Times,* tracing the origin of his industry's malaise to the 1999 launch of Napster.[3] Dubious though this claim is, it remains a vital element in the music industry's narrative of its own decline, which in turn is foundational to the industry's calls for more sweeping copyright powers, as well as enhanced surveillance and censorship of digital communications platforms.

Yet the case against P2P and online music sharing in general, like many of the music industry's claims, is not nearly so damning as it may appear on the surface. It is manifestly true that for some sharers, under some circumstances, P2P is used as a replacement for legal music sales and therefore has a negative economic impact on record labels, publishers, and some recording artists and composers. More broadly speaking, P2P has also been one of several factors that have undermined the market value of traditional music distribution formats such as CDs, by rendering the social practices, modes of listening, and economic models inherent to these older technologies obsolete. But, as it turns out, music sharing has had beneficial effects as well, both economically and socially. For some P2P users, it provides the opportunity to sample music freely before spending money on it. For businesses, it provides a valuable channel for marketing and research. Socially, it provided the first broadly accessible platform for people to gain access to a significant volume of music beyond their "comfort zones," contributing to a more sophisticated musical culture that transcends the generic boundaries imposed by the economics of mass production and mass media. And for a great many musicians and composers, it has provided a powerful platform for self-promotion and independent distribution that has allowed them to catapult into broader awareness and to take a more active role in their own careers than they would have had in the twentieth-century music industry.

Given the range of factors at work, it would be impossible to judge P2P and online music sharing as "net positive" or a "net negative" for the music industry or musical culture overall. Any claims in either direction are likely to be so limited in scope as to be irrelevant, or so biased as to be disinformative. Yet it is possible to take a close look at the technology's many pros and cons, and in so doing, to understand better its uses and threats to specific parties under specific conditions.

How Does P2P Work?

Before exploring the social and economic ramifications of peer-to-peer file sharing, it would be helpful to review some of the key concepts and components of this platform. There is no single technology, protocol, or architecture underpinning P2P, nor is there even a clear boundary separating P2P from other forms of online information-sharing. Although it typically gets represented as a kind of digital black market, a shady back alley where contraband and counterfeits flourish free from the prying eyes of the authorities, this representation is wrong on at least two important counts. First, P2P isn't a "place" any more than e-mail or instant messaging is a place. It is simply a collection of diverse and often competing technologies, any of which may enable two or more users (or "peers") to share digital information, encoded in a file of any kind. Like e-mail, this platform may be accessed via a web site or via a stand-alone application, yet it is independent of these avenues of entry. In the parlance of computer developers, these websites and applications are "front-ends," and the P2P protocol or network in question is the "back-end."

Second, there is nothing necessarily shady or illicit about the material being shared on these networks—at least, no more than is the case for any other communication network, such as e-mail, telephone, or the US mail. And, though some P2P networks are "closed," requiring invitations or other credentials for participation—a safeguard typically used for quality control as well as privacy—the vast majority of file sharing takes place on "open" networks, which are as accessible and subject to surveillance as the web, and far more transparent than e-mail or instant messaging.

Not only are there dozens of rival back-end technology platforms for P2P file sharing and hundreds of front-ends via which to access them, there is also a wide range of different architectures for the networks themselves.[4] Some platforms, such as the original Napster, are centralized, meaning that all the information about who is searching for what travels through a single server, which has a kind of god's-eye-view on the activities of each peer. Other networks, such as Gnutella, are unstructured; there is no center to the network, and each peer has only a limited view of the network based on information from the other peers to which it is randomly connected. While Napster and Gnutella facilitate the exchange of complete files, such as MP3s, between any two given peers, BitTorrent (currently the most popular P2P protocol) breaks down files into their component bits, and requires that users go through a somewhat complex process to collect and reassemble those bits into a complete file. A peer enters the network by opening a "torrent"—a small text document containing information about the file in question, generally hosted on a website and discoverable through a specialized search engine called an "index." The torrent then directs the user's software to a "tracker," which is a database containing a list of other peers that currently have all or part of the file. The user's computer then collects bits of the file from each of these other peers and, once it has all of the file's bits, reconstructs them into the file itself. At no point does an individual peer deliver an entire song, movie, document, or other file directly to another individual peer, nor is there a central node from which a god's-eye-view of the network is attainable. There are several other variations on P2P network architectures, but currently these are the three primary flavors—the vanilla, chocolate, and strawberry of file sharing.

These distinctions are neither academic nor sheer computer science geekery. They have profound implications for the degree of culpability, surveillance, and censorship the networks themselves can be legally assigned or subjected to. Napster, owing to its centralized architecture, was the most vulnerable to both legal and technical challenges. Because the service was capable of identifying copyrighted files on its servers and restricting their transfer, it was found liable for "contributory infringement" and "vicarious infringement" for the unlicensed sharing behaviors of its users.[5] Once its servers were shut down, the service became unusable.

The same could not be said of more decentralized file sharing services such as Grokster and LimeWire.[6] Because these file sharing services lacked network oversight and therefore could not be found liable for contributory or vicarious infringement, they were ultimately found liable for "inducement" of copyright infringement, a new legal standard that emerged from the US Supreme Court's decision in the Grokster case.[7] Yet despite these rulings, the networks were not as easy to shut down as Napster was. For instance, even though LimeWire stopped publishing its software and remotely disabled many of its users' copies via a "back door" in the program's code, an open-source "Pirate Edition" of the software emerged two days later and remains fully functional and active at the time of writing despite the efforts of LimeWire and the RIAA to shut it down.[8]

BitTorrent is the most difficult "flavor" of P2P to prosecute or contain successfully. Because the BitTorrent protocol is freely available for programmers to use, there are many open-source software front-ends based on it, each of which operates completely independently of its developer, BitTorrent Inc. And because the sharing process is broken up into so many moving parts and reduced to the scale of bits, issues of legal liability become far more complex. Is hosting or contributing to an index a violation of copyright, even though the torrent file is only a text file *about* a copyrighted work, rather than the work itself? Is joining or maintaining a tracker a violation of copyright, even if the tracker is neither contributing to nor inducing infringement, in a legal sense? Is there a *de minimis,* or a minimum number of digital 1s and 0s that need to be shared by a given peer before they constitute an infringement? Would sharing a single bit of data, technically indistinguishable from any other bit of data on the Internet, constitute infringement if it were related to a torrent for a song or a film? These questions have yet to be addressed definitively by either legislation or case law, although the music and film industries, as well as several governments around the globe, have taken legal and quasi-legal action against many parties including scores of trackers and hundreds of thousands of individual BitTorrent users.

In short, P2P file sharing is not simply a piece of "rogue technology" that enables "pirates" to infringe on copyrights. It is a diverse assortment of technologies and platforms with a broad range of uses in a variety of different contexts. While some specific P2P architectures are vulnerable to some varieties of legal challenges and technological restrictions, others are technically legal or as yet untested, and many remain impervious to any kind of legal or technological regulation except perhaps total surveillance or closure of all digital communications networks. And, as network technologies continue to evolve in the coming years, it is likely that the range and complexity of P2P platforms will increase as well. There is no preordained path for social or technological development, but it seems very likely that in the near future, our mobile devices will be able to establish ad hoc, locally aware P2P networks[9] that eschew Internet traffic altogether and remain virtually undetectable and beyond surveillance by centralized authorities. Torrent tracker The Pirate Bay has already made moves in a similar direction, announcing plans on its blog to launch low-orbit drone airplanes hosting its servers.[10] Given the likelihood that technological developments such as these will continue to outpace efforts at policing and enforcement,[11] any economic or legal strategy that attempts to contain P2P rather than accept and embrace it is very likely to fail.

Does P2P Hurt the Music Industry?

One of the primary reasons that the traditional music industry views P2P as such a threat is because it disrupts conventional power relations. During the twentieth century, the major labels built their empires on the basis of a distribution cartel; only the "big six" (as things stood in 1999, before recent waves of consolidation) had the economic might and the political heft to saturate retailers and airwaves alike with their music. Independent artists and labels were either left out in the cold, or charged an exorbitant rate to participate in the marketplace. And music fans were essentially left with a choice between musical Coke and Pepsi; unless they were fortunate enough to live near an indie music retailer or a free-form radio broadcaster, their options were limited to whatever the major labels were promoting at that moment.

P2P changed this dynamic profoundly, by leveling the playing field and lowering the barriers for music distribution. Although this process didn't erase the strategic benefits accruing to large industrial organizations (marketing still costs a fortune), it did undermine one of the core mechanisms by which they accrued and retained market power. Yet when the music industry critiques P2P and decries the "piracy" that takes place on file sharing networks, it rarely does so by complaining that its distribution cartel has been compromised. Instead, it argues a more direct economic threat, that consumers use file sharing networks as an alternative to paying for music and therefore that every download on a P2P network can be viewed as a "lost sale."

Clearly, this notion is absurd if it's taken literally; so much music is downloaded freely from the Internet that if each downloaded song were sold at market value the total amount of money spent would outstrip the music industry's revenues, even in the best of years, by orders of magnitude. US District Court Judge James P. Jones, adjudicating a case brought against Daniel Dove, a member of a BitTorrent tracker site called Elite-Torrents, has pointed this out as well. In his decision, he faults the music industry's logic, observing that the "RIAA's request problematically assumes that every illegal download resulted in a lost sale," and pointing out that "it is a basic principle of economics that as price increases, demand decreases. Customers who download music and movies for free would not necessarily spend money to acquire the same product."[12] Yet logic would dictate that if not every download represents a lost sale, at least some of them must. And doesn't this subset of downloads directly hurt the music industry's bottom line?

Researchers have been grappling with this question—attempting to assess and quantify the impact of P2P on music sales revenues—at least since Napster's debut. I was among the first to publish findings on this subject, as an analyst for Jupiter Research in 2000. At the time, my clients included the RIAA and all of the major labels, so my purpose was to help the industry assess whether a genuine threat existed, and to develop market strategies that would mitigate or accommodate these new technologies. We employed a robust methodology, fielding a survey of over two thousand US "online music fans."[13] At one point in the survey, we asked whether respondents' purchasing habits had increased, decreased, or remained consistent since they first started visiting music sites. At another point, we asked whether they had ever used Napster. Given the range and order of questions on the survey, there was no way respondents could know that we were looking for a statistical relationship between these two factors.[14] Our results were surprising, even to us:

> No segment of respondents was more likely as a whole to have increased its music purchasing than the segment of Napster users was. . . . Napster users were 45 percent more likely to have increased their music purchasing habits than online music fans who don't use the software were. This trend holds true regardless of factors such as age, income, online tenure (the number of years that an individual has been using the Web), and overall music purchasing level.[15]

In other words, we found that, among online adults who liked music, *Napster was actually helping music sales.* Although some were no doubt using the service as a replacement for traditional music retail, others were using it as a vehicle to discover and sample new music, increasing their enthusiasm about music products and driving them to purchase more. In 2002, I published follow-up research, based on a newer Jupiter survey, showing that file sharing continued to have a mixed effect on music purchasing habits, with a net positive effect overall. This time, we found that file sharers were 75 percent more likely than the average online music fan to have increased their music purchasing habits since they started visiting online music sites.[16]

In the decade since then, dozens of researchers worldwide have published scores of studies on this subject in both academic and commercial venues, and the results have run the gamut from positive to neutral to negative for the industry. A thorough review of all the relevant literature is beyond the scope of this chapter, but there are several recently published meta-analyses that attempt to summarize and integrate this literature. The business professors Felix Oberholzer-Gee and Koleman Strumpf have been among the most active in this area, publishing a number of frequently cited articles on P2P and media economics since 2004. As they argue in their most recent work on the subject, "because the theoretical results are inconclusive, the effect of file sharing on industry profitability is largely an empirical question." Yet, reviewing the empirical literature, they find that "the results are decidedly mixed." While "the majority of studies find that file sharing reduces sales," there are several that "document a positive effect," and "an important group of papers reports that file sharing does not hurt sales at all."[17] In short, there is no research consensus on the subject, either theoretically or empirically. Similarly, the technology journalist Drew Wilson has recently published an extensive series on the P2P news website *ZeroPaid* analyzing twenty published research reports related to P2P's economic effects. He has found that a great deal of the research undermines the RIAA's claims, and that some of the corroborating research uses spurious logic or questionable methodologies.[18]

If we can conclude anything at all from the research in this field, it's that the relationship between P2P and music economics is anything but simple. Studies have produced variant findings in part because different groups of people share music in different ways, at different times, under different circumstances, for different reasons. Similarly, the music industry has undergone significant changes in recent years owing to a variety of factors, many of which are so closely related to P2P that it's hard to control for one and measure the impact of the other independently (I discuss these other factors in chapter 5).

Even framing the question introduces difficulties. If we look only at music "sales," are we ignoring revenues that accrue from non-retail sources such as licensing and subscriptions? If we look at "industry profitability," which firms count as "industry" and which don't, and whose numbers are we going to use to assess profit and loss? If we are interested in the total "economic impact" of P2P, do we take into account second-order effects such as sales of concert tickets and merchandise, or word-of-mouth marketing? To my knowledge, nobody has yet addressed these questions definitively, and it's entirely likely that a definitive answer is downright impossible. Far from being an unmitigated threat to the bottom line for artists, composers, labels, and other stakeholders in the music economy, P2P is more of a digital Rorschach test; any assessment of it is far more likely to reflect the viewer's biases and preconceptions than to represent an objective measure of its total impact on the marketplace.

Economic and Social Benefits of P2P

Although the net economic impact of P2P on the music retail marketplace is an open question, there is ample evidence to suggest that, in many cases, it contributes substantially to record label bottom lines and has a positive effect on the broader music economy, and that it has other beneficial social and cultural effects that can't be quantified. Even the major labels have come to recognize many of these benefits, repositioning themselves to take advantage of the newly energized, P2P-driven fan base for their artists. In recent years, traditional artist contracts have been largely supplanted by "360 deals," in which a record label or other institution (e.g., the concert promoter LiveNation) will participate in all artist revenue streams including recordings, concerts, merchandise, publishing, endorsements, and licensing. Because of the diversification and control that 360 deals offer labels, they are so lucrative and low-overhead that they've come under heavy fire from pro-artist advocates. In the words of the industry analyst Bob Lefsetz, who advised aspiring artists against signing such deals, "they want more of YOUR money for doing less work."[19]

Between these 360 deals and a host of other emerging revenue streams, record labels have significantly offset the decreases in album retail revenues over the past decade or two. These new revenues typically aren't reflected in the infamous figures depicting the music industry's precipitous decline, and are rarely mentioned in the industry's piracy crusade rhetoric. Some of the most significant new revenue sources for labels include:

Performance rights royalties. This category includes the licensed use of music in broadcast, specifically royalties from satellite, digital and Internet broadcasting. A decade ago, these revenues were virtually nonexistent, because AM/FM radio in the United States pays royalties only to publishers. But in 2011, according to the IFPI, global performance rights from these new, digital broadcast platforms yielded $905 million in revenue for labels.[20] It is important to note that, unlike sales revenues, the labels are not required to pay artist royalties on this income; an additional $905 million in royalties (or thereabouts) were paid directly to artists and unions by collection societies.

Synch rights royalties. In addition to the licensing revenues described above, record labels receive synchronization or "master use rights" revenues whenever their songs are used in television shows, video games, movies, or commercials. The music industry only began reporting revenues from this source in 2012, when it claimed $342 million for the previous year. The IFPI, which bases its estimates on revenues reported by member labels, may be underestimating the actual figure considerably. In 2011, the music licensing attorney Steve Gordon (a former major label executive and widely read author)[21] told me that "in the last 20 years, master use licensing has gone way up and become a new, important income source for the labels."[22] Overall, Gordon estimates that this market brings the labels closer to $1–2 billion per year.

Live events. The live music events sector has climbed steeply in value over the past decade, as ticket prices have escalated and audiences awash in digital recordings increasingly crave live contact with their favorite artists. Today, this sector is worth well over $20 billion annually, roughly three times what it was a decade ago. It's difficult to say what percentage of this accrues to labels through 360 deals, but a conservative estimate would be over $1 billion and growing, compared with zero a decade ago. There is little question that free online music sharing has played a significant role in driving these gains; as Lady Gaga told the *Sunday Times* in 2010, she "doesn't mind about people downloading her music for free, 'because you know how much you can earn off touring, right? . . . Make music—then tour. It's just the way it is today.'"[23]

Sponsorships and endorsements. Traditionally, many popular musicians have turned their noses up at corporate sponsorship, viewing it as a form of "selling out" that reflected poorly on their perceived authenticity. This attitude has changed in recent years, as the amount of money spent on music sponsorship in North America alone has climbed to $1.17 billion in 2011,[24] up from $867 million in 2007.[25] Again, it is difficult to specify a specific percentage of this figure that flows into record label coffers, but the amount is probably in the high tens or low hundreds of millions of dollars a year.

Hardware royalties. In various countries worldwide, record labels earn royalties on the sale of various forms of storage media (e.g., CD-Rs, DATs) and hardware devices (e.g., MP3 players, CD burners), which are both markets driven by free music sharing. It's difficult to establish exactly the volume of revenues accruing to labels from this sector, but given that these product categories represent tens of billions of dollars in sales each year, the figure must be considerable.

Thus, while the amount of money accruing to large record labels from the direct sale of music to consumers has dropped significantly over the past decade, these losses have been mitigated to a great degree by a variety of new and rapidly growing sources of revenue, driven in part by the free distribution of music via online channels. Although it's very difficult to establish whether this nets positively or negatively for any given record label or even for record labels as a sector, there are a number of recent analyses by researchers around the world that provide compelling evidence that free music sharing has contributed to an increase in revenue for musicians themselves and for the music economy overall.[26] For instance, based on a variety of sources, the editors of *techdirt,* a prominent media and technology blog, have shown that the musicians' share of the overall US music economy grew 16 percent between 2002 and 2010, to $16.7 billion, while the overall entertainment economy has grown by 50 percent in the past decade.[27] Even the IFPI's own figures show that an economic index it calls "the broader music industry" (an amorphous and changing category including some forms of consumer spending that don't directly affect the labels' bottom lines) has grown from $132 billion in 2005 to $168 billion in 2010. A great many prominent recording and performing artists have acknowledged this publicly as well. As 50 Cent told an interviewer in 2007, "What is important for the music industry to understand is that this really doesn't hurt the artists. . . . A young fan may be just as devout and dedicated no matter if he bought it or stole it."[28]

These findings have already had policy implications that contrast sharply with the recommendations of the IFPI and other piracy crusaders. For instance, immediately following the 2011 release of a report it had commissioned on the subject, the Swiss government announced that it would allow its citizens to download copyrighted content freely, from unlicensed channels, for personal use. The Swiss report found that money saved by consumers via P2P was being reinvested in newer, more innovative entertainment products and cultural practices, while anti-piracy efforts simply cost more than they saved, both economically and socially. As the authors of the report argue, the process is necessarily one of Darwinian adaptation: "Winners will be those who are able to use the new technology to their advantages and losers those who missed this development and continue to follow old business models."[29]

In addition to the more quantifiable dimensions of P2P's economic impact, it offers several widely acknowledged benefits for artists, labels, and musical culture in general. One of its most valuable roles for the industry at large is as a conduit for marketing and promotion, providing a platform for new and emerging musicians to find a listener base, for established artists to deepen their relationship with their fans, and for record labels and other industry organizations to defray some of the costs of traditional media. Terra Firma, the private equity firm that owned EMI at the time, acknowledged this in its 2007 Annual Review, writing that "historically, the industry has viewed digital principally as a piracy threat. In reality, it offers new possibilities across the value chain, from discovering and producing through to promoting music."[30] In fact, the labels have exploited the user bases of online file sharing networks for marketing and distribution for years, partnering with platform providers like SNOCAP, QTrax, and Grooveshark to place commercial tracks within peer-to-peer environments and relying on consumers to promote and distribute both free and for-pay digital music on their behalf. Many of the world's best-known recording artists have embraced this principle as well, either explicitly leveraging P2P as a marketing and distribution platform or simply acknowledging its value as a conduit for fan relations. As Shakira told the *Daily Mail* in 2009, "I like what's going on [with file sharing] because I feel closer to the fans and the people who appreciate the music. . . . It's the democratisation of music in a way. And music is a gift. That's what it should be, a gift."[31]

Online music-sharing platforms and social media have also proven a vital platform for artists, labels, and other content providers to research the marketplace more effectively. This is hardly a new idea; in 1999, I published a research report advising entertainment companies to track the usage of downloaded material "to better understand their markets in aggregate and to build closer relationships with individual consumers,"[32] and even back then, popular acts like Rage Against the Machine[33] and Tom Petty[34] were already leaking tracks online both to gauge and to stoke consumer demand (and also to cash in on the inevitable press coverage). In the years since then, first a cottage industry and then a mature market research sector have emerged around delivering "intelligence" to record labels, movie studios, and software publishers based on the analysis of free sharing, commenting, and linking on social platforms including P2P.[35] Today, both newer firms such as MusicMetric, Next Big Sound, and BigChampagne (perhaps the first to track actual P2P behaviors in aggregate for a market research product), and established research titans such Nielsen and NPD offer such products, and they are used widely throughout the media and entertainment industries.

Beyond the business and economic spheres, P2P also serves some important social functions. One effect has been to broaden significantly what we might call the "musical public sphere." In the pre-Internet music industry, there were only three channels providing an opportunity for recording artists to share their work with potential fans: retail, radio, and television. Each of these channels was, and continues to be, highly concentrated in its ownership structure, as in the record label sector. This high concentration, along with the native technological limitations of traditional media (e.g., limited shelf space and airtime) drastically diminishes the number and range of artists who are able to share their work through such channels. Internet-based distribution, especially P2P file sharing, eliminated these bottlenecks. While a commercial radio station may play fewer than a hundred artists' work in a given week, and Walmart's shelves may carry a few hundred at best, millions of artists have the capacity to reach their audiences around the world via the "long tail"[36] of P2P networks.

These networks are also largely immune to the influence of payola[37] and other anticompetitive forms of promotion that have plagued traditional broadcast media virtually since their inception. As a result, music fans are able to develop their tastes based primarily on their social connections to other fans instead of being dependent on media gatekeepers who have been paid to keep most artists and styles out of the public eye (and ear). Thus, as several researchers have shown, P2P has both improved the accuracy with which consumers are able to match music to their tastes and broadened those tastes.[38] For musical culture in general, P2P increases the prevalence of diverse and innovative music and also allows songs, artists, and styles to remain in the public ear far beyond their traditional market lifespan. As the music blogger Eric Lumbleau, editor of *Mutant Sounds,* argued in a recent *Wire* magazine article, free music sharing serves an important social function: "File sharers uploading rare and out of print records challenge official histories of music." This activity has not only helped to democratize musical culture but has also made the marketplace more sensitive to diverse tastes and helped it to thrive by catering to those tastes. Lumbleau boasts that "numerous reissues have come to market as a direct result of those albums having first been discovered on *Mutant Sounds* and / or made viable enough to reissue because of the increased profile that a previously obscure album has received by being posted on *Mutant Sounds.*"[39] This is not a self-serving claim; many high-profile musicians have made similar arguments. In the words of Pink Floyd's Nick Mason, "File sharing means a new generation of fans for us. It's a great thing to have another generation discovering your music and thinking you're rather good. File sharing plays a part in that, because that generation don't do it any other way."[40]

Of course, "pirates" have been responsible for keeping obscure and out-of-print music in the public sphere for generations, and perhaps since the dawn of the recorded music industry itself. As Adrian Johns argues, music bootleggers in the 1950s who sold jazz and opera records "wanted to make money, but they were in business for more than profit alone. They justified their actions in terms of furnishing a public archive of classics" that the recording industry was overlooking in search of larger markets.[41] Other musical traditions benefited similarly. The ethnomusicologist Harry Smith, whose groundbreaking compilation *Anthology of American Folk Music* more or less single-handedly inaugurated the 1960s folk revival—and in so doing forever changed the tenor of American music—included dozens of songs still under copyright, without permission. As he argued in his liner notes, "Only through recordings is it possible to learn of those developments that have been so characteristic of American music," and therefore the power of such recordings to "make historic changes" rests in their "making easily available [to a broader audience] the rhythmically and verbally specialized musics of groups living in mutual social and cultural isolation."[42] To put it simply, Smith believed that, by uniting the diverse ethnic and regional recordings in his collection, he was somehow uniting America as well. Far from being branded a criminal for his blatant rejection of copyright, Smith was celebrated throughout his life, and was even awarded a Chairman's Merit Award, shortly before his death, at the 1991 Grammys. In his acceptance speech, he told the smiling crowd of music industry executives and major label artists that "I'm glad to say my dreams came true. I saw America changed by music."[43]

Many Artists Support (And Are Supported by) P2P

I have already mentioned several high-profile recording artists who have publicly voiced their support for P2P and free music sharing for a variety of reasons, but these are only the tip of the iceberg. In my expert report for *Arista v. Lime Group*,[44] I cite dozens more, and a now-defunct blog called *Pirate Verbatim* collected over a hundred such quotes between 2010 and 2011.[45] Of course, not every artist supports file sharing; several prominent musicians, such as Bono and Lily Allen, have come out strongly against the practice, and others who had expressed support (such as Shakira)[46] have recanted or repositioned at the behest of the industry. But a great many (perhaps the majority of) working musicians continue to support the practice, and an increasing number of both independent and major label recording artists are embracing P2P as a positive dimension of their fan relations and business strategies.

Several prominent artists, such as Steve Winwood,[47] Counting Crows,[48] Green Day[49] and Heart[50] have actively released their new music to P2P networks, some of them prior to the official release date. Many others have experimented with innovative distribution and revenue models that rely on P2P either tacitly or explicitly as a central element. A great example is Nine Inch Nails. For his 2008 album *Ghosts I-IV*, frontman Trent Reznor parted ways with his label, Interscope, and released the music on his own website under a Creative Commons license, allowing his fans to freely redistribute the music in a noncommercial capacity, on file sharing networks and elsewhere. In addition to freely available digital files, NIN also released the music under a number of premium packaged formats, including multi-track DVDs, heavy duty vinyl, and an "ultra-deluxe limited edition" box set costing $300.[51] The 2,500 ultra-deluxe box sets sold out in a day,[52] and within the first week, NIN had grossed over $1.6 million in sales revenues across all formats.[53] Retail distribution was handled by Sony Music's RED division, as well as Amazon MP3. The album's CD release was successful enough to win it fourteenth place on the *Billboard* 200 chart, as well as the number 1 position on the Dance/Electronic Albums chart. For his following album, *The Slip*, Reznor pursued a similar strategy.[54]

Another excellent example is the band Radiohead. In 2007, the band, which had recently parted with longtime label EMI over financial and strategic disputes, self-released its album *In Rainbows* on its own website, offering fans the opportunity to pay anything they liked for the songs in DRM-free MP3 format. Despite making the music effectively free and freely shareable, the band had a significant commercial success. Although official sales figures for the album have never been announced, the band's publisher, Warner Chappell, reported that sales of the new album on the band's site during its first twelve weeks of release yielded more income than total online and off-line sales of their prior, major-label album.[55] Roughly two months after the self-release, the band shipped a retail CD version of the album via major label distribution deals. In its first week of official release, sales of the CD format pushed *In Rainbows* to first place on the *Billboard* 200, as well as the UK Album Chart.[56]

A third example is the rock/R&B megastar Prince. More than almost any other popular recording artist, Prince has shown an enthusiasm from the Internet's earliest years to experiment with new forms of distribution, sales, and marketing. Although his stated position has been subject to numerous shifts and reversals (not long ago, he declared that the Internet is "completely over"),[57] he has benefited immensely from innovative distribution strategies based on free distribution and redistribution. In 2007, for instance, he released his new album *Planet Earth* as a CD included free in three million issues of Britain's *Mail on Sunday* tabloid newspaper. In addition to being paid a reported half million dollars plus royalties by the paper's publisher, Prince went on to play a twice-extended, sold-out, twenty-one-night engagement at London's 02 arena during the subsequent two months, which grossed over twenty-two million dollars in revenues.[58] A copy of *Planet Earth* was also given away free to every ticket purchaser. This newspaper distribution strategy was so successful, he repeated it three years later with his *20Ten* album.[59] Although Prince has been a vociferous opponent of file sharing at times (and has sued torrent tracker The Pirate Bay), there is little question that his financial success as a touring artist owes some of its longevity to his efforts to make his music freely available for people to access and share.

Although Nine Inch Nails, Radiohead, and Prince were pioneering innovators who could not have predicted the successful results of their experiments in the late 2000s, countless other artists have followed confidently in their footsteps, and improved on their models, in the years since then. Singer-songwriter Sufjan Stevens sold over ten thousand copies of his 2010 EP, *All Delighted People,* from his artist page on Bandcamp.com in a single weekend, despite making the album available for free streaming and only promoting the release via a single e-mail, a single Twitter message, and a single Facebook post. Based on these sales alone (the album wouldn't be released on CD for over three months), it debuted at number 48 on the *Billboard* 200 chart, and climbed to number 27 in the following week. As Stevens explained in an interview, he considered offering free access to the music to be an integral element of his success. In his words, "I think it really helped that people could stream the whole album. My personal theory is that people can stream anything in its entirety anyway [via YouTube]. . . . The question for record labels and musicians is how far the buy button is from that stream."[60]

A year and a half later, indie punk musician Amanda Palmer (formerly of the major-label band The Dresden Dolls) financed her new album and tour via the crowd-funding website Kickstarter.com, raising almost $1.2 million in a single month from 24,883 individual backers[61] without any corporate funding or marketing support, and becoming an overnight blogosphere "DIY" sensation in the process. She charged only one dollar for a digital copy of the entire album in DRM-free format (tacitly acknowledging that its market value is practically nil), while offering more unique formats and merchandise (such as signed art books and custom-painted turntables) for larger pledges. While the costs to provide these additional incentives were high, she still anticipated netting more revenue than she would from a major label contract for the same music.[62] Palmer didn't simply stumble on a million-dollar accident; this was a well-considered strategy tailored to the post-P2P media and economic environment. As she explained nearly two years earlier, in a speech at Harvard University:

> Now with content being freely available, as we know, in the cloud, there has to be a massive shift [in the way musicians are remunerated]. With everyone screaming that the music business is collapsing and 'Oh my god, everyone's torrenting and this is terrible for business,' I think we should be celebrating the fact that while music is free and content is free, we also have the technology for artists to

stand up on their boxes, in their virtual street corner, in their place in the Internet. And you, as the audience, if you're moved by what an artist does, if you're moved by a song that I put out for free, you can put in a dollar. And you can know that you've had a very real exchange with me, with no middlemen, and no label, and no promoter, no nothing—it's just you and me.[63]

These cases, though celebrated, are becoming the rule rather than the exception; collectively, over five thousand music projects raised nearly $35 million in crowd-funding on Kickstarter alone in 2012, and that number is sure to skyrocket; the amount of money raised via the site more than tripled from 2011 to 2012.[64] Similarly, in December 2012, Bandcamp achieved the milestone of distributing over a million dollars to its artists in a single month.[65]

In addition to the many famous musicians using P2P and digital music sharing to extend and grow their careers, there are also many recent examples of obscure or emerging musicians whose careers were propelled into the stratosphere via free online distribution. One widely celebrated example is teen pop sensation Justin Bieber. After his mother posted home videos of the Stratford, Ontario, fourteen year old singing (unlicensed) pop R&B songs to YouTube, he was "discovered" accidentally on the site by a former label marketing executive, who helped him sign a recording contract with Island Records.[66] By the time his first single was released in 2009, the singer was already the twenty-third-most-popular musician on YouTube. After his commercial release, Bieber continued to grow in popularity, fueled by free sharing on YouTube (where, at the time of writing, he has the second most popular video of all time, with over 819 million views), Twitter (where he is the currently second-most-popular account, with over thirty-two million followers), and P2P networks (where he is consistently among the most shared musicians, according to BigChampagne). None of this free sharing kept Bieber's first two albums from selling like gangbusters (each earned RIAA-certified Platinum status in the United States and Canada), and it's clearly only helped fuel the "Bieber fever" driving millions of fans to buy his merchandise and attend his live concerts for nearly half a decade thus far.

Another example of an artist climbing from obscurity to fame on the coattails of free Internet distribution is the Gregory Brothers, a Brooklyn-based indie band best known for their YouTube video series *Auto-Tune the News* (*ATTN*), in which they remix and harmonize television news footage. Although *ATTN* has enjoyed significant traffic (millions of views per video) and press attention since its debut in spring 2009, the band was catapulted to mainstream success with the July 2010 release of *ATTN* episode 12b, "BED INTRUDER SONG!!!!" This video, which remixed a Huntsville, Alabama local news story about an attempted rape and featured the colorful personality of the victim's brother, Antoine Dodson, garnered over fifty million YouTube views within its first four months of release.[67] Additionally, within a month of its first appearance, thousands of other YouTube fans had posted their own interpretations of the song, accounting for tens of millions of additional views. This viral success translated to a degree of market success beyond the confines of YouTube; the song was made available for paid download on iTunes and charted on the *Billboard* Hot 100, a rare accomplishment for an iTunes-only song by an unknown act. The Gregory Brothers shared 50 percent of writing credit and revenues with Dodson,[68] who has also used the video to sell merchandise and music of his own and has reportedly used the revenues to move his family out of the projects to a safer home.[69]

As these two examples make clear, P2P alone cannot take all the credit for launching new musicians' careers; social media and online video sites such as YouTube (both of which also qualify as "free online distribution" and frequently lack licenses from copyright holders) have played an increasingly important role since the mid- to late 2000s. Recently, the Internet researcher Alex Leavitt reported on Twitter that a major record label had seen 42 percent of its new musical acts originate as YouTube cover artists.[70] This statistic, though anecdotal in nature, reflects an evident truth: namely, that sharing unlicensed versions of commercial music freely via the Internet has replaced the traditional "demo tape" as the primary vector for amateur or independent performers to shop their wares to the music industry and to a broader audience. While Bieber is the best-known example of this phenomenon, my personal favorite is Arnel Pineda.

Pineda served as the lead singer of The Zoo, a popular classic rock cover band in his native Philippines. After the band posted several cover versions of songs by Journey to YouTube, Journey cofounder and guitarist Neal Schon contacted him to ask whether he'd be interested in auditioning to be the band's lead singer. Pineda got the job; the resulting album, *Revelation,* sold a million copies within six months of its release in June 2008,[71] and their tour that year grossed over $35 million. Fortunately, Schon and Journey saw something of value in The Zoo's YouTube covers; had the copyright holders simply censored or prosecuted the cover band for its "piracy," Pineda might have been bankrupted,

Journey might have missed out on an ideal lead singer (and a $35 million paycheck), and Journey fans around the world might not have been able to enjoy their new album and live concerts.

P2P vs. Traditional Music Economics

In December 2011, the digital "storage locker" service Megaupload (a website that enabled people to store, transfer, and share large media files and which has been vilified by the RIAA and others for encouraging piracy) unveiled a new marketing campaign featuring a cavalcade of popular and major label musicians such as Macy Gray, Sean "P. Diddy" Combs, and Kanye West singing the service's praises both literally and figuratively. Predictably, the video became a viral hit; within hours, "#megaupload" was a trending topic on Twitter, and millions had viewed the video.[72]

Then something interesting happened: the video disappeared from YouTube, which offered an explanatory note that "this video contains content from UMG [Universal Music Group], who has blocked it on copyright grounds." In other words, the largest record label in the world had filed a DMCA takedown notice,[73] claiming that it owned some of the video's contents. The problem is, the record label had no legal basis for its actions; while artists such as P. Diddy have recording contracts with UMG, these contracts don't typically prohibit them from appearing in advertisements. The labels control copyrights to recordings, not to the artists themselves.

Within a week, YouTube had reinstated the video,[74] after finding that UMG's copyright claims were baseless. Yet, in the course of that week's outage, the label successfully interrupted a viral marketing campaign, halting its ascent and probably preventing it from being viewed by millions of people. Ironically, UMG resorted to false copyright claims in order to do battle with a site it accused of abusing intellectual property. The following month, Megaupload's founder (and the star of the censored video) Kim Dotcom was arrested in his home country of New Zealand and indicted by the US Department of Justice for "running an international organized criminal enterprise allegedly responsible for massive worldwide online piracy of numerous types of copyrighted works."[75] At the time of writing, the case is still pending. After six weeks in jail, Dotcom was released on bail. He is currently confined to an 80 km radius around his home, and is prohibited from using the Internet, out of concern that he has "the ability to use it for wrong purposes."[76]

Why did UMG invoke false copyright claims to prevent the video from being seen? Was it simply a matter of using any means necessary to combat a website it considers a dangerous pirate? Perhaps so, but I believe the company was equally concerned with the video's actual contents, which consisted of major label artists celebrating the site. A foundational element of the recording industry's anti-piracy narrative is the argument that label-backed music distribution "support[s]"[77] artists, while its efforts to crack down on unlicensed distribution "protect[s] artists."[78] So it's problematic when some of the best-known and best-selling major label artists publicly extol one of the very services the industry has identified as a threat.

The truth of the matter is that, historically, the major labels have done a fairly poor job of supporting and protecting artists, and therefore artists today have little incentive to fight for the status quo on behalf of companies that are routinely criticized for unfair or unethical business practices. Most notably, major label record contracts typically include clauses whose primary effect is to diminish actual royalties paid to the recording artist. As the Future of Music Coalition, a pro-musician advocacy group, argues in a lengthy critique of these contractual hijinks, "Outside of the major label music world many of these clauses are seen as an affront to basic logic."[79]

Several economic analyses have demonstrated the effects of these practices on actual artist revenues. The celebrated rock producer Steve Albini (Pixies, Nirvana, PJ Harvey) wrote a widely read and reprinted 1993 article in *The Baffler,* demonstrating how such clauses, and other economic factors, could conceivably lead to band members signed to a $250,000 contract taking home roughly $4,000 apiece for their work.[80] More recently, in 2010, the online magazine *The Root,* in conjunction with Don Passman, author of *All You Need to Know about the Music Business,*[81] conducted an economic analysis corroborating this point, demonstrating that "for every $1,000 in music sold, the average musician makes $23.40."[82] These economic disparities pertain even in the digital music economy; according to court documents filed in 2011 by rapper Chuck D, artists signed to UMG get paid $80.33 for every 1,000 iTunes downloads sold.[83]

Even the more justifiable contractual elements can be damaging to artists' bottom lines. For instance, "recoupment" clauses require that labels make back their expenditures for producing, distributing, and marketing the music before any royalties are owed to the recording artist. As the RIAA has admitted on its own website, fewer than one in ten of its constituents' album releases ever make back the money the label has spent;[84] therefore, by this logic, more than 90 percent of major label artists never see royalties beyond the initial advance.

Aside from these contractual considerations, the major labels have historically fought to diminish the degree of power, ownership, and revenue recognized by recording artists, in the interest of maximizing their own profitability. One fairly recent example is their lobbying effort to insert four words into the text of the Satellite Home Viewer Improvement Act of 1999, thereby with one tiny stroke reclassifying all recording artists' labor as "work-for-hire" under copyright law. The practical effect of this maneuver was to eliminate artists' rights to recapture control of their work via "term reversion" after their contracts had expired. Although President Clinton signed this bill into law, subsequent Congressional testimony by major label artists such as Sheryl Crow and Don Henley led to its repeal by the Senate. Despite this highly visible reversal, however, the major labels and publishers have continued to fight copyright term reversion. Most recently, a federal judge ruled in favor of Victor Willis, composer of the song "Y.M.C.A.," in a test of this principle in 2012. Yet, this story has only begun; it seems likely that the music industry will continue to push the matter by any means necessary to avert a "ticking time bomb" of mass copyright reversion from taking effect.[85]

Another highly visible, high-stakes battle between the major labels and their artists has revolved around the issue of whether digital downloads (such as those available from iTunes) are technically retail or licensing. According to traditional artist contracts, retail royalties are significantly lower (by a factor of about 3-to-1) than licensing royalties, which means that the answer to this question could be worth billions of dollars to either labels or artists. Recently, this battle has been waged in the form of a lawsuit between rapper Eminem and Universal Music Group[86] (the US Supreme Court has declined to revisit an Appeals Court ruling in favor of Eminem),[87] as well as an ongoing class action suit brought against UMG by a variety of musicians including Rob Zombie and Rick James.[88]

In short, the relationship between the major labels and the artists they purport to represent has historically been a fraught one, and continues to be contentious. Although many benefits, such as fame, legitimacy, and the chance of riches, accrue from a major label relationship, it is no surprise that even successful artists continue to express support for P2P and other forms of free online music sharing, as, in their eyes, the benefits must far outweigh the risks. For the labels, this support has led to numerous public defections and embarrassments—a consequence I discuss in greater detail in chapter 6.

Peer-to-peer file sharing and other forms of free online music distribution have played a complex and contentious role in the ongoing transformation of musical culture and economics. While the recording industry decries these services as "rogue technologies" and has painted their hundreds of millions of users as "pirates," research shows that it is difficult if not impossible to ascertain whether P2P has a positive, negative, or neutral effect on music sales. The evidence also suggests that, in many ways, free sharing grows the overall music economy, empowers and enriches recording artists, and contributes to a more vibrant musical culture. These benefits, which contrast with the historical powerlessness and poverty faced by most musicians in the traditional music economy, help to explain why so many artists today publicly support and actively employ P2P and free online sharing as crucial elements in their business and marketing strategies.

Yet there is no arguing that traditional music sales have plummeted in recent years and, as the music industry is quick to observe, that the downturn coincided with the introduction of Napster. But if P2P can't be blamed for whatever misfortunes the music industry has faced in recent years, what is a more plausible explanation? As I argue in the next chapter, the reality is more complex, and more interesting, than simple scapegoating would suggest; although digital media play a role, the precipitous drop in music sales during the first decade of the twenty-first century can best be understood as the result of an unprecedented bubble punctured in a perfect storm.

CHAPTER 5

Bubbles and Storms

The Story behind the Numbers

WE ARE ALL familiar with this story: Everything was going swimmingly for the music industry until Napster hit. Sales were on the rise, and the future looked brighter still. But since that fateful day in the summer of 1999 when P2P file sharing was unleashed on the world, music sales have plummeted and a once-vital industry has been reduced to a shadow of its former self. As Cary Sherman, RIAA chief executive, lamented in the *New York Times* in 2012, "music sales in the United States are less than half of what they were in 1999, when the file-sharing site Napster emerged, and [as a result] direct employment in the industry ha[s] fallen by more than half since then."[1]

That P2P is squarely to blame for this turn of events is rarely questioned. The recording industry maintains that "widespread piracy is the biggest factor undermining the growth of the digital music business," and continues to push for "cooperation from online intermediaries" such as ISPs and search engines (largely in the form of surveillance and censorship) as a remedy, or at least a bulwark, against the tide of P2P and other "unauthorized channels" of music distribution.[2] Stanley Liebowitz, an economics professor whose research on file sharing has been funded[3]—and often cited[4]—by the RIAA, even claims that "file-sharing has caused the *entire enormous decline* in record sales that has occurred over the last decade."[5] The news media tend to reproduce this frame of analysis without critique, routinely referencing "losses from file sharing" or speaking of sectors "avoiding what happened to the music industry" in their business coverage.

If this narrative has succeeded in becoming "common knowledge," a truism repeated in classrooms, boardrooms, and at cocktail parties around the world, it has been aided in large part by the Chart. This

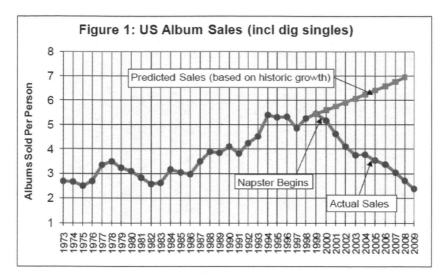

Figure 3. Chart by Stanley Liebowitz depicting the purported effect of P2P on music sales.

graphical argument has appeared in various forms, in hundreds of blogs and publications, but each version tells essentially the same story: a market peak, followed by the introduction of P2P, followed by a long and steep decline. An excellent example is the version of the Chart provided by Liebowitz in his testimony on behalf of the plaintiffs in *Arista v. Lime Group* (fig. 3), which has been reproduced in the *Hollywood Reporter*[6] and elsewhere. Liebowitz's chart shows that music sales in the United States, measured in terms of albums sold per capita, did indeed reach a historical market peak shortly before the introduction of Napster, and have fallen significantly since then. He also asserts that music sales would have continued to climb linearly, without leveling off or falling, had P2P not undermined this growing consumer demand (a claim that seems to defy the basic tenets of logic). As he argued in *Sony BMG v. Tenenbaum,* another file sharing case in which he was retained as an expert witness by the major label plaintiffs, "the clearest and probably the most compelling evidence for file-sharing's impact on sound recording sales is the timing of the rise of file-sharing with the decline in sound recording sales."[7] In other words, according to the music industry, the coincidence of these two events is the greatest proof that the former caused the latter.

I maintain, however, that the Chart and its accompanying narrative, although they contain elements of truth, amount to little more than a convenient fiction, scapegoating music fans and media innovators for the recording industry's own strategic failures and ascribing responsibility to "pirates" and "piracy" for trends and events that are beyond anyone's control. While the introduction of Napster does correlate conveniently with the beginning of a downward trend for music retail, so do a number of other factors, and furthermore, as any statistician can tell you, correlation doesn't necessarily imply causation. As one statistics textbook puts it, "an observed correlation between two variables may be spurious. That is, it may be caused by the influence of a third variable."[8] In this chapter, I describe many other variables that have played a role in the transformation of the music economy over the past few decades, demonstrating that any part that P2P plays is relatively minimal. The larger story involves a "perfect bubble"—a confluence of economic, political, and technological forces that drove the aggregate value of music sales to unprecedented heights at the end of the twentieth century—followed by a "perfect storm," which punctured this bubble and undermined the music retail market. I briefly discuss the music industry's often-cited figures regarding the economic impact of piracy on jobs and productivity, showing that independent research has debunked many of these claims.

Before I take up these points, however, I offer a chart of my own, depicting the IFPI's own published figures for the global music sales market (fig. 4). It parallels Liebowitz's in many respects, although it represents actual money spent on music rather than unit sales per capita. Most salient, there is a steep two-decade climb, followed by a peak around the turn of the century, followed by a steep decade-long dip. Also like Liebowitz's and every other version of the Chart, *this is as much a work of art as a work of science.* All data and methods of analysis have their biases and inconsistencies, and market research published by the music industry excels in both of these respects. Therefore, any researcher working with the data must necessarily use his or her judgment in developing a meaningful set of figures as a basis of analysis. (If you aren't keenly interested in the detailed challenges of working with music industry market data, feel free to skip to the next section).

There is no definitive tally of music industry market data. The IFPI, the RIAA, and other official organs of the music industry regularly publish statistics, and these are often supplemented, cited, and reliant upon data from third-party research companies, such as Nielsen SoundScan. Yet there is rarely agreement even between two publications from the same source let alone among these many sources. There are a variety of reasons for this disparity. First of all, organizations such as the IFPI and the RIAA routinely revise previously published figures, for a variety of

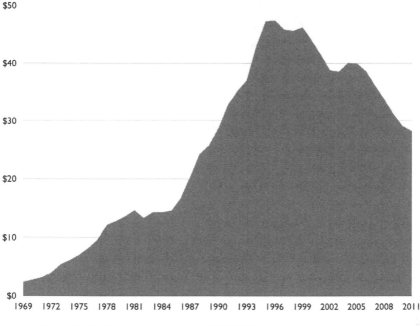

Figure 4. Global music sales revenue, 1969–2011 (inflation-adjusted $US billions).

reasons including changes to their internal data, analyses, and methodologies.[9] Second, inflation makes longitudinal data difficult to compare. Some of the difficulty is due to confusion (it's not always clear which year's dollars are represented in a given publication's figures), and some of it is genuinely thorny math (inflation is not consistent from region to region, market to market, and currency to currency). A separate but related challenge is the fact that exchange rates between currencies differ on a daily basis; therefore, globally reported market figures in US dollars are difficult to assess for a single year and a guesstimate at best for longitudinal data. As the Organisation for Economic Co-operation and Development (OECD) warned in its own analysis of IFPI data, "Global sales figures in USD . . . must be used with caution due to fluctuating US dollar exchange rate [sic] which can make year-to-year comparisons difficult."[10]

In addition to these macroeconomic challenges, many of which pertain to any global marketplace, there are additional idiosyncrasies about recording industry data that make them even knottier to unravel. For one thing, there is a methodological inconsistency between some figures, which are based on analysis of *retail sales data* (e.g., SoundScan, which the IFPI uses), and others (e.g., RIAA publications), which are based on *shipments*, or the number of units record labels report sending to retailers, which are then extrapolated to dollar figures. Each of these methods of assessment has its strengths and weaknesses, but there is invariably a significant quantitative gap between the two.

Another challenge is that the music industry sometimes reports sales data in terms of "trade value," or wholesale price, and at other times in terms of retail value, or the price paid at market. Moreover, the conversion rate between retail and trade value differs from format to format, region to region, and year to year. For instance, the IFPI recently reported figures that suggested an 83 percent retail markup for physical goods and a 59 percent markup for digital goods in the United States in 2008, while reporting a 107 percent markup for physical and a 73 percent markup for digital in Austria in the same year.[11] Given that the IFPI's older publications report retail value, while the newer ones tend to report trade value, this makes longitudinal market analysis even more difficult.

Finally, there is the question of what the object of analysis is. Historically, the music industry only reported revenues accruing from the global sale of physical goods in brick-and-mortar stores. As the industry's revenue model has diversified, some additional income sources have slowly been added, though others have not. For instance, global IFPI figures have included performance royalties and digital sales (including ringtones) for most of the past decade, and in 2012 began to include synch license royalties. Given that these aren't technically "sales," and have no retail markup, the process of comparing current to past global market figures is a bit of an apples-to-oranges-to-watermelons process.

I discuss these challenges not to bemoan my job as a researcher or to besmirch the integrity of the recording industry, but simply to point out that it is theoretically impossible to describe the historical global music marketplace with total accuracy, and that any market data that appear in any publication must be understood as fundamentally interpretive in nature. Nor are the resulting inconsistencies sufficiently small as to be of academic interest only; they bear directly on the questions I address in this chapter: namely, when and why did the music industry's fortunes reverse? According to an IFPI publication from 2000, the global music retail market peaked in 1996, followed by a market contraction, with a 2 percent drop in 1999.[12] By 2005, the IFPI was reporting two sets of figures: in terms of "variable" dollars (at same-year exchange rates), the market peaked in 1996, but in terms of "fixed" dollars (all years calculated at a 2004 exchange rate), the peak came in 1999.[13] Today, all IFPI publications show a 1999 peak, and there is no discussion of fixed vs. variable dollars. Perhaps the industry changed its analytical methods because it believes fixed dollars are a more meaningful measure. Perhaps they just make for a better story.

For my own version of the chart, I rely on data from two recent IFPI publications. For 1969–2004, I use the variable-dollar figures reported in the *Recording Industry in Numbers 2005*. I chose these figures because they are the most recent official data going back that far, because they reflect retail rather than wholesale, and because variable dollars more accurately reflect the role of macroeconomic factors (such as buying power) in shaping the music economy over time. For more recent years, I use the IFPI's numbers published in 2012 (which use fixed dollars). Because these are reported in terms of trade revenue, I adjusted for retail based on an average 70 percent markup across different regions and formats. As I discussed above, the IFPI doesn't use a single conversion rate, but this figure is both conservative relative to the range of percentages the industry uses, and consistent in its results with many additional published market data.[14] All of my figures reflect inflation-adjusted 2011 US dollars.

The Perfect Bubble: 1985–2000

As the chart shows, global music sales revenues began to climb steeply in the mid- to late 1980s. In the decade between 1985 and 1995, adjusting for inflation, the market expanded by 324 percent—more than it had in a generation, and far outstripping any previous gain in terms of actual dollars spent. This explosion wasn't simply the result of people liking music more than they had in the past, or of the product improving (say what you will about the relative merits of '80s pop and metal, and '90s grunge and hip-hop). To the contrary, it was the result of a combination of factors, including a highly successful (and expensive) new recording format, the consolidation of the music retail and broadcasting sectors, a new generic strategy that focused on aggregating mass audiences, and a booming consumer economy.

One of the biggest boons to the recording industry during the last two decades of the twentieth century was the market success of the compact disc. As I discussed in chapter 2, one of the primary reasons the music industry has historically updated its distribution formats each decade or two is to reinvigorate the marketplace, both renewing interest in recorded music as a consumer product and driving fans to upgrade their existing collections. The CD has been the most successful physical distribution format of all time by many measures, including the speed with which it achieved market dominance and the total number of units sold at its peak. First introduced to the market in 1983, retailers were already touting the CD's potential to spark a replacement cycle by 1984.[15] CDs outsold microcassettes globally for the first time in 1993, and remained the dominant sales format, in terms of revenues, through 2010. Only in 1998–1999 did *Billboard* magazine first raise the specter of diminishing sales due to the "maturing of the CD-replacement cycle,"[16] suggesting that it had played a significant role in driving revenues for the past 15 years (fig. 5).

Another important factor in the expansion of the recorded music market during the 1980s and '90s was the transformation and consolidation of the music retail sector. Until the 1970s, most people bought their music at independent record shops or general merchandisers. While there were some regional "music specialty" chain retailers such as Sam Goody and Camelot Records, they were still a far cry from the global superstores and megastores typified by Tower Records, HMV, and Virgin a decade or two later. By the early 1980s, the head of the National Association of

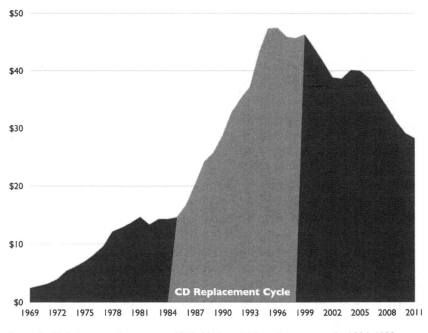

Figure 5. Global music sales revenue, 1969–2011, and CD replacement cycle, 1984–1999.

Recording Merchandisers (NARM) was confidently predicting the imminent death of "mom and pop operations" in the wake of "further consolidation of the large retail chains."[17] His words proved prescient; coasting on the larger wave of industrial consolidation and the general transformation of retail into a mall-based, entertainment experience, the music sector reinvented itself under the auspices of its new corporate owners, forcing most independent retailers out of operation and streamlining and standardizing the music shopping environment.

In the short term, this was a boon to music sales; it increased retail space and foot traffic overall, brought many innovations in "end-cap" promotion and other forms of in-store and cooperative marketing, and made price competition less likely. It also helped fuel sales for the industry's biggest acts; with a single deal, a record label could effectively promote its top artists in thousands of stores across the country and around the world. In the longer term, however, consolidation had a strategic downside; with the mom-and-pop stores out of the picture, there was little basis for customer loyalty, not much diversity in terms of music selection, and a strict, short-term bottom line driving all strategic decisions.

Within another decade, a new breed of big-box retailers such as Best Buy, Circuit City, and Walmart began selling a significant amount of music. Like the Towers and HMVs of the world, they were large corporate chains with little to differentiate them. But unlike the music-only megastores, these retailers could afford to sell music at break-even point, or even as a "loss leader," with the assumption that a portion of consumers lured to the store with the promise of $9.99 CDs would end up splurging on $299.99 stereo systems and $499.99 televisions. The effect, according to one music chain executive, was "like a neutron bomb has gone off," instantly undermining sales at nearby music-only stores by up to 50 percent.[18]

While the lower prices offered by big-box retailers temporarily helped boost sales volume, they also augured ill for the industry. By the mid-1990s, the music specialty stores, forced into a losing price war with Best Buy and Circuit City, began to see their retail margins erode steeply. Together with the record labels, which had initially ignored their plight on the grounds that greater volume meant a better bottom line, they came up with a plan to stanch the blood flow. In exchange for the labels' financial cooperation in music advertising, retailers would adhere to a strict "minimum advertised pricing" (MAP) policy—essentially fixing the price of CDs at a level high enough for the music retailers to retain some profit.[19] This policy lasted from the mid-1990s until 2000, arguably

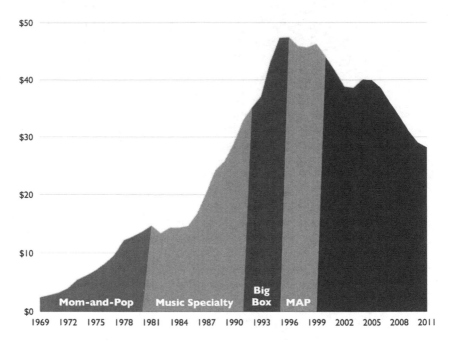

$50

$40

$30

$20

$10

$0

Mom-and-Pop   **Music Specialty**   **Big Box**   **MAP**

1969 1972 1975 1978 1981 1984 1987 1990 1993 1996 1999 2002 2005 2008 2011

Figure 6. Twentieth-century music retail transformation and global music sales revenue.

maintaining an artificially inflated value for the compact disc market beyond its expiration date (fig. 6).

The 1980s–90s also saw the emergence of a "blockbuster economy" in the music industry, in which an increasing portion of the record labels' fortunes rested in the market performance of a dwindling number of megastar artists with increasingly short shelf lives. Several factors were responsible. First, beginning in the late 1970s, major labels entered into a bidding and poaching war over some of the industry's biggest acts, inflating the advances paid on royalties to stratospheric heights. James Taylor, Michael Jackson, and Bruce Springsteen were three of the initial beneficiaries of these deals, which paid them millions of dollars before they had recorded a single note.[20] In order to recoup these unprecedented expenses, the labels had to sell an unprecedented number of units, which meant spending more on marketing and promotion, which in turn eroded their margins and required a higher volume of sales to achieve profitability.

This dynamic was compounded by an increasingly concentrated, integrated, and expensive marketing and promotional system. Beginning with the 1981 launch of MTV, television became a (possibly *the*) dominant element in bringing new songs and acts to the public's attention, and successful artists were increasingly required to be triple threats—good musicians, good dancers, and good-looking to boot—which naturally depressed the number, range, and diversity of potential pop stars. After Viacom bought MTV in 1985, it began to expand its music television offerings rapidly, building or acquiring nearly every major music cable channel, including VH1, BET, and CMT. With the deregulation of the US radio industry in the mid-1990s, media conglomerate Clear Channel went on a buying spree of its own, expanding from the legal maximum of 40 stations in 1996 to over 1,100 by the end of the century. Together, Clear Channel and Viacom accounted for the majority of the music marketing opportunities on US radio, television, and outdoor media (e.g., billboards), as well as the nation's largest events promotion company.

These corporations wielded their consolidated power as a form of leverage over artists and labels, requiring all-or-nothing commitments to national tours, marketing, and promotional campaigns (often, all three). For labels, this dynamic further undermined the value proposition for investing in mid-level artists who may have a loyal following of a few hundred thousand, but would never be able to sell a platinum album or fill stadiums across the country. It also meant that there was a higher-than-ever risk associated with artist development; beginning in this period, if an artist didn't have a hit with his or her first radio single, a full album could very well never be released. Gone were the days when artists like Bob Dylan or Simon & Garfunkel could struggle through a few albums' worth of obscurity before hitting it big.

Naturally, the rise of the blockbuster economy could be heard aesthetically in the music itself, which had to aim for larger audiences, often sacrificing depth of resonance for breadth of appeal. One example of this trend was the emergence of "boy bands" such as New Kids on the Block, the Backstreet Boys, and 'N Sync. With their youthful bravado, carefully coiffed images, and even more polished sound, these groups were ideal vehicles to sell a few platinum albums, sell out a few tours, unload a ton of merchandise, and then put out to pasture (or, on rare occasion, develop into successful solo acts). If many of these groups sounded the same, it was often because much of the music was written and produced by the same people. Labels and artists during this time increasingly came to rely on the pop expertise of a handful of "super producers" such as Max Martin, Rami Yacoub, and Rodney Jerkins,[21] who developed consistent songwriting and studio techniques that could be applied to any popular artist of the day.

The true value of such producers to the music industry is reflected in their economic remuneration; while most major label artists wait a lifetime without ever seeing a royalty check, successful producers typically receive high production fees *plus* royalties on sale, without having to wait for the labels to recoup their expenses. In fact, in many cases, the producer's cut is paid out of the artist's piece of the pie, rather than the label's—meaning that the more expensive a producer is, the smaller the chance is that the artist will ever earn a dime.

Despite the many business risks of the blockbuster economy (greater upfront expense, less diversified risk, lower customer loyalty, slimmer margins), its short-term effect was to increase record sales volume, and therefore revenue. Thus, while only two of the top-selling albums of all time, according to the RIAA, were produced between 1990 and 2000,[22] suggesting that the artists promoted during this period tended to lack the longevity of those from earlier eras, eight of the seventeen albums to surpass one million copies sold in a single week were released during this period, and the Backstreet Boys, 'N Sync, and Britney Spears were the third, fourth, and fifth to achieve this milestone, respectively.[23]

The final element of the music industry's "perfect bubble" was an excellent economy. The decade between March 1991 and March 2001

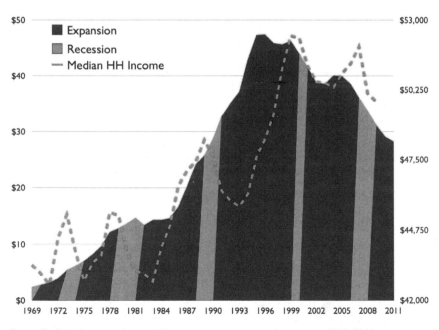

Figure 7. Global music sales and US economic expansion and recession, 1969–2011.

was characterized by a consistent economic expansion unprecedented in American history.[24] This had a direct impact on the ability of consumers to purchase music products, as it was characterized by a similar expansion in median household income[25] (fig. 7). Meanwhile, following the end of the Cold War and other geopolitical changes of the era, new global markets emerged, increasing worldwide demand for entertainment industry products. This buoyed the creative economy as a whole; according to research published by the United Nations, creative exports nearly doubled from $227.5 billion in 1996 to $424.4 billion in 2005.[26]

To summarize, the last decade and a half of the twentieth century—a period during which the global music sales market grew to more than three times its former size—amounted to a perfect bubble for the recording industry. Between the ascendance of the CD format, the evolution of the music retail market, the rise of the blockbuster model, the consolidation of broadcasting, and the unprecedented expansion of the US and global economies, it is little surprise that the market fared so well. Yet in many of these factors, short-term success was paired with long-term instability. All bubbles eventually pop, and the music retail market was no different in this respect. The "perfect storm" that ensued was complex, severe, and had very little to do with P2P or any form of "piracy" by music fans.

The Perfect Storm: 2000–2011

The year 2000 marked a turning point for the music industry; on this much, everyone can agree. Sales began to descend from the heights reached between 1995 and 1999, with a rapidity that justifiably alarmed artists and labels alike. With very few exceptions, each year since then has marked a continuation of this dismal trend, and by 2011, global sales amounted to only about 68 percent of what they had been a decade earlier. While these losses were mitigated to a degree by the rise of new revenue models and sources (as I discussed in the previous chapter), music sales remain the "bread and butter" for record labels, and, accurately or not, are seen as a barometer of the broader industry's overall health.

One of the most important factors underpinning these changes is a profound shift in consumer psychology. The recording industry tends to promote a simplified version of this process, arguing that, in the wake of P2P and other forms of sharing, consumers have come to "simply believe that online music, books and movies should be free."[27] Yet the major labels have, on occasion, acknowledged that there's more to the story than mere freeloading. As the EMI owner Terra Firma Capital explained in its 2008 Annual Review, the label's "revenue had been declining due to the structural shift in the consumer music market and to a slow response, both by the industry and the company, to the move towards digital consumption. . . . This shift has been particularly detrimental to the consumer-facing Recorded Music business."[28]

What does this "structural shift in the consumer market" consist of? We can understand it in the same terms that apply to any vibrant and competitive marketplace: convenience, quality, and value. Digital music provided fans with an unprecedented degree of choice over the mode, method and context of music consumption, control over their music listening experiences, volume of content to choose from, and portability in their music-listening venues. Whereas physical music formats such as LPs, cassettes, and CDs required consumers to carry around a bulky plastic object in order to listen to ten or fifteen songs by a given artist in a predetermined order, MP3s and Internet streaming enabled them to compile their own tailored listening experiences, suited to their individual preferences, habits, time frames, and locations.

Once this shift occurred in consumers' behavior and psychology, they could no longer recognize the same use value in the CD format, and were therefore unwilling to accord it the same degree of market value. This process was accelerated by the massive distribution and adoption of CD "ripping" and "burning" technologies (some of which are created and manufactured by parents and affiliates of the record labels themselves, for example, Sony), which took place independently of online sharing activity. Moreover, as the Terra Firma report acknowledges, the labels themselves can be faulted for taking a decade to absorb the significance of this shift in market demand (despite early research published by me and others), and for failing to accommodate it sooner, despite the existence of willing retailers, distributors, service and technology providers, and, of course, consumers. To put it simply, the recording industry has always benefited economically from promoting consumer adoption of new music distribution formats; in the case of digital music, it chose to ignore and fight the new format instead, and lost out on the potential rewards.

This failure on the industry's part to exploit new digital technologies and modes of consumption dovetailed with the end of the CD replacement cycle (see fig. 5). By 2000, nearly every Beatles fan in the world owned the "White Album" on CD, and yet it wasn't until late 2010 that this classic recording finally appeared on iTunes, available for legal download for the first time ever.[29] Naturally, music sales lagged during this interim. And again, despite the prevalence of the "P2P killed music" narrative, major labels have occasionally acknowledged the role that format replacement plays in maintaining and growing their market size. Warner Music Group (WMG) has been one of the most vocal labels on this subject, consistently acknowledging in its public filings between 2006 and 2010 that "negative growth rates on a global basis" can be attributed in part to the fact that "the period of growth in recorded music sales driven by the introduction and penetration of the CD format has ended."[30] Lyor Cohen, then WMG's North American chief executive, acknowledged this fact as well, calling the end of the CD replacement cycle the "biggest challenge" facing the company in the early years of the twenty-first century. In a 2006 interview with the *Los Angeles Times,* he argued that

> Warner's infrastructure was way too expensive. Throughout the 1980s and early '90s, the success of the compact disc format allowed music companies to build enormous, expensive staffs. When the industry began to decline in the late 1990s, most companies decided that rather than cut staff, they would take shortcuts to sell more records. That's why Britney Spears, the Backstreet Boys and 'NSync appeared, because labels had to find huge pop hits to pay for their staffs, no matter how short-lived those hits were.[31]

This exceptional candor on Cohen's part suggests another important factor affecting music sales at the turn of the century: the waning of the "blockbuster economy" and the collapse of the boy band/pop aesthetic. The same blockbuster processes that contributed to an inflation of the music market in the 1990s undermined its value a decade later: by cutting down on aesthetic diversity, the labels put too many of their eggs into a single basket. P2P, and other forms of digital music, played a role here. While music promotion and distribution channels were highly concentrated in the 1990s, it was unnecessary for labels to diversify their offerings, and unlikely that most consumers would develop the expectation of greater variety. But as innovations like MP3, portable digital devices, and streaming music gained widespread market traction, music fans began to experience the "long tail"[32] through metaphors like "custom radio," "playlists," and "shuffle," listening to a wider range of musical styles in a broader array of contexts. By the same token, the promotional stranglehold maintained by the monolithic gatekeepers of radio and television was loosening thanks to the growing popularity of independent online music sites and services, both licensed and unlicensed. By the mid-2000s, there was neither the economic necessity nor the market demand for the kinds of blockbuster acts the recording industry had emphasized in the 1990s. Yet the labels were essentially stuck with this model, having jettisoned both the artists and the infrastructure to accommodate smaller, more targeted markets. As a result of this mismatch between the expectations of music buyers and the capacities of music sellers, the market suffered.

Another major factor in the contraction of the global music market was the "unbundling" of songs. As I discussed in chapter 2, the introduction of the LP vinyl music format after World War II contributed to the ascendance of a new product category—the album—in which songs were bundled together and essentially sold at a discount relative to their aggregate price. By the 1960s, the album had become more than just an economic and technological convenience: it had become the dominant paradigm through which recording artists and their fans communicated. Programmatic recordings like the Beach Boys' *Pet Sounds* (1966) and the Beatles' *Sgt. Pepper's Lonely Hearts Club Band* (1967) conceived of the album as a contiguous suite of interrelated songs, rather than a more or less random assortment of radio hits. Increasingly elaborate and well-designed album cover art and packaging helped to communicate this aesthetic to fans, and to establish a sense of the work as a discrete category.

Yet not every album was like *Pet Sounds*. A significant portion of album releases continued to contain mostly "filler" material punctuated by a handful of hits. This was an economic calculation on the music industry's part, tailored to make consumers pay more relative to the number of songs they genuinely wanted to hear, and it inflated the value of the music retail industry above the level of actual demand. As iTunes, Amazon, and other retailers began to offer digital "singles" in the 2000s, and as iPods and other new digital music players offered fans the ability to create their own playlists and to listen in "shuffle" mode, consumers began to spend their money more strategically, purchasing only the individual songs they wanted to hear. Naturally, this deflated the music retail market by cutting out the portion spent on filler. As Bob Pittman, the cofounder of MTV, former AOL Time Warner COO, and current Clear Channel CEO, acknowledged a few years ago, the reversion to digital singles as the dominant sales format has had a far more ruinous effect on record industry revenues than file sharing has. In Pittman's words, "Stealing music is not [what's] killing music. . . . When I talk to people in the music business, most of them will admit the problem is they're sell-

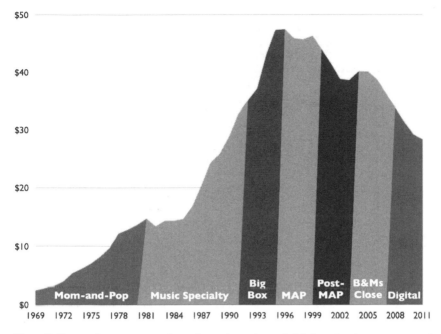

Figure 8. Twenty-first-century music retail transformation and global music sales revenue.

ing songs and not albums. I mean, you do the math."[33] After doing the math, the Harvard Business School professor Anita Elberse concurred with Pittman, concluding that it is indeed a significant factor in decreased sales revenues: "I find strong support for the hypothesis that revenues for [albums] substantially decrease as music is increasingly consumed digitally. While the demand for individual songs is growing at a faster rate than the demand for albums is declining, the dollar amounts gained through new song sales remain far below the level needed to offset the revenues lost due to lower album sales."[34]

Sales have also declined over the past decade as a result of the continuing evolution of the music retail sector. Beginning in the mid-1990s, as I mentioned above, MAP pricing schemes artificially sustained the sales price—and therefore the aggregate sales value—of CDs. This practice ended abruptly in 2000, when attorneys general from forty-three states launched an investigation into its potential anti-competitive implications (fig. 8). Two years later, the suit against the labels was settled for $143 million in cash and donations, with no admission of wrongdoing by the labels. However, then–attorney general of New York Eliot Spitzer announced that the agreement was "a landmark settlement to address years of illegal price-fixing." In the eyes of regulators, there was little question that this scheme had impacted music spending. In fact, Robert Pitofsky, former chairman of the Federal Trade Commission, estimated that consumers had overpaid roughly a half billion dollars for music during the half decade that MAP was in place.[35]

With the end of MAP, CD price points plummeted in the United States, and so did retail margins. This decline happened at just the moment when real estate costs began their greatest climb in American history, causing home values to double in less than a decade,[36] and as retail space underwent a similar escalation in cost. Big-box stores like Walmart and Best Buy could absorb these losses, but music specialty chains began to turn belly-up. HMV scaled back its operations, closing its last American store in 2004. Tower Records and the Musicland Group (owner of Sam Goody) both filed for bankruptcy in 2006. In 2007, Virgin Group sold its North American megastore business to a real estate conglomerate, which then decided to close every store.

These closures had a profound effect on the music retail market, beyond the mere loss of brick-and-mortar square footage. By 2003, owing in large part to its massive, post-MAP discounts on CDs, Walmart had become the top music seller in the world. Yet, because its focus was solely on bringing in foot traffic, its music selection was far more limited than those of Tower or HMV. Why waste valuable shelf space on "niche" music when Shania Twain marked down to $9.99 is all you need to bring in hordes of potential big-ticket shoppers? As the music chains disappeared, so did the music from off the beaten track and below the Top 40. This inevitably undermined music sales overall; although popular music is, by definition, the most popular, independent record labels have historically made up at least 20 percent of the marketplace, and major label "back catalog" (typically older releases and former hits) made up about 30–40 percent of the remaining sales. In other words, by 2003, the world's biggest music retailers were selling only a tiny fraction of the commercial music library, and even the popular titles they did carry addressed only about half of total market demand in terms of volume.

This winnowing of the brick-and-mortar music selection didn't sit well with music buyers. Some shifted their purchases to online CD retailers like Amazon, which had (virtually) infinite shelf space and therefore a broader range of music for sale. Others began to buy their music from digital retailers such as iTunes (which was still burdened by the yoke of DRM). And others shifted their music discovery and acquisition onto online sharing platforms like P2P, or streaming platforms such as

Pandora. As real estate prices continued to climb and consumers became more comfortable with buying their music online, this process began to accelerate. By the end of the decade, big-box retailers had scaled back their already limited music shelf space to make way for other low-consideration entertainment goods (such as movies and games), while iTunes surpassed Walmart as the world's top music seller in 2008. Given that digital goods tend to have a lower retail margin than physical ones, in addition to the unbundling process, this change, like each new development in music retail over the past fifteen years, only further undermined the total value of the music retail market.

There has also been a less quantifiable, but in many ways far more valuable, casualty: the sense of localized music community, best represented by independent record stores and celebrated in books such as Nick Hornby's *High Fidelity* and films such as *Empire Records*. This community has been slowly eroding ever since the "mom-and-pop shops" came under siege in the 1970s, but the total commoditization of music at the hands of Walmart and its consequent dematerialization in the digital ether were the final nails in the coffin. There are many social and cultural benefits that accrue from online music sharing, but none of them can exactly replace what's been lost.

Despite the death of the mom-and-pop shop, the digital age has been a massive boon to the sale of *used* and *independently distributed* music— neither of which appears in the IFPI's market figures (because they don't generate revenue for the member labels). These markets have never been conclusively measured, to my knowledge. There is compelling evidence, however, that both have grown significantly in the past decade, competing with RIAA and IFPI constituent recordings for consumer music expenditures. According to a 2007 *Billboard* article, for instance, the market for used recordings may have doubled or even quadrupled during the early years of the new century. Among the retailers they interviewed, "used CD sales have grown from about 5 percent to sometimes 10–20 percent of overall CD revenues."[37] While this may be a relatively short-term phenomenon, a self-limited consequence of the commoditization of CDs and the shift of the marketplace to digital distribution, the same can't be said for independently distributed music, which has no reason to halt its ascent.

For one thing, there's simply more of it. With cheap music production tools such as Apple's GarageBand, as well as thousands of free and open-source audio production programs, the sheer volume of independently produced music has escalated dramatically over the past decade. A recent report by media researchers Michael Masnick and Michael Ho shows that the music metadata company Gracenote has increased its database of recorded music tenfold in the new century, from eleven million songs in 2001 to over a hundred million in 2010.[38] Although not all of these new entries are necessarily newly released, they largely represent songs that are newly available in the marketplace. For another thing, "long tail" economics have leveled the playing field somewhat, allowing independent music to share virtual shelf space with the biggest sellers on iTunes, Amazon, and Spotify.

It's impossible to quantify the total size of the independently distributed music market, but there are some market indicators that suggest its size is growing significantly. First of all, independent music isn't just *available* on digital music services—people actually listen to, stream, download, and purchase it. Chris Anderson showed this to be the case in his book *The Long Tail,* in which he demonstrated that 45 percent of sales revenue at the digital music seller Rhapsody could be accounted for by "products not available in [the] largest offline retail stores."[39] Similarly, Pandora founder Tim Westergren recently testified before Congress that 70 percent of the artists whose music is played on the digital radio provider (generating performance royalties) are independent.[40] We can also see hints of this market's size by looking at individual aggregators of independent music. CD Baby, a rapidly growing company that sells over four million songs by more than three hundred thousand independent musicians, reports on its website that it has paid out over $250 million to its artists to date,[41] suggesting a retail value in the range of $350 million. Similarly, the independent digital music distributor TuneCore, founded in 2005, currently accounts for about one-tenth of the songs—and 4 percent of the revenues—on iTunes, or about $70 million annually from that source alone. According to its founder, Jeff Price, as of mid-2012 the company had already paid over $300 million in royalties to its member artists.[42] Likewise, as mentioned, the crowdfunding company Kickstarter raised $35 million for independent musicians in 2012, and Bandcamp .com is generating roughly $1 million per month in artist revenues. In short, there are hundreds of millions—or even billions—of dollars spent on music purchases each year that don't figure into the IFPI's official tally, and this number appears to be increasing sharply. At least a portion of these expenditures are doubtless responsible for diminishing major label music sales through competition.

Finally, just as the booming economy of the 1990s inflated the value of music sales during that period, the sagging economy in the twenty-first century has deflated the market, a factor exacerbated by increased competition for consumer discretionary spending from the growing sectors of home video, video games, Internet access, and mobile applications.[43] After a decade of unprecedented expansion, the US economy suffered two major recessions in the course of a decade, while median household income dropped from its historic peak (see fig. 7). Although these factors aren't typically acknowledged by piracy crusaders seeking to place most or all of the blame for their misfortunes on P2P and online music sharing, the major labels have occasionally acknowledged that their market, like any, is subject to the vagaries of the global economy. Predictably, this has happened more frequently in the discussion of good news than bad. For instance, in a 2005 press release, the IFPI acknowledged that improvements in the music economy over the past year had been due in part to "economic strength and strong releases help[ing] CD volume growth."[44]

In short, we cannot blame P2P—or any single factor—for the heavy decline in global music sales over the past decade. However convenient it may be to scapegoat online music fans for the industry's woes, the preponderance of evidence points to a far more complex, and interesting, picture. If "piracy" played a role at all, it was likely in the form of massive commercial CD duplication (primarily in emerging markets), which according to the IFPI has grown from roughly 165 million units in 2000[45] to 1.1 billion units in 2008, accounting for $4.6 billion in sales that year.[46] Nor are the many factors of the music industry's perfect storm discrete. We can't confidently ascribe 10 percent of the market contraction to one and 20 percent to another. To the contrary, they are deeply interrelated; the bad economy helped to drive the housing bubble, which helped to push brick-and-mortar retailers out of business, which helped drive consumers to digital goods, which accelerated the unbundling process, and so forth. At the end of the day, all we can say is that these many factors, taken in aggregate, represent the conclusion of an economic cycle for the music industry, and inaugurate another, with its own threats and opportunities.

Mommy, Where Do Piracy Loss Estimates Come From?

I have spent the bulk of the last two chapters deconstructing myths about "piracy"—specifically, the crusaders' claims that online music sharing is antagonistic to musical culture and industry, and the major labels' attempts to pin the blame for recent sales declines on P2P. Before I conclude this chapter, there is another myth that must be addressed:

namely, oft-quoted figures purporting to tally the total economic impact of "digital piracy," in terms of both lost revenues and lost jobs. Nor is the music industry solely responsible for this myth; similar claims have been made by the film industry and the software industry, who often partner with the IFPI and the RIAA to lobby for stricter copyright, surveillance and censorship laws, and in their legal and extralegal efforts to shut down unlicensed content distribution and punish those responsible.

The news media, government reports, and scholarly articles are rife with quantitative estimates of the economic impact of unlicensed goods and content, most of them attributed to seemingly reputable sources, including trade groups, government departments, commercial research firms, and academic researchers. The most commonly repeated claims are those that the US Chamber of Commerce (USCC) has promoted on its website at least since 2007, namely that "counterfeiting and piracy costs the US between $200–250 billion in lost sales each year [and] have resulted in the loss of 750,000 jobs in the United States."[47] More recently, the USCC has commissioned a research report by self-described "brand protection" company MarkMonitor, which finds (unsurprisingly) that "the worldwide economic impact of *online* piracy and counterfeiting" amounts to $200 billion annually.[48] It is not clear from either organization's publications whether this "staggering" online problem is a very large subset of, or an addition to, the $200–250 billion in annual costs the USCC had previously ascribed to piracy in general. If the former (which seems more likely), it doesn't leave much room for the economic impact of off-line piracy.

Elsewhere, the USCC cites a different study, authored by research firm Frontier Economics and commissioned by the International Chamber of Commerce (ICC), which found that "approximately 2.5 million jobs [annually] have been destroyed by counterfeiting and piracy." This report also claims that the "global economic value of counterfeited and pirated products" was $650 billion in 2008, and is expected to grow to about $1.2 trillion by 2015. The portion of this figure ascribed specifically to "music digital piracy" was "between $17 billion and $40 billion in 2008, and was most likely closer to $40 billion."[49] In other words, according to the ICC, the value of music piracy actually significantly exceeds the value of the entire recorded music industry.

The ICC report itself takes some pains to explain that the music industry hasn't actually lost more to piracy than it earns. The authors emphasize that their figures "provide an estimate of the *total value* of unlicensed digital files available on line [but] are not an estimate of the *business losses* associated with digital piracy, and *should not be interpreted as doing so,*"[50] explaining that such losses would be methodologically impossible to capture. Predictably, these numbers have been consistently misinterpreted in exactly the way the report's authors warn against. For instance, US Senator Chuck Grassley recently gave a statement at a Senate hearing on intellectual property claiming that the "global impact of counterfeiting and piracy" is $650 billion—in other words, painting this figure as representative of costs, rather than value. Even the USCC has misrepresented the ICC's findings, citing the report on its website to support the disingenuous claim that "counterfeit and pirated products account for $360 billion in losses in international trade annually."[51] (This is actually the figure the ICC report describes as the maximal *value* of internationally traded counterfeit and pirated products, a subcomponent of their $650 billion estimate).

Other figures abound as well. For instance, The Institute for Policy Innovation, an archconservative think tank founded by US Congressman Dick Armey, still prominently promotes a 2007 report it published called "The True Cost of Sound Recording Piracy to the U.S. Economy." According to this report, "the U.S. economy loses $12.5 billion in total output annually" (or nearly half of the global recorded music industry's total sales) due to "piracy of sound recordings."[52] The report, which was authored by an economist who, according to his bio, has "been instrumental in furthering the global efforts of the World Intellectual Property Organization,"[53] also claims that Americans lose over 71,000 jobs annually from music piracy. This number is difficult to reconcile with RIAA chief executive Cary Sherman's claim that "direct employment in the industry" has fallen by only about 10,000 in the past 13 years,[54] or with a new report from the International Intellectual Property Alliance (IIPA),[55] penned by the *same author* as the IPI's, which claims that the "core copyright industries" (defined as music, filmed entertainment, software and publishing) only lost a total of 4,000 jobs between 2007 and 2011.[56] Yet the IPI's report has been widely repeated without critique in the press, and is called a "credible study" on the RIAA's own website.[57]

Despite the consistency with which these contradictory and often illogical figures get repeated in the press and elsewhere, I am hardly the first researcher to call the various claims of piracy's economic impact into question. *Ars Technica* journalist Julian Sanchez published an in-depth investigative piece in 2008, concluding that the $250 billion and 750,000 jobs figures promoted by the USCC are "at best, highly dubious. They are phantoms. We have no good reason to think that either is remotely reliable." He also points out that, despite recent reports apparently validating these numbers, they are both "seemingly decades old, gaining a patina of currency and credibility by virtue of being laundered through a relay race of respectable sources." Apparently, they have no foundation whatsoever in concrete economic analysis. When he contacted the government agencies which ostensibly served as the sources of the dollar figure, for instance, he was told that they couldn't "find any record of how that number was computed."[58] Sanchez has revisited this subject over the years; in an extensive blog post for the Cato Institute in 2012 titled "How Copyright Industries Con Congress," he connects the dots between research and policy, demonstrating that his "phantom" numbers were a central element in the recent efforts to legislate Internet censorship via the Stop Online Piracy Act (SOPA).[59]

The US Government Accountability Office (GAO) has also taken pains to identify the sources of many of these figures, pursuant to the Prioritizing Resources and Organization for Intellectual Property (PRO-IP) Act, which was signed into law in 2008. Interestingly, the GAO's findings were somewhat at odds with the rhetoric of the law's proponents. Specifically, the authors found that "[t]hree widely cited U.S. government estimates of economic losses resulting from counterfeiting [including the $200–250 billion figure cited by the USCC] cannot be substantiated due to the absence of underlying studies." Even further, the report conceded that any such figures cited in any context are most likely spurious, given that "it is difficult, if not impossible, to quantify the economy-wide impacts" of piracy.[60]

Ultimately, then, the entire case for the economic impact of digital "piracy" is a castle built on quicksand—or perhaps a more apt metaphor would be the mythical Ouroboros, a snake that devours its own tail. A lobbyist (RIAA) aims to amplify its credibility by citing a study produced by an independent consultancy (Frontier Economics) and funded by the International Chamber of Commerce.[61] Frontier's study repeatedly explains that it is "building on the OECD methodology" and "building on the OECD's work,"[62] thereby increasing its own credibility by resting its case on the findings of a multigovernmental economic organization. The OECD, in turn, gains credibility by basing its analysis in part on figures sourced to government agencies—specifically, the US Federal Trade Commission (FTC). The US government's own Accountability Office investigates these figures and finds that FTC officials "were unable to locate any record or source of this estimate within its reports or archives, and officials could not recall the agency ever developing or using this estimate."[63] Yet, regardless of this fundamental absence of substantiation, the RIAA successfully lobbies Congress, the White House, and international treaty organizations to aggressively promote legislation based on their claims, and to police, arrest and punish those allegedly responsible for the phantom damages. Dissenting voices are systematically excluded from the debate and erased from the news coverage. The cycle, unchecked, repeats itself *ad nauseam*.

As I HAVE argued in this chapter, most of the claims underpinning the piracy crusade have little or no basis in reality. The music industry has indeed undergone a radical economic transformation since the turn of the century, but to the extent that P2P and online music sharing played any role, it was minimal, and can't reasonably be said to have "caused the entire enormous decline," as Liebowitz and his sponsors at the RIAA have claimed. The industry, which was buoyed to unprecedented heights by a "perfect bubble" in the 1990s, shrank again a decade later, due to a "perfect storm" exacerbated by the recording industry's own self-admitted failure to adequately provide their consumers with a functional digital music market.

The industry's quantitative assessments of market harm from P2P and other forms of digital "piracy," though widely repeated, have little or no basis in fact, and analysis by the federal government has debunked some of the claims that are integral to its own trade and copyright policies. In fact, according to the IIPA's own recent analysis, value added to the US economy by the "core" copyright industries increased by $27.5 billion, and the sector itself grew by 1.1 percent annually in real value, between 2007 and 2010. With these metrics, according to their 2011 report, "the U.S. copyright industries have consistently outperformed the rest of the U.S. economy" in recent years.[64] These findings seem fundamentally irreconcilable with claims of large-scale damages due to piracy, especially considering that file sharing traffic has continued to grow, and is projected to nearly triple between 2010 and 2015, according to analysis by research firm GigaOM.[65]

Despite (or because of) the continued growth of online music sharing, there is significant reason to believe that the music industry economy is beginning to stabilize, which would make the "perfect storm" years of 2000–2011 seem transitional in retrospect. Not only is the rate of decline in global music sales slowing considerably (in fact, the market grew in the US and elsewhere in 2011, and preliminary data show US music unit sales volume at an all time high in 2012), but the labels and publishers have finally begun to license their content for use in innovative new business models premised on abundance rather than scarcity, such as Spotify and iTunes Match, offering the prospect of higher revenues—and higher customer satisfaction—than the sales of "a la carte" digital singles alone could accomplish. To put it another way, the industry appears to be recognizing that its market has transformed, and is applying genuine efforts toward meeting its consumers halfway.

We are not out of the woods yet, however. Labels are still more likely to litigate than to license when confronted by a genuinely innovative music distribution platform, and there's the minor matter of a decade of lost opportunities and ill will to overcome. In my next chapter, I will discuss the recording industry's lingering goodwill problem and continuing strategic missteps, and discuss the extent to which its piracy crusade has exacerbated these problems.

CHAPTER 6

Is the Music Industry Its Own Worst Enemy?

IN 1896, the British House of Lords adjudicated Trego vs. Hunt, a suit involving two business partners who had parted ways, Hunt selling his share to Trego. After pocketing Trego's money, Hunt hired a clerk to copy down all the names and addresses of the firm's clients, so he could start a new business and poach them. Ultimately, Hunt was found to be in the wrong, the reason being that when he sold his share of the company, he had also given up his rights to the "goodwill"—the business reputation and customer relations—that went along with it. As Lord MacNaghten, one of the adjudicators, reasoned: "Often it happens that Goodwill is the very sap and life of the business, without which it would yield little or no fruit. It is the whole advantage, whatever it may be, of the reputation and connection of the firm, which may have been built up by years of honest work, or gained by lavish expenditure of money."[1]

Much in culture, law, and finance has changed since the late nineteenth century, but goodwill remains the "very sap and life" of business, and, if anything, has become only more vital in our brand-driven, media-saturated information economy. Today, goodwill is a standard element of business accounting and formally refers to the intangible reputational factors that increase a company's value above the "book value of its identifiable or physical assets."[2] Although there are established methods for valuing goodwill (and its loss, or "impairment"), this process is still considered by many finance professionals to be "more art than science."[3]

Because of its heavy reliance on marketing and promotion ("lavish expenditure of money"), as well as its extensive business-to-business dealings ("years of honest work"), goodwill is even more important in music than in most other fields. The authors of the industry bible, *This Business of Music,* declared, "One cannot overemphasize the value of names in the music industry, [and] the goodwill attached to names in the music business is even more important in music industry circles [than among consumers]."[4] Naturally, then, any impairment or tarnishing of the major labels' brands and reputations is a serious threat to their market value and to their ability to do business (according to recent analysis by Echo Research, the average company can attribute 26 percent of its market cap to its reputation).[5]

Has the music industry lost goodwill in recent years? It's an interesting question, and even the major labels themselves don't seem sure of the answer. Warner Music Group, which was a publicly traded company from 2004 to 2011, was required to disclose any goodwill impairment in its public financial filings during that time period. According to its annual reports (form 10-K), the results of its own tests showed that "no impairment occurred" in 2008, 2009, or 2010. Yet when the IFPI—of which Warner is a constituent member—sued The Pirate Bay torrent tracker in 2009, it specifically claimed that "the damages sought should cover not only record sales lost to the Pirate Bay, but the loss of goodwill and other harm caused by file sharing."[6] In other words, the major labels were suing for the damage done to their goodwill by P2P despite claiming no such damage in their official accounting records.

A clue that the recording industry has, in fact, suffered from some goodwill impairment came in 2007, when the RIAA was voted the "worst company in America" by readers of popular blog *The Consumerist,* consigning the previous year's winner, Halliburton, to second place.[7] Thus, I tend to agree with the IFPI that there has been substantial damage to the industry's brands and business reputation, but differ when it comes to the cause. Far from blaming file sharing services or their users, I believe the industry itself is largely the engineer of its own reputational misfortunes. To the extent that P2P or digital technology in general have played a role in the process, it is only by (a) providing consumers, artists, and innovators with an alternative to the industry's historically cartelized distribution practices and therefore bringing the fundamental unfairness of those practices into sharp relief, and (b) providing a target for the music industry's ruinous piracy crusade, which has engendered an unyielding torrent of public relations debacles since the turn of the century. Additionally, the industry's continuing strategic failure to develop a proactive digital business model (as I discussed in chapter 3) has undermined its credibility among potential partners and investors, further diminishing whatever goodwill remains.

The Industry's Chickens Come Home to Roost

This is hardly the first era in which the music industry's reputation has been challenged. The payola scandals of the 1950s and 2000s suggested to many observers that the industry was more concerned with raking in profits than with releasing good music. The 1985 Senate hearings on profanity in popular music spurred nationwide hand wringing over the nefarious effects of heavy metal (and other forms of "audio pornography") on America's youth. Sensationalistic challenges to religious authority by Madonna, Sinéad O'Connor, and other performers and the association of underworld violence with gangsta rap sent god-fearing, law-abiding citizens into apoplexies during the 1990s. In every era, it seems, the industry has struggled to keep its nose clean, barely skirting the edge of propriety and keeping only one step ahead of the proverbial torches and pitchforks.

Given this colorful history, it would be tempting to see any current challenges to the music industry's goodwill as simply another iteration of a well-established pattern. Yet there is something distinct about the industry's present reputational straits. In the past, its primary critics and detractors tended to fall into two (somewhat overlapping) categories: social conservatives opposed to the sex/violence/permissiveness exhibited and championed by youth-oriented musical genres like rock and rap, and "high culture" types like Theodor Adorno,[8] concerned that popular music was junk food for the soul and corrosive to the political process. Even the payola scandals, which were technically about unethical market manipulation, were initially spurred by concerns about the role of rock music in promoting racial integration and otherwise undermining the foundations of white American hegemony.[9] In nearly every case, the music industry was able to turn the outrage to its advantage, developing a romantic aura of danger and mystique, and a reputation as a boundary-pushing force for social change, in cahoots with the youth, the artists, and the revolutionaries of the world.

By contrast, the music industry today faces its greatest criticism from its former allies: its own artists, business partners, and consumers. Ironically, its staunchest supporters today are government regulators (instead of holding investigative hearings, for instance, Congress now promotes legislation aimed at granting the industry ever-greater power), and its chief allies include religious groups, police organizations, and conservative social and political advocates.[10] What accounts for this sudden shift in polarity? How did the music industry lose its mojo and its cred, and why does it seem to have become the very image of its putative nemesis, what in the counterculture era it would have called "The Man"? The answer has little to do with some foundational shift in industry ethics or practices and can be better understood as a powerful cartel's long-wandering chickens coming home to roost.

First of all, the music industry has a history of unfair and exploitative labor practices. In addition to the legislative and contractual wrangling I described earlier, the major labels have often reached beyond the liberal scope of their allotted power, violating the terms of their own contracts and functionally robbing their artists of their entitled dues. For instance, a recent legal suit brought by country music legend Kenny Rogers against Capitol Records[11] offers a litany of alleged violations, including

> taking two years to respond to an audit request
>
> refusing to account for, or pay a share of, the substantial fees collected in lawsuits against P2P companies such as Napster, Kazaa, and Grokster
>
> holding over $76,000 in unprocessed royalties in a "suspense file" with no apparent right or cause
>
> non-payment of royalties from sales of music via record clubs
>
> non-payment of royalties on "free goods" distributed overseas, in violation of Rogers's contract
>
> inconsistent documentation, "in that some accounts showed earnings for certain albums in certain periods, but other accounts . . . failed to reflect those earnings"
>
> withholding foreign taxes even though they were offset by tax credits
>
> incorrect royalty rate calculation in some foreign territories
>
> charging over $12,000 to Rogers without any explanation of those charges
>
> charging Rogers 100% of video production costs, even though his contract stipulated a 50% charge
>
> failing to account for or pay royalties based on radio performance royalties[12]
>
> paying Rogers a far lower royalty than his contract required for "non-disc records" such as digital downloads and ringtones
>
> failing to remedy any of these oversights financially once the audit had revealed them

True, these are *alleged* wrongs in a legal complaint, but they are consistent with those described in other recent lawsuits and with widespread criticisms from artist advocates over several decades. (The University of

Ottawa law professor Michael Geist, quoting another lawsuit brought by artists against major labels alleging $6 billion in damages *by the labels,* attributes what he calls their "rampant infringement" to a routine policy of "exploit now, pay later if at all.")[13] And if these are the kinds of liberties major record labels are willing to take with the accounts of popular, established acts such as Kenny Rogers, it seems likely that less experienced or less powerful artists are apt to be exploited to an even greater degree and have less recourse. Indeed, chroniclers of African American musical culture have observed in depth the degrees to which the music industry has systematically denied black musicians an ownership stake—or even a living wage—for the profound range of musics they have contributed to the marketplace, from ragtime to rap and beyond.[14] As Q-Tip rapped in A Tribe Called Quest's classic 1991 song "Check the Rhime": "Industry rule number four thousand and eighty / Record company people are shady."

In addition to its exploitative labor relations, the music industry has also historically had problematic dealings with its partners and competitors, and has consistently been accused, and at times convicted, of anti-competitive, collusive, coercive, or dishonest relations with other firms and organizations. As I discussed in chapter 1, this predates the recorded music industry; as early as the mid-nineteenth century, the largest American music publishers colluded to set prices for printed scores. Since then, virtually every consolidated sector of the industry, from broadcasters[15] to radio promoters[16] to event promoters[17] to television networks[18] to music retailers[19] to the major labels,[20] has conformed to this pattern, facing lawsuits, government investigations, and regulatory actions aimed at curtailing such behaviors or even dismantling the cartels. By the turn of the twenty-first century, the music industry rested on an uneasy détente between these highly concentrated, deeply interdependent oligarchies (in the words of the veteran pop guitarist and author Steve Lukather, it was, at this point, "the most corrupt business—next to politics—in the world").[21]

The third area in which the music industry has historically undermined its goodwill is in its relations with its consumers. Price-fixing of musical scores and CDs continued into the digital age, with the launch of the major label–owned, DRM-backed digital music subscription initiatives MusicNet and PressPlay in 2001, which required consumers to pay $240 per year—far more than the median music buyer typically spent—just to listen to digital music from all five major labels.[22] The US Department of Justice soon investigated these services for potential anticompetitive practices,[23] and at the time of writing, there is still a pending antitrust suit[24] against the majors for their involvement in these businesses (the US Supreme Court declined to hear an appeal by the labels in 2011). Another practice that engendered some bad blood was the recording industry's effort to phase out the "single" format while injecting the typical album-length release with more filler than hits. This widely recognized practice (*Billboard* once reviewed an album as "remarkably filler-free")[25] was an affront to consumers, who were forced to pay for several songs they didn't want in order to own the two or three they actually cared about. Numerous other examples could be cited, from the FTC-investigated "negative option" billing practices[26] used by label-run record clubs to the self-scalping, service charges, and other methods by which music event ticket prices have been jacked up over the years.[27] A full accounting could easily fill a chapter on its own; suffice it to say that the music industry has historically overcharged and under-delivered for its own consumers, across a range of products and sectors. If we also consider the industry's periodic attempts to demonize its own customer base (e.g., "Home Taping Is Killing Music"), it is little surprise that the long-simmering pressure cooker of consumer resentment would explode once the lid was lifted.

The digitization of music, and musical culture, proved the necessary catalyst to bring the music industry's tensions with its artists, business partners, and consumers to a crisis point. By giving artists the tools and technologies to take charge of their own production, marketing, and distribution, digitization underscored the disequilibrium of traditional record contracts and offered what for many is a preferable alternative. Why agree to a 12 percent royalty rate (pre-recoupment, and pre-shenanigans) when an online self-distribution platform like Tunecore enables an artist to keep 100 percent of sales revenues for a fixed fee of a few dollars per track per year? True, a major label–backed album might sell more units, but, as the old business adage holds, you can't make up for negative margins on volume.

Digitization has also challenged traditional music cartels, and the anti-competitive practices they embrace, largely by virtue of its dematerializing effect on recorded music itself. Historically, the cartels were built by tightly controlling distribution of physical scores and recordings to retail environments, and by restricting music on the airwaves to "clear channels" owned by broadcasting conglomerates. Both methods were forms of manufactured scarcity, inflating the market value of what would otherwise have been a ubiquitous resource through a constellation of technological and legal constraints. Digitization largely eliminated these technological barriers, by enabling songs to be reproduced and redistributed infinitely at no cost, by providing online retailers with limitless shelf space, and by enabling webcasters to offer as many different programs and playlists as there are listeners.

These changes provided greater leverage both to innovative businesses and to consumers. For instance, independent musicians and record labels no longer had to pay a premium to share shelf space or air time with the majors; most digital retailers and subscription providers now boast libraries of 15–20 million songs, as does Clear Channel's custom webcasting product, iHeartRadio (though many of the company's terrestrial broadcasting stations still offer playlists of 100 or fewer songs). Nor are consumers nearly as beholden to the dictates of the marketplace; if commercial music products and services don't offer appealing features at reasonable prices, they will seek out their music through other means, such as P2P.

Not only have these newfound freedoms highlighted by contrast how unfair the twentieth-century music business was, they have allowed artists, music businesses, and consumers a measure of independence from the major labels, publishers, retailers, and broadcasters. This independence in turn has allowed a greater degree of criticism without fear of reprisal. In the meantime, the burgeoning blogosphere and other outlets of social media have amplified the conversation, bringing once arcane legal and economic arguments into the public realm. Whereas the industry once operated behind a veil of chic professionalism, today its inner workings are subject to the judgments and voluble opinions of millions of armchair business analysts and cultural commentators. Even this book, which once would have been written in a solitary vacuum and read by a select group of academic researchers, has been "pre-published" freely online and already read by thousands of people, many of them presumably from outside of the academy and music industry. With this greater degree of overall scrutiny has come a broader acknowledgment of the industry's faults, its errors, and its foibles; even if the industry transformed itself today into a global charity focused on curing AIDS and ending poverty, it seems likely that its uncharitable past would continue to haunt it.

Battling Customers: A Recipe for "Badwill"

Unfortunately, the music industry did not view digitization as a sign that its historically anticompetitive business practices needed revamping, or that its bully image required rehabilitation. Instead, the major labels and their allies tacked in the opposite direction. With the physical mechanism of cartelization quickly evaporating, the industry redoubled its focus on its legal mechanism—namely, copyright. Now, instead of erecting toll booths outside of retailers and broadcasters, and excluding or overcharging potential competitors seeking admission, the major labels and publishers wielded the threat of crippling and sustained litigation to prevent upstarts and innovators from gaining market share and industry influence. The strategy appears to have worked, at least to a degree; as an unidentified industry insider recently told Rutgers law professor Michael Carrier, "from 2000 to 2010, even to this day, there really hasn't been new innovation in digital music other than iTunes."[28]

With the renewed focus on copyright as the saving grace of the legacy music cartels came an amplification in the rhetoric and propaganda surrounding unlicensed uses of music online. Innovative sites and services were branded as "rogues," and their millions of users classified as "pirates." These changes were neither coincidental nor reflexive, but rather the result of what the IFPI called an "intense global information campaign [beginning] in 2003, with the aim of explaining the illegality of unauthorised online music distribution." By the recording industry's own account, the campaigns had an immediate and "decisive impact in raising public awareness on the issue internationally."[29] Available data appear to bear this out; a search of international news sources on the research archive Westlaw shows the use of the term "illegal downloading" escalating from 80 stories in 2002 to 315 in 2003; similarly, uses of the term "music piracy" grew from 363 to 908 during the same year (fig. 9). Yet despite these apparent successes, the campaigns also brought some negative consequences, namely a groundswell of "badwill" (the opposite of goodwill, in business jargon) among the industry's consumer base. While such consequences may have been unintended, or even underevaluated by the industry, they were hardly unforeseen; as an article in *Businessweek* warned in January 2003, at the outset of the campaign, "Branding too many customers [as] criminals could incur the wrath of the larger music community."[30]

Vitriolic and effective though it may have been, the "piracy" rhetoric was only half of the industry's "awareness" effort. As the IFPI described it, the campaign was "coupled with the launch of extensively publicised lawsuits against major copyright offenders in the US," which were conceived of not as a means to recoup lost revenues or even to punish wrongdoers, but rather as "a crucial public deterrent" against copyright infringement. In other words, these "major copyright offenders," who

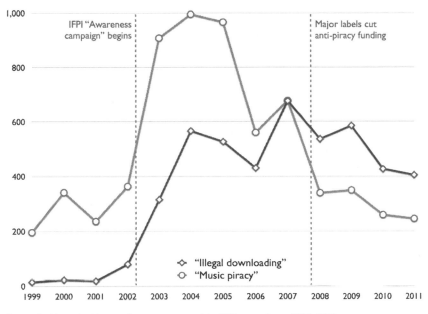

Figure 9. News incidence of terms promoted by IFPI campaigns, 1999–2011.

by the IFPI's own definition were those who had shared "hundreds" of song files via P2P, were targeted for litigation primarily as a media stunt. Again, by the IFPI's own accounts, the policy was immediately effective; according to its tally, "awareness of the illegality of unauthorised file-swapping in the US rose from 37% before the lawsuits to 64% in December 2003."[31]

Like those of the awareness campaign, the litigation initiative's measurable short-term successes were easily matched by long-term strategic failures. If calling its own customers criminals had spurred some negative backlash, suing them by the thousands, after explicitly pledging not to do so,[32] officially put the music industry at war with the population at large. And like some actual military interventions, this quickly became a classic "quagmire"; even as the evident costs to goodwill mounted, the industry remained far too invested to cease operations and withdraw. The initiative began with a splash, with 261 lawsuits filed against alleged P2P users in September 2003 and the promise that "thousands more" suits would follow if need be.[33] The RIAA lived up to its word; five years later, the major labels had sued over 35,000 Americans.[34]

The badwill associated with the RIAA lawsuits wasn't simply a matter of freeloaders grousing at the consequences of their own wrongdoing.

An unprecedented wave of mass litigation by an industry against its own customers was a pretty ugly story to begin with. Forcing these tens of thousands of defendants to settle for thousands of dollars apiece or face mounting legal costs and the threat of millions of dollars in damages was worse; it was widely (and accurately, in my opinion) perceived as bullying. Failing to compensate musicians for the revenues collected from these suits[35] cemented this perception, and undermined the labels' claims that they were motivated primarily by the desire to "support" their artists. But the greatest blow to the recording industry's reputation was in its seemingly callous disregard for the lives of its defendants, many of whom were either so clearly innocent, or so severely challenged by circumstance, as to warrant leniency—a consideration they received belatedly, or not at all.

Several publications have examined these cases in far greater detail[36] than I can here, so I will simply mention a few notable examples. One of the initial 261 "major offenders" to be sued was Brianna LaHara, a twelve-year-old honors student living in a New York City housing project. Despite her parents' financial straits, and the fact that her mother had actually paid $29.99 to use the KaZaA P2P service, the RIAA demanded (and received, in less than a day) a $2,000 settlement and a public apology.[37] In addition to targeting minors, the industry has also sued the elderly, and even the deceased. In 2005, the RIAA sued an eighty-three-year-old, technologically illiterate woman named Gertrude Walton for allegedly sharing over 700 songs via P2P—a week *after* it had received a copy of her death certificate from her daughter in response to a warning letter.[38] This case was wisely dropped once the press caught wind of it. Similarly, after a P2P defendant named Larry Scantlebury died in the midst of litigation, the RIAA requested that the case be stayed for sixty days "to allow the family additional time to grieve," then resumed the suit by deposing his children.[39] The RIAA has also sued apparently innocent people without even alerting them to the situation. When the *Rockmart Journal,* a local paper in Georgia, called nearby resident James Walls to ask for comment on his being named as a defendant, he seemed taken by surprise. "I don't understand this," he reportedly responded. "How can they sue us when we don't even have a computer?"[40]

College students are a natural target for the RIAA, but sometimes its choice of students and methods of addressing them have seemed almost calculated to produce badwill. In November 2002, as the "war on terror" was gearing up in Afghanistan and elsewhere, the organization goaded the US Naval Academy into raiding one hundred of its own midshipmen, confiscating their computers in the middle of class and threatening to court martial those found guilty of infringing copyright.[41] In 2006, an MIT student named Cassi Hunt, who had been sued for file sharing, called the RIAA's "settlement negotiation hotline" and tried to explain that she couldn't afford either a sustained legal defense or the $3,750 settlement they'd requested. As she reported in an article in campus paper *The Tech,* the negotiator told her that "the RIAA has been known to suggest that students drop out of college or go to community college in order to be able to afford settlements." Hunt's analysis of the situation aptly summarized the message communicated by the litigation campaign: "The Recording Industry of America would rather see America's youth deprived of higher education, forever marring their ability to contribute personally and financially to society—including the arts—so that they may crucify us as examples to our peers. To say nothing of wrecking our lives in the process."[42]

Finally, the RIAA has on several occasions targeted severely ill or disabled people for litigation. According to the Electronic Frontier Foundation (EFF; a nonprofit group that advocates for civil liberties in cyber space), one defendant, a "fully disabled widow and veteran," was sued for downloading five hundred songs she already had copies of on CD. In her case, P2P was used purely for accessibility; she wanted to listen to her music collection in the room where she spent most of her time. The RIAA offered a $2,000 settlement, on the condition that she share "a wealth of private information regarding her disability and her finances."[43] In 2007, the labels sued John Paladuk, a former railroad worker who had recently suffered a stroke that paralyzed the left side of his body, and whose sole source of income was his disability check. The alleged infringements had taken place in Michigan, and Mr. Paladuk had lived in Florida at the time they took place.[44] After nearly two months of litigation (and negative coverage in publications including *BoingBoing,* the *Consumerist,* and the *New York Times*), the RIAA agreed to dismiss the case, leaving "each party to bear his its/his own fees and costs." In another case, the recording industry aggressively pursued Rae J. Schwartz, a Queens, New York, mother suffering from multiple sclerosis, who could only travel aboard a motorized scooter and who maintained that she had never downloaded anything illegally. Her lawyer requested that the case be dropped, the plaintiffs declined, and the suit went forward, with the court assigning a legal guardian to stand for Ms. Schwartz. After more than two years of harrowing and expensive litigation, the parties settled out of court for undisclosed terms.[45]

It's perfectly reasonable to assume that the cases I've outlined above are the exceptions rather than the rule; most P2P defendants aren't quite so unfortunate, and it's possible that the majority of them are, in fact, liable (although Ray Beckerman, a defense attorney who knows more about these suits than anyone else outside of the RIAA, holds otherwise).[46] Yet, from the standpoint of goodwill and public relations, these questions are irrelevant. The recording industry inaugurated this policy as part of a "public awareness" campaign, and by the end of its five-year run,[47] the public was painfully aware that the industry seemed hell-bent on protecting its assets at any cost. In the words of a 2009 article in the *Minnesota Journal of Law, Science & Technology,* the industry's strategy to counter "digital music piracy" has "embittered or calloused a substantial portion of the public. In particular, the lawsuit component of the industry's approach, besides being ineffective, has proven highly repugnant."[48]

Toward the end, even some record industry executives and organizations publicly acknowledged that the strategy had backfired. For instance, EMI threatened to leave the IFPI over the "bad public image" resulting from the suits,[49] and Jennifer Pariser, an attorney for Sony Music, admitted under oath that the lawsuits represented a "money pit" for the labels.[50] Yet when RIAA president Cary Sherman—the definitive industry spokesman—was interviewed by Declan McCullagh of *CNET News,* he showed neither remorse nor trepidation about the litigation tactics or their ruinous effects on defendants. In response to the question "Do you view your lawsuits, even ones where you sued a 12-year-old girl or a Boston grandmother, as a success overall and do you think the process is working?," Sherman responded, "Yes. We're feeling pretty good."[51]

Insult to Injury: Further Piracy Crusade Debacles

In addition to the significant badwill engendered by the music industry's past business practices and its recent litigious fervor, the piracy crusade has been repeatedly marked by public relations debacles that have presented the industry as duplicitous, corrupt, and/or clueless. Ultimately, it is irrelevant whether these characterizations, like the lawsuits, reflect the industry's typical conduct or demeanor; the important thing is that the labels' reputations have been further tarnished.

An early example of this propensity for bad PR took place in 1997, when the industry was just ramping up its efforts to combat MP3-hosting websites. The RIAA identified ParSoft Interactive, a game design company from Plano, Texas, as one such online infringer. Instead of calling the company and asking it to stop, "RIAA lawyers stormed in 'like the Men in Black,'" the Parsoft business manager told a reporter soon afterward. They threw down "a huge swatch of legal papers and said, 'You're running an illegal site.' . . . "It was a week of hell and $10,000 down the toilet." After ParSoft was forced to retain both an attorney and a public relations firm to defend the suit and the company's reputation, it turned out that the files hadn't been posted by anyone at the company, but rather by an employee of their Internet service provider.[52]

While the Parsoft incident can be written off as a regrettable but somewhat humorous case of mistaken identity, other anti-piracy fiascos have not been quite so benign. For instance, as early as 2002, the RIAA and its frequent partner in the piracy crusade, the MPAA,[53] successfully convinced Congress to introduce a bill that would have indemnified both groups against all state and federal laws in their attempts to stop a "publicly accessible peer-to-peer file-trading network"—essentially granting them carte blanche to hack into and destroy any private or commercial computer suspected of hosting unlicensed content. Given the obvious risks of false accusations and the lack of legal checks and balances, there was little doubt among its critics that such a law would have led to significant, unrecoverable damages sustained by innocent parties. Moreover, there was legitimate concern (considering the industries' histories) that such power could have been used as an effective tool for anticompetitive tactics. Consequently, the Berkeley law professor Mark Lemley characterized the bill as a "nightmare,"[54] Will Rodger of the CCIA[55] referred to it as "vigilante justice for the 21st century,"[56] and the tech policy analyst Hal Plotkin, writing on the *San Francisco Chronicle* website, called it "an incredibly vivid example of how easily government officials can unintentionally screw up the economy."[57]

Unsurprisingly, given the backlash it generated, this particular bill died in subcommittee. But that didn't stop the music industry from experimenting with computer hacking as a piracy deterrent. On Halloween 2005, a blogger and tech researcher named Mark Russinovich posted a lengthy analysis[58] of a new security risk he had discovered: "copy-protection" technology installed on a CD manufactured by Sony BMG had, without his knowledge or consent, installed a rootkit on his computer. In Russinovich's words, rootkits are "cloaking technologies that hide files, Registry keys, and other system objects from diagnostic and security software, and they are usually employed by malware attempting to keep their implementation hidden." In other words, even without Congressional carte blanche (or suspicion of infringement, for that matter), Sony BMG had gone ahead with its hacking plan. In the weeks that followed, it turned out that tens, if not hundreds, of millions of discs contained the software, which not only opened a "back door" in users' computers, exposing them to malicious hackers, but also slowed down and in many cases crashed their computers. Some consumer electronics, such as car stereos, were also affected (in fact, my own Sony car stereo became unusable after I tried to play a Sony Music CD in it). After a tsunami of negative publicity, several class action lawsuits,[59] and several investigations by state and federal regulators, the CDs were recalled, and Sony BMG published uninstallers for the software—which, sadly, presented new security threats when used.[60]

After this colossal debacle, one would think the major labels would take greater care to ensure their customers' privacy and security. Yet security problems related to the piracy crusade have continued to crop up—for example, in 2009 it was discovered that BayTSP, which policed online copyright infringement on behalf of the RIAA and MPAA, was storing all of the data about the identities of suspected infringers in an unsecured Internet database, permitting it to be searched via Google and "allowing anyone with hackerish leanings ample opportunity to create all kinds of mischief."[61]

Finally, there have been several instances of apparent "piracy" and corruption by the piracy crusaders themselves. Some of this is predictable, garden-variety hypocrisy, as when sixty television shows (worth $9 million in damages, according to statutory rates) downloaded illegally via BitTorrent were tracked to the RIAA's headquarters,[62] or when executives at "nearly every major entertainment industry company in the US" were caught downloading both music and movies via P2P.[63] But sometimes the stories have taken a darker turn. For example, there is the case of Melchior Rietveldt, a freelance music producer who was commissioned to compose a soundtrack for an anti-piracy video released by BREIN (the Dutch entertainment industry trade association) in 2006. The following year, Rietveldt bought a DVD of a *Harry Potter* movie and was shocked to find that the video had been included on the disc, in direct violation of his contract with BREIN, which limited its use to a local film festival. After doing some research, the composer discovered that the video had been included on tens of millions of Dutch DVDs without his knowledge, consent, or remuneration. In other words, his anti-piracy song had been pirated by the piracy crusaders.

Rietveldt soon contacted the music rights organization Buma/Stemra in search of what he estimated were about a million euros in unpaid royalties. The organization, which according to its website[64] "represents the interests of music authors" and "help[s] enforce copyright," was not immediately forthcoming with either royalties or advice. After years of effort, Rietveldt finally heard back from a Buma/Stemra board member named Jochem Gerrits, who offered to help him recover the unpaid royalties. But the offer came at a steep price: Gerrits demanded that he personally be paid 33 percent of whatever money was recouped. Fortunately, the Dutch television show *PowNews* recorded Gerrits's extortion request in a phone conversation with Rietveldt's financial adviser, and Gerrits was exposed and forced to "temporarily" resign. Whether Rietveldt ultimately prevails in his lawsuits against BREIN and Gerrits, the damage to the industry's goodwill has been done. The scandal has been called "corrupt," a "money grab," and "mafia-like" by prominent politicians and musicians,[65] and has been covered by media outlets around the globe.

THAT THE music industry's reputation, both among consumers and within the business community, has taken a beating in recent years is clear. And though digital technologies such as P2P have certainly played a role, the developers or users of these technologies are not necessarily to blame. To the contrary, it is the piracy crusaders themselves—primarily, the major labels—who have ruined whatever goodwill the industry once enjoyed.

In part this results from the public airing of years of "dirty laundry"—poor labor relations and questionable business practices—in the wake of digitization, which has both shifted the industry's balance of power and provided an outlet for the industry's critics to collect and share information. But, ironically, the bulk of the badwill can almost certainly be attributed to the recording industry's efforts to curb what it calls "digital music piracy." By insulting and litigating against its own consumers, and pursuing several highly publicized suits against seemingly innocent, unfortunate, or otherwise sympathetic defendants, the RIAA and its constituent labels have come to be seen as intransigent bullies, big businesses willing to "pick on the little guy"[66] in order to enforce obedience through fear. And by tolerating P2P usage and worse hypocrisies within its own ranks, the industry has further eroded any moral high ground it might have sought in the arena of public opinion.

What's more, these highly publicized lapses amount to far more than a mere embarrassment or black mark on the industry's reputation. Because goodwill is so central to the music economy, the greatest damage can be measured in the industry's bottom line. Although it is impossible to quantify precisely, there can be little doubt that the impairment of goodwill is a primary factor in defections among artists, mistrust among potential partners and business clientele, and indifference or hostility within the customer base.[67] According to a recent survey in Britain, nearly half of all music fans now believe it's "acceptable to download music free of charge."[68] The recording industry would probably interpret this fact as a sign that its awareness campaigns and antipiracy efforts need to be improved upon and amplified. As I have argued in this chapter, the opposite conclusion is far more reasonable—the music economy has suffered *because of,* not despite, the piracy crusade.

PART III

Collateral Damage: The Hidden Costs of the Piracy Crusade

IN THIS FINAL section, I address the social and economic costs of the industry's piracy crusade and consider some of the longer-term dangers we face if the crusade is allowed to continue.

Given the pro-business veneer of the music industry's rhetoric, it's ironic that one of the principal victims of the piracy crusade is the music business itself. The major labels' unwillingness to license their music to innovators on viable terms, combined with their inability to innovate on their own, paralyzed the industry at exactly the moment when new technologies offered the greatest amount of promise and when consumers expressed the greatest enthusiasm for new products and services. Similarly, the anti-piracy laws and policies promoted by the industry seem tailored to keep established oligopolists firmly in place, while eliminating the market conditions that allowed upstarts (and the major labels and broadcasters themselves) to reinvent the music industry in the past.

Far more troubling than the piracy crusade's commercial effects, however, are its social effects. An underlying political agenda that privileges the short-term interests of media cartels over the long-term health and viability of our democratic institutions has prompted the music industry and its allies to promote an increasingly draconian set of laws and policies in the United States and around the world. Collectively, these laws and policies threaten to stifle free speech and the open public sphere, and provide ample opportunity for exploitation by anti-competitive business interests, repressive political regimes, and organized criminals alike. These threats will only grow as networked communications become ever more pervasive and as the piracy crusade successfully promotes ever stricter laws governing the flow of information via these networks. Ultimately, neither musical culture and industry nor democratic society can thrive until the crusade is ended and its policies are dismantled.

CHAPTER 7

"This Sounds Way Too Good"

No Good Idea Goes Unpunished

IN MOMENTS of quiet reverie, I often return to a favorite fantasy of mine—one most likely shared by many media and technology enthusiasts of a certain age. I have been transported back in time to visit my teenage self, equipped with the latest twenty-first-century gadgetry. I watch as fifteen-year-old me familiarizes himself with the smooth contours and intuitive interface of my MacBook, tests his mettle in the multiplayer mode of the latest Halo installment on a sixty inch HDTV, and reminisce with him about our childhood as we retrace the geography of our shared past via Google Earth. All of this, naturally, blows his little analog mind. But the thing that gets his heart—and mine—racing the fastest is the music technology.

I amaze my younger self with Shazam's ability to identify any song just by listening to it for a few seconds. Together, we search for rare Bob Dylan concert videos on YouTube. I set up GarageBand on an iPad and help him cut a demo of his latest peace-punk anthem. But I save the crowning achievement of my era for last. Holding up a sleek little box about the size of a half deck of cards, I tell him "this device holds up to forty thousand songs!" His interest seems piqued, but the ecstatic response I expected fails to materialize. I watch him do some mental calculations, and then he frowns. "I don't get it," he tells me. "How can anyone afford to fill one of those things?"

Unfortunately, I have no legal answer to this question. Nor does the music industry. Over the past two decades, thanks to Moore's law, massive capital investment, and the loving labor of thousands of independent developers, innovations in hardware, software, interface design, and communication networks have profoundly altered musical culture and practice. Today, there is little we can imagine doing with music that can't be realized through some kind of digital intervention—and our imaginations are growing more adventurous with every passing year. Yet, despite (or because of) this rapid change, the music industry seems unwilling or unable to match its pace by developing new business models that take advantage of these innovative technologies and emerging cultural behaviors.

"Now, wait a minute," you may be thinking. "Every day, I read about some hot new digital music startup. And I get all the music I could ask for, legally, from services that didn't even exist a decade ago. What more could I want?" This is a perfectly reasonable objection. Yet if we look at the digital music companies that dominate today's industry, they are precisely those that offer the least innovation, and are therefore the most viable partners for an inflexible recording sector. As I discussed in chapter 3, part of the reason iTunes was able to dominate the music market for much of the past decade is that it replicated the traditional wholesale / retail relationship with the labels, requiring very little adaptation on their end. The price, as I discussed in chapter 5, was the "unbundling" of the album, which has simultaneously depressed music sales revenues and limited consumers' ability to fill their own iPods with legally obtained music (as my younger self noted, it would cost $40,000 at a dollar a song). Pandora, the reigning titan of the webcasting sector, innovated as much as it could without crossing the line into "interactive webcasting" as defined by copyright law. This way, the company could go about its business using statutory licenses and without ever having to negotiate with the labels or publishers.[1] The result isn't quite traditional radio, but it's certainly not the most functional or adventurous service that the company's "music genome" technology (now more than a decade old) could support—nor is it yet profitable.[2] By the same token, Spotify, the newest darling of the digital music business, is essentially relying on a business model first proposed at the dawn of the digital music era[3]—yet it took the company five years from its founding and three years from its European launch to become available commercially in the United States, largely because of licensing difficulties. Moreover, the company's CEO acknowledged at the end of 2012 that, although recording artists have complained loudly about getting short-changed by the company, it has yet to become profitable[4]—at least in part because its licenses with the labels still treat each song streamed by the service as a unique financial transaction, rather than settling for a fixed percentage of revenue.

Thus, while digital technology has certainly played a transformative role in the music industry, this transformation has been hindered to a considerable degree by the difficulties faced by innovators in their dealings with the legacy cartels. Unlike iTunes and Pandora, most new digital music services must face a choice between entering into extended, and likely fruitless, negotiations with the major labels before launching, or being branded as "piracy" enablers and litigated out of existence. Either way, only a small fraction of the good ideas ever make it to market, and only a handful of those become stable, revenue-generating (let alone profitable) businesses. This isn't simply an annoyance to those of us hoping to impress our inner adolescents with the wonders of the digital future—it's a significant hindrance to the development of the industry, and a serious drain on economic growth. As the business professors Jeff Dyer, Hal Gregersen and Clayton M. Christensen write in the introduction to their book *The Innovator's DNA,* innovation is "the lifeblood of our global economy and a strategic priority for virtually every CEO around the world."[5] In other words, an industry incapable of adapting to—and capitalizing on—technological change is doomed to obsolescence.

Unfortunately, innovation has never been one of the music industry's strong points; even in the pre-digital era, the labels' attitude toward new technology always mixed optimism and distrust in equal measure. In a blog post, Steve Blank, a tech entrepreneur and the author of the Silicon Valley bible *The Four Steps to the Epiphany,*[6] explained how the music business has often innovated in spite of itself: "The music and movie business has been consistently wrong in its claims that new platforms and channels would be the end of its businesses. In each case, the new technology produced a new market far larger than the [negative] impact it had on the existing market."[7]

This resistance to new ideas has only increased in the digital age, as the gap between the innovators and the industry has widened. The resulting stalemate has essentially ground the wheels of progress to a halt, hurting businesses old and new, as well as consumers and musicians. The Rutgers law professor Michael Carrier, who published an extensive study on this subject, argues that the music industry is largely to blame for its own economic collapse because of its single-minded focus on "preserving an existing business model and ignoring or quashing disruptive threats to the model" and its consequent reliance on "overaggressive copyright law and enforcement, [which] has substantially and adversely affected innovation."[8]

In the remainder of this chapter, I tell the stories of five promising digital music businesses that suffered as a result of such policies.[9] Although these are only a handful among hundreds if not thousands, each is in its own way emblematic of the dysfunction at the heart of the music industry in the digital age. Through their stories, I hope to provide a glimpse of what's been lost and what the costs have been to both musical industry and culture, as well as a sense of the human toll, measured in terms of wasted hours and diminished dreams.

Putting the "Play" in Playlist: Uplister

In 1999, few record label executives were more in touch with the brewing digital music revolution than Jeremy Silver. As vice president of new media at EMI, Silver was charged with granting licenses to deserving innovators. In his words, "I had every single music Internet company that had a new business model for music coming in to see me and putting their business plan across my desk."[10] From his office on the ninth floor of Los Angeles' iconic Capitol Tower, he could see Hollywood spread out beneath him, and he was excited when he thought about the changes that would soon transform its business landscape.

The problem was, not everyone in the business, or even within his own company, was as excited as Silver was. As he told me, he'd been "experiencing a degree of frustration with EMI at that point," because even though he'd been busy granting licenses, often in exchange for big cash advances or equity stakes in the companies themselves, "we weren't actually developing our side of the deal to be able to really play ball." Silver might be granting innovators *permission* to use their content, but the label was dragging its heels when it came to providing these companies with access to the *content itself*. There was no in-house infrastructure to digitize and distribute songs, nor were any of the associated assets, such as videos and metadata, readily available to licensees, and there was no effort to bring the bands themselves to the table to help augment and promote the services. It was as though the company were partially paralyzed, with Silver's department intent on moving forward and the rest of the organization refusing to budge.

One day, a group of engineers came to his office, and though they didn't have much of a business plan, their technology piqued his interest. He decided that even if "the music industry was visibly missing the boat," it didn't mean that he had to be left on the shore. In May 2000, Silver tendered his resignation at EMI, and signed on as the executive vice president for the engineers' digital music startup, which was called Uplister.

Uplister's basic premise was simple: if digitization was going to unbundle the traditional album (a fact that was already evident to many in the industry), music could be re-bundled by the listeners in the form of playlists, which could then be searched and shared among the service's user base. Music itself might become ubiquitous and commoditized, but the service of providing access to songs, combined with a social platform catalyzing musical community through the act of sharing, would still be a valuable—and potentially profitable—enterprise.

When Uplister launched in September 2000, it had almost every piece in place: powerful and intuitive software for creating, sharing, and searching playlists, an enthusiastic early adopter community ready and willing to pay for the ability to use the service, and enough venture capital to last a year without revenues or additional cash infusions. The only things missing were licenses from the major labels. Without them, the service could legally provide only thirty-second clips of each song[11]— a good proof-of-concept, but hardly a compelling proposition for music fans.

Silver knew the licenses would be a make-or-break for his company. Without them, he acknowledged, the service would be "hugely inferior. It was much more exciting once you were able to turn all the music on." Yet, he wasn't terribly concerned; as a recent EMI executive, Silver had little doubt that he would be greeted with "open arms." After all, these executives were his friends and former colleagues. And besides, who knew better how to approach negotiations than someone who within recent memory had sat on both sides of the table?

Silver now realizes that this expectation was evidence of his "incredible naiveté." True to the old saying, he found that he couldn't go home again. "As soon as I'd crossed that bridge and became someone in a technology company," he remembers, "everything that we did was viewed with suspicion." Not only did the labels have "fundamental business concerns" regarding Uplister's ability to distribute music profitably based on an untested model, Silver also believes that personal feelings got in the way. In his words:

> There was this idea that "these guys might go out and make a load of money that we're not making. And they might make a load of money on the back of our content. And *he* might make a load of money that he wasn't making with us." . . . And I knew that because I'd sat there in plenty of meetings from the other side of the table, feeling exactly like that about all these guys coming in. Thinking, "Well, hang on, this sounds way too good." Which is why I started wanting to become part of it.

In the end, the major labels never quite said no to Uplister. They simply never got around to saying yes, demanding millions of dollars apiece in advances, and refusing to negotiate for a lower fee, even though the sums they asked would bankrupt the fledgling enterprise. Nor did they respond to Silver's appeals with any kind of enthusiasm or alacrity. As he described it, the "major labels' attitude . . . when there was a problem was 'this is too difficult, we'll go really slowly.'" And for a venture-funded startup with a high burn rate in a rapidly evolving business and technological environment, this amounted to the kiss of death. Things were a bit better with the indie labels, who were "much more interested, much more engaged, much more willing to experiment," and thus granted licenses to Uplister only a year or so after the company launched.

Unfortunately, this proved too little, too late. By September 2001, Uplister had about 750,000 users, six weeks of cash left in the bank, and zero major label music on its site. As Silver recalls, "It was like we were in this race car, although someone had disabled the brakes, and we were headed for a wall. It was horrible." The dot-com bust earlier that year had made investors far more cautious, and venture capitalists (VCs) were unwilling to pour more money into the company if it didn't have a fully functional service. Then came the attacks of September 11, which froze investment entirely. Silver was forced to lay off his thirty-five employees, his wife and young children returned to their native England, and Uplister shut its doors permanently. Although Silver soon moved on to become the CEO of the music composition software company Sibelius, his experience at Uplister had left him with a lingering sense of personal regret that starkly contrasts with his earlier optimism and enthusiasm. "Actually, it's quite painful thinking about it," he told me. "It wasn't fun."

Putting the "Play" in Playlist: Muxtape

Nearly seven years after Uplister closed its doors, a twenty-four-year-old designer and DJ named Justin Ouellette, who had never heard of the company, came up with a similar idea. For years, he had been using the Internet to keep track of his college radio playlists, both as a public service and as a personal diary of sorts. Having been an avid Napster user in high school, Ouellette knew that the Internet was a powerful medium for music distribution, and to him it "seemed like an incredibly tragic disconnect"[12] that there was no simple way to turn his curated list of songs into an active, on-demand digital playlist. So he set out to remedy the problem. "I just became sort of obsessed with why that couldn't happen," he told me. "Why can't I just click on these songs, and hear them right now?"

Because Ouellette's primary expertise was in design and his computer programming skills were only at the hobbyist level, and because he had a full-time job at the video sharing site Vimeo, he initially viewed his pet project "strictly as a user interface experiment." After working nights tinkering on his playlist software for some time, he suddenly realized that it was "two or three weeks away from being releasable." He quit his day job and buckled down, spending most of March 2008 in full-time development. Even at this point, however, he didn't view it necessarily as a career move. It was more of a creative challenge, a test of his minimalist design principles. "I want the whole site to be music," he told himself. "Literally, the surface area of the site should [have] very few areas you click on" without hearing something.

After three weeks of "intense" work on the project, which he dubbed Muxtape (a portmanteau of "MUX," an electronic device that manages the flow of audio or video signals, and "mixtape"), Ouellette was ready to share his creation with the world. Because it wasn't initially intended as a commercial project, there was no marketing or promotion involved with its launch, though he was certainly optimistic about its social impact. He posted a screenshot of the Muxtape logo to his Tumblr blog, and told his readers, "I'm proud to introduce Muxtape, a new way to share, discover, and listen to hand-picked music online. . . . My goal is nothing short of changing the way we consume, distribute, and discover music."[13]

The response was sudden and overwhelming, in part because some of Justin's Tumblr readers were themselves influential bloggers. Within four and a half hours, a thousand people had signed up for the service. Within twenty-four hours, thirty-five thousand people had visited the site, and about a quarter of them had signed up to use it, posting nearly twenty thousand songs. His post was the most "reblogged" item on Tumblr, and his site "melted" under the heavy strain of its exponential growth.

Music fans weren't the only ones who responded quickly to Muxtape's release. The day after he launched the site, Ouellette started hearing from record labels. Universal Music Group was the first to contact him. The label's general counsel called Ouellette directly ("how they got my contact information is still a mystery"), and "asked where he should send the summons." Independent labels also e-mailed him, but unlike the majors, they were "mostly inquisitive, not hostile or anything."

"Wow, I'm really onto something," Ouellette thought to himself. "I should get a lawyer immediately." So he found a prominent music attorney willing to take him on a deferred-compensation basis, and immediately entered into negotiations with labels big and small. He spent the entire summer in negotiations, all the while tending to his rapidly growing site. He found the process simultaneously fascinating, frustrating, and absurd. "It was real Jekyll and Hyde," he told me:

> It was weird, because I'd have the business development people on one side of the table. And then on the other side of the table is the legal side. And the meeting would start, and the business side would say, 'Justin, thanks for coming in. We love Muxtape. We use it in the office, it's so cool. Let's talk about some possibilities.' And then I'd turn my head to the right, and the lawyers would be like, 'We are going to sue you into the ground. We want the site shut down by the weekend. This won't stand. We're going to destroy you.' And I'm like, 'You guys gotta talk to each other. Decide whether you want to quash me or do a deal. But it's like literally having two different meetings at the same table.'

Ouellette was savvy enough to understand that this Jekyll and Hyde routine was essentially the labels' version of good cop / bad cop; the threat of litigation, while real, wasn't immediate. Instead, the labels appeared to be using it as a form of leverage. This wasn't a problem, as far as he was concerned; once the licensing terms were worked out, and he paid appropriate retroactive royalties for the site's first months of operation, everybody would get along just fine. His attitude toward the labels at the time, he told me, was "you guys are snakes, but, you know, I can respect the game."

It was clear to Ouellette that the four majors had conferred about terms prior to their separate negotiations with Muxtape. They each offered essentially the same deal: the service would have to pay anywhere from a half cent to two cents each time a song was played on the site, it would have to share 50 percent of its revenues (Ouellette anticipated selling ads to music-related companies) with the majors, and it would have to give each major an ownership stake in Muxtape ranging from one to five percent. Against these terms, the labels collectively required cash advances amounting to ten or fifteen million dollars. Although he considered them onerous, Ouellette was willing to accept the labels' terms, as long as they'd allow him to go about his business in peace. "I'm not interested in being a millionaire," he told me. "What I really wanted was to build the best music experience."

The problem, from Ouellette's perspective, was that even if he agreed to the financial terms, he still couldn't build the "best music experience" as he envisioned it. Some of the major labels also insisted on having "some say in the project," for instance, demanding that Muxtape's front page dedicate a certain portion of its space to promoting major label bands. For an obsessive design geek, this was simply beyond the pale. "I started to get freaked out a little bit," he recalls. "What I want for my money is to be able to develop this product exactly the way I want to and with total transparency. I'm not gonna turn this into a new payola. This is not going to be a new thing where the record industry gets to fuck it up just like they've fucked everything else up."

Meanwhile, Ouellette had another problem on his hands. While he was theoretically willing to let the labels "drink me dry, in terms of money," potential Muxtape investors were not so sanguine about the proposed financial terms. As he discovered, "there's a lot of music-loving venture capitalists in New York who just could not stomach the idea of paying that much money to a bunch of robber barons." Without the major label licenses, Muxtape would have cost a half million dollars to become a viable business. With them, he needed to raise thirty times that amount just to get off the ground. Once Ouellette realized that he was essentially stuck between the rock of the major labels and the hard place of the VCs, it started to dawn on him that maybe "this isn't going to work out."

Unfortunately, Ouellette never made it past this point in the negotiations anyway. Out of the blue, he received an e-mail from Amazon Web Services, which hosted the Muxtape site, saying it was going to shut down the server in twenty-four hours, pursuant to legal action by the RIAA. He immediately called Amazon, with whom he'd been in acquisition talks, but they claimed to have no influence over their corporate sibling. He confronted the labels with whom he'd been negotiating, and though "none of them would cop to" having ordered the closure, "none of them were willing to make the call to the RIAA to stop it, either."

At this point, Muxtape was less than six months old, it had six hundred thousand active and enthusiastic users, it was the darling of the blogosphere and mainstream media alike, and, as far as Ouellette was concerned, it was dead in the water. Once the site was taken off-line, it would lose the momentum it had enjoyed since its debut, and it would become "toxic for any investor" because of the cloudy legal outlook. And, most important, Ouellette told me, "I felt betrayed. I was like, this is not a negotiation in good faith." The labels had failed to live up to even his diminished expectations of how "the game" was played. So he pulled the plug on negotiations, closed down the site, and replaced it with a brief note saying that "Muxtape will be unavailable for a brief period while we sort out a problem with the RIAA."

After spending "a long weekend feeling sad," Ouellette dedicated a few months to developing a new version of Muxtape, in which bands and labels could voluntarily post music as a form of self-promotion; that way, licenses wouldn't be necessary. After six months, he closed the doors on that, as well. "My heart wasn't in it the same way anymore," he confessed. "It just wasn't as interesting to me as a product." Today, Ouellette works at Tumblr, the site where the Muxtape story began, and says he "love[s] working there. . . . If there's anywhere that the spirit of Muxtape is alive, it's in Tumblr."[14] Despite his own venture's disappointing outcome, he acknowledges that "that'll probably go down as the best year of my life. . . . I don't have any real regrets." Nonetheless, he told me, there is one thing that continues to bother him: "I still wish the state of music on the Internet was better."

Music in the Cloud: MyPlay

In early 1999, while Jeremy Silver was still sitting at his desk in the Capitol Tower and Napster was just a germ of an idea in Shawn Fanning's mind, David Pakman was already fed up with the state of digital music. As vice president of business and product development at the online music retailer N2K (which had recently merged with its competitor CDnow), he realized that the newly popular MP3 format represented the future of his business and the writing on the wall for the CD format. Yet, as it stood in those days, the digital music experience was "hugely frustrating."[15] There were only a few, low-capacity portable MP3 players available on the market (the iPod was still almost three years away), and the process of "ripping" CDs and transferring songs to such a device was "very cumbersome, it wasn't very elegant. A layperson couldn't really do it."

Pakman and his former Apple colleague Doug Camplejohn decided that there was good money to be made in streamlining the process, using the Internet's growing speed, capacity, and ubiquity as the foundation for people's personal digital music libraries. The basic value proposition was simple. In Pakman's words, "if you're going to be ripping CDs, you should store your music in the sky[16] so you can get to it from any device." So they created a prototype, which they called a "digital storage locker," and cofounded a new company around the concept, which they named MyPlay.

Although the service represented a significant step forward for digital music users, it wasn't quite as powerful as Pakman and Camplejohn wanted. The problem was getting all of the ripped digital music into the locker in the first place. At dial-up broadband speeds (typically 28.8 or 56.6 kilobits per second), which were standard at the time, a single song could easily take fifteen minutes, and a library of a hundred CDs could take over two weeks (assuming constant transfer, which would mean no outages and no telephone usage on the dial-up line). In other words, there was virtually no way that MyPlay users could store their entire music libraries on the service.

There was a simple engineering solution. MyPlay could create its own library of music, allowing its users to stream the songs that corresponded to their CD collections without having to rip them and then transfer the files themselves to their lockers. But this solution entailed some problems of its own. Although there was a strong argument that "fair use" provisions[17] of copyright law covered self-transfer of files, Pakman believed that the automatic streaming solution "was not something we could employ without licenses. And so we didn't go that route, although it's more elegant." This was a considerable compromise; as former Apple product developers, "elegance" was almost a religion for MyPlay's founders. Yet, as experienced music industry executives, they also "knew it was a litigious and dangerous place to play, and so [they] carefully designed a solution that was not copyright-infringing."

Thus, when MyPlay launched in October 1999, it was legal, but inelegant. Pakman and Camplejohn immediately set out to rectify this situation, reaching out to copyright owners in order to build a "more streamlined, licensed version." Yet despite "constant conversation with the record labels," they were not successful in achieving an accord. As Pakman recalls:

> They required huge advances. They wanted all sorts of changes in the product to conform to whatever their views were about how the product should behave, which was a problem for a bunch of Silicon Valley guys, who frankly knew a lot more about how to design products than record company execs. They wanted all sorts

of promotional guarantees ('you're gonna use your inventory to promote our stuff, this often and this much space'). They wanted equity
in the company, they wanted the advances, and obviously a piece of
revenue as we built the service up. . . . [I]t was just all not practical.

In other words, the major labels made the same set of crippling demands on MyPlay that they would make on Muxtape a decade later.
And, like Ouellette, Pakman found the pill too bitter to swallow. In his
words, "we never signed any deals because the terms were so onerous."

By the spring of 2001, the company had managed, despite spending a
year and a half in fruitless negotiations, to attract eight million users. But
the service was still inelegant (especially in comparison to the booming
unlicensed P2P services), and revenues were paltry. Then, soon after a
proposed $200 million acquisition by Yahoo imploded because of dis-
agreements over a preexisting partnership with its rival AOL, the tech
bubble burst, and MyPlay's horizons narrowed. Without major label licenses, there was little chance that newly cautious investors would continue to support MyPlay's business.

So Pakman and Camplejohn sold the company (for considerably less
than $200 million) to the only buyer still on the market—Bertelsmann
eCommerce Group, the sister company to major label BMG.[18] Presumably, the company would now have an easier time obtaining licenses,
and the plan was to integrate its locker service with the soon-to-be-
obsolete CD subscription service BMG Music Club. Although Pakman
was disappointed about the earlier setbacks, he was still optimistic about
MyPlay's future at Bertelsmann. He was "excited to work for" his new
boss, Andreas Schmidt, and "thought he was going to do great things."
Unfortunately, Schmidt was fired three months later (owing largely to
his "great vision" of a post-retail, digital future for music), and "the new
guy had no vision." So Pakman left Bertelsmann as soon as his contract
expired, a year to the day after the acquisition. Soon thereafter, the
eCommerce group itself disappeared beneath the waves, taking MyPlay
down with it.

Today, Pakman is a partner at Venrock Associates, a New York venture capital firm, and is still an influential thinker when it comes to the
music industry (*Billboard* magazine considers him one of the "music
industry characters you need to follow"[19] on Twitter). Yet despite his
love of music and his history in the business, he says he won't invest
in digital music startups and has "not found a single investment in the
space worthy of our capital." In fact, when he meets promising young

tech entrepreneurs, he actively "tries to steer them away" from music. The problem, he says, is that the record labels are incapable of providing licenses on equitable terms, because "no one [at the labels] is rewarded for cannibalizing the existing business," even if it means building a better long-term strategy and ensuring the continuance of the sector. Consequently, "getting licensed is death" for startups, Pakman holds. "The economics do not allow you to build a business that's sustainable. . . . And you end up scarred and broke at the end of it, before you even have your product to market. To know whether consumers care." Which is, of course, all that any innovator truly wants.

Music in the Cloud: MP3.com

In 1997, when the web was still in its infancy, Michael Robertson was a thirty-year-old Internet entrepreneur running a fledgling search engine business called the Z Company. One day, he was looking at the most popular search terms on the site, and saw a curious new entrant: "MP3." Robertson recognized this as "the first clue that there was a new trend to look at,"[20] promptly registered the MP3.com domain, and decided to reposition his business as an online music directory under the new name.

Before long, MP3.com had expanded beyond its search engine origins to become one of the first hosting services for online music ("The concept was, we're gonna be a music site that, crazily enough, actually has music!"). Anyone was free to upload a song to the site and to make it available to other visitors (after it was vetted by site staffers to make sure it wasn't copyrighted by another party). Tens of thousands of artists, including many major label musicians, uploaded hundreds of thousands of songs to the site. While there were "a few little skirmishes" between the digital marketing professionals at the labels (who wanted their artists' music posted for promotional purposes) and the legal departments (who wanted the music taken down), there were no serious legal entanglements; by and large, the marketing factions won out, given the growing site's powerful role in generating online publicity.

MP3.com went public in 1999, raising over $370 million and setting a new record for Internet IPOs. By this time, it was also the biggest music website on the Internet, with over six million visitors per month. Yet Robertson envisioned even more for the company, akin to what MyPlay had started doing the same year. "My vision of the future was, all music's gonna live in the cloud," Robertson remembers. "But it was a big data problem—how do you get a person's music collection into the cloud?"

Although MyPlay's Pakman and Camplejohn had rejected the "elegant" concept of automatic streaming because they believed it would require licenses from the major labels, Robertson wasn't so sure. Why should consumers need permission to listen to the music they already owned, and why should a company need permission to help them do it? In his words, "you should have a right to do whatever you want for your personal needs with your personal property." So in January 2000, six months after the company's IPO, Robertson launched a service called My.MP3.com, powered by a technology called "Beam-it." The service, which was otherwise similar to MyPlay, allowed consumers to unlock a free streaming version of any song or album merely by putting a CD into their computer's CD-ROM drive, thereby obviating the need to populate their online libraries by uploading their collections song by song.

In Robertson's opinion, the service was a boon to the music industry despite its lack of licenses. In the face of digital dematerialization and unbundling, he was extending the value, and therefore the market lifespan, of the CD, providing an incentive for consumers to continue to buy them in the digital age. He had good reason to believe this was true; MP3.com also licensed a private-label version of Beam-it, called "Instant Listening," to three online music sellers, enabling people who purchased CDs on their sites to listen to the music via the Internet while they waited for the CDs to arrive. According to Robertson, all three retailers saw "an immediate boost of twenty to forty percent in their sales, overnight."

Robertson wasn't concerned about his service abetting "piracy." Because MP3.com required that people have a physical recording in order to gain access to music on the site (or purchase a CD from a participating retailer), there was even less risk of fraudulent use than one would expect in an upload-based service such as MyPlay. As Robertson reasoned, "you had to have the CD, with all the audio. Well, you can't ask for better security than that."

Unfortunately for MP3.com, the recording industry didn't agree with his assessments about the service's legality or its market effects. A few weeks after the service launched, the company received cease-and-desist orders from the major labels, soon followed by a lawsuit.[21] Robertson still believed his company was legally in the right, but he pulled the plug on the new service, "just to show good faith to the record labels." Nonetheless, they persisted in the litigation, which is unusual; typically, the industry seeks to avoid the possibility of a precedent being set against them. Robertson attributes this change of strategy to his company's unusually deep pockets: "We had gone public, we had raised a bunch of money in the capital market, and they wanted to take it all. It's that simple. . . . They know they have big statutory damage award laws, and they can crush people with it, and that's what they do."

In May 2000—a scant four months after the service had launched—US District Judge Jed S. Rakoff found for the plaintiffs, deciding that, because MP3.com had made copies of the labels' music in order to stream to its customers, and because these copies did not merit fair use protection, it had therefore infringed their copyrights and was liable for statutory damages, which were eventually tallied at $53.4 million.[22]

What happened next was both predictable and absurd. Having sued the company to the brink of bankruptcy, Vivendi Universal (the owner of Universal Music Group, the largest major label) purchased it. The media conglomerate paid only $5 per share for MP3.com—less than a fifth of the IPO price of $28 and less than a twentieth of its peak price of $105, despite the fact that the company had revenues of $80 million per year and (unlike most Internet companies) was actually profitable.

Although Robertson ultimately was able to walk away from the company with a considerable portion of the acquisition money and the knowledge that his technology would live on in some form (it was used, in part, to power PressPlay, a major label initiative to sell digital music directly to fans), the experience left him bitter. Not only had he been branded a pirate in the court of public opinion (as well as in a court of law) and seen a substantial percentage of his net worth evaporate, but he had lost control of his company before he could finish building it. More than a decade later, he still evinces both regret and anger when he talks about the sale to Universal. "It was a sad day, really," he told me. "Because I had all these great plans, visions, and we weren't really able to achieve it."[23]

"A Covenant Not to Sue": The Curious Case of Choruss

Not all of the innovative business ideas in the digital era came from outside the traditional music industry. In fact, one of the most interesting and potentially transformative initiatives began in 2008 as a project within Warner Music Group. The brainchild of Jim Griffin, a veteran music industry technologist, the aim of this project, named Choruss, was to grant Internet service providers and their users immunity from major label litigation in exchange for a fixed monthly fee. This "covenant not to sue," as Griffin and his team called it, would cover any kind of unlicensed distribution, including P2P. The fees would be collected and redistributed to rights holders based on analysis of aggregate user activity on the unlicensed networks themselves. As long as there was "a pool of money, and a fair way to split it," as Griffin was fond of saying, everybody could be happy.[24]

The Choruss team had its work cut out for it. In addition to Griffin, who served as chief proselytizer and liaison to WMG chief Edgar Bronfman Jr. (who had earmarked about $3 million for the project), the group also included current Warner executives (and former Gartner business analysts) Max Smith and Jack Foreman. Smith's job was to get other labels on board, and Foreman's was to pitch the idea to ISPs. Given the labels' abhorrence of unlicensed distribution and the ISPs' existing legal immunities under the DMCA's "safe harbor" provision, it was going to be a tough sell on both fronts.

The team decided that "because the music industry was so horrified of this kind of stuff," it made sense to target university ISPs before the major broadband providers, "because they were like China": lawless, self-contained, and low-revenue to begin with. They cobbled together some non-binding "memoranda of understanding" (MOUs) from the other majors, essentially saying they had permission to enter preliminary negotiations on their behalf, and set out to cut some deals.

At this point, Foreman recalls, "I had no technology, I had no service, I had no way to collect the money." All he did have to offer his potential university ISP customers was "a promise on the part of the labels" not to litigate against the schools or their students if they were willing to pay up. To sweeten the deal a bit, he also pitched it as an experiment worthy of formal research. As he describes it, he told the universities that it was a chance to "participate in something that is an academic study that we think you can get a lot of mileage out of." The responses from universities were promising, ranging from "sounds interesting" to "Hey, you've gotta talk to me now!" Out of a pool of about fifty initial targets, there were seven schools that showed sincere interest and were willing to engage in negotiations (and in at least one case, to conduct formal academic research on the business model).

Almost immediately, the negotiators ran into some serious conceptual problems. There were pricing questions, privacy questions, and questions regarding scope of immunity (Would it apply to overseas students? Students on vacation? Non-matriculated students?). Undergirding all of these issues was the foundational question of whether Choruss would be opt-in (allowing students to pay voluntarily for immunity), or opt-out (adding the Choruss charge as a line item on students' university bills).

"That was a big, big, big, big, big debate," Foreman recalls, and "one thing that never got solved."

If the service was opt-in, then the universities didn't have much to gain; the non-participating students would still be subject to litigation, which would continue to pose legal and technological hassles for the schools. If the service was opt-out, then the schools would have to justify what amounted to a tuition increase even for students who had never used P2P. Furthermore, at the public universities, their state governments would have to ratify any across-the-board rate increases, which could take years of complex political wrangling. On top of all this, the labels insisted on pegging pricing to this negotiation point. If the service was opt-out, they would agree to accept $5 per month per student (which was more or less universally agreed to be a fair and feasible sum throughout the music industry); however, if the service was only opt-in, the labels would expect something closer to $20 per month (which is more or less universally viewed as excessive, and anathema to consumers).

Time was of the essence. As Foreman recalls, Choruss felt like a "house of cards." If they didn't get the project moving forward quickly, the house would collapse, and Bronfman's support would evaporate. Yet, in addition to the seemingly intractable impasse with the schools over opt-in vs. opt-out, the other labels appeared to be dragging their heels on the business affairs side.

It wasn't that they weren't willing to talk. "We had lots of meetings over a very long period of time," Forman told me. "We had lawyers on the phone, had contracts drawn up, all this stuff. And we were negotiating on finer points." Yet something always seemed to prevent the contracts from getting finalized. At one point, he says, Bronfman and Universal Music Group CEO Doug Morris failed to meet to discuss the project because they couldn't agree on whose office they would meet in. When they did manage to meet, each label brought its own set of concerns to the table. Universal was worried that Choruss would set a legal precedent validating P2P, and specifically objected to partnering with LimeWire to track music downloads while they were litigating a high-profile case against the file sharing company. Sony was worried about a different kind of precedent—specifically, that granting immunity to P2P users would establish a degree of legal ownership over the music they'd downloaded tantamount to that conferred by a retail sale.

The ultimate sticking point, Foreman says, was Choruss's foundational premise. "If you ask me why did we fail," he told me, it was "the covenant not to sue." Even the indie labels and the publishers balked at the idea. There is no way Choruss could have worked without it; trying to license every single track, by every single artist, composer, label, and publisher, for all possible forms of distribution was just not logistically possible within a reasonable time frame. Therefore, promising not to sue for unlicensed usage was the only feasible workaround.

Yet the legal departments at the labels and publishers were loath to give up the power to litigate. It wasn't just an essential form of business leverage for their employers, it was also the attorneys' primary function within the organizations, and therefore their job security itself was on the line. Foreman sees this as one of the key problems facing the music business in the digital age. "Lawyers are the hardest part of the industry," he told me. "Our impression is that they were working against [Choruss] the whole time." Nor did the universities care for the deal as Foreman pitched it—to them, it sounded too much like extortion, a classic protection racket. At best, it sounded like vapor: everyone at the universities kept asking, "What am I *getting* with my $5 per month?"

"So it was a balancing act, and ultimately, it all came down," Forman recalls. "If we could have gotten a covenant not to sue from the majors that was signed, then we could have maneuvered our way into the schools. Then we would have been able to set everything up." Unfortunately, it was not to be; at the eighteen-month point, it became obvious to everyone, including Bronfman, that Choruss had run its course. Griffin and his crew approached some VCs (including the music-averse David Pakman at Venrock) about turning it into a privately funded project, but everyone concerned realized that once it lost its affiliation with WMG, Choruss would have an even lower chance of bringing all four major labels on board.

The project never officially shuttered its doors, but without Bronfman's financial and political support, Choruss more or less disintegrated. After a year and a half of promising, cajoling, and placating, Foreman was forced to call his would-be customers at the universities and tell them the deal was off the table. "They're probably not all happy with me," he acknowledges, "but I did the best I could. It brings a tear to my eye."

"Why license them and make a little, when you can sue them and make a lot?"

The rapid developments in digital media and networking technology over the past fifteen years have contributed to a golden age of experimentation in music production, distribution, and audition akin to (and possibly outstripping) the early days of electromagnetic storage and transmission. The concepts I have discussed in this chapter, playable playlists, cloud music services, and blanket immunity for peer-to-peer distribution, are three excellent examples of ways in which developers and entrepreneurs have tried—and failed—to create business models around these experimental innovations. Though not all five of the companies I profiled would necessarily have become profitable enterprises given full participation from the music industry, there can be little doubt that stonewalling by the major labels prevented each of them from testing their full market potential.

An interesting theme that emerges from my interviews is how consistently these innovators are inspired by aesthetic, or even altruistic, motivations. From Ouellette's desire to solve the "user experience problem" to Pakman's focus on producing "elegant software" to Griffin's "proselytizing," these initiatives were driven primarily by enthusiasm for music and technology rather than by either calculating avarice or antipathy toward the industry. "I definitely didn't start out to disrupt anything," Ouellette told me; nor was he "interested in being a millionaire." Similarly, Foreman says that in his opinion, Griffin is still so selflessly committed to the spirit of Choruss that he "would die penniless if he knew that there was a pool of money and a fair way to split it."

Yet if these innovators harbored neither ill will nor evil intent toward the music industry (at least at the outset), why were the labels so reluctant to work with them? I asked Larry Kenswil, who worked in business affairs at Universal Music Group for fourteen years and then ran eLabs, UMG's digital licensing and business incubation unit, from 1997 to 2008. As he described it to me, one of the labels' primary motivations for refusing to license on reasonable terms, if at all, was their desire to cut out the middle man completely and sell music directly to online customers (this is something they have attempted a number of times, most spectacularly with their failed subscription initiatives, MusicNet and PressPlay, in the early 2000s). In Kenswil's words, "there was a general reluctance to outsource by licensing if you could do it yourself."[25] Furthermore, the labels feared that, if a third party successfully developed a business selling their content, they would "just become licensing entities like the music publishers" and lose the position and power they had enjoyed in the days of cartelized distribution.

As to why the majors wouldn't even do business with Choruss, which was itself a division of a major label, Kenswil (who was "involved with" the initiative) said that "if Choruss came out of Warner, that would mean all the other labels would be immediately suspicious of it, because of the not-invented-here problem." This happened frequently, he told me: "One label would sort of invent something, the other labels would hate it immediately. Down deep, they hate each other."

Kenswil and Silver also offered some valuable insight into the labels' negotiating (or anti-negotiating) methods. For example, the massive cash advances the labels requested of companies like MyPlay and Muxtape served many different functions. At their core, they served the purpose that one would expect: namely, to mitigate the risk involved in doing business with an untested licensee, and to guarantee that the labels would see at least some money for their efforts. Yet, this doesn't explain why the advances were often set so high as to cripple or chase off would-be licensees. One of their secondary purposes was apparently to provide startups with what Kenswil calls an "entrance ticket." As Silver explained to me, "we needed to make sure that we didn't do deals with companies that had no means. So by making sure that we sucked a ton of money out of them, in theory that meant they had means."

Silver never particularly believed this rationale. In his opinion, the huge advances were motivated primarily by the fact that "we liked cash." Specifically, the labels viewed venture capital–funded digital startups as a source of easy money with few strings attached. When he was at EMI, he told me, "we talked very regularly about 'shaking the VC tree,' and that the dollar bills would fall very readily from the branches. And we felt no compunction about doing that whatsoever." Similarly, Kenswil said that labels can be very "cynical" in their approach to cash advances:

> If they think this company has no chance of ever succeeding, and there's some stupid money behind it, they're just gonna pull as much of that money out up front as possible. Because they figure there's never gonna be anything on the back end. And there's been enough advances paid for companies that never launched, that it becomes something they look for: "Wow, is this a company we can just fleece an advance out of, and never have to have to worry about it again?" But when that becomes the only way you're doing business, it's very cynical and not very productive.

During the Internet boom years, Silver told me, this practice got so out of hand that "many of the majors introduced quotas," requiring executives in charge of licensing to reach revenue targets on an ongoing basis. "So if you didn't get two million dollars a quarter in business, on the back of all these startups, there was something wrong with you," he recalls. "And there are individuals who are now the head of digital for large corporations who were very successful in doing that." Nor was this money simply "gravy" from the labels' perspectives; in at least one financial year, Silver claims, digital music advances at EMI "made the company's budget when the retail sales would have failed . . . so the appetite was pretty keen."

Along similar lines, Kenswil confirmed what many of my other interviewees alleged regarding the motivations driving the major labels to litigate against digital music innovators. While there are certainly instances in which the labels legitimately feel as though it's the most effective method of curbing unlicensed distribution, there are other cases in which it serves more as a form of leverage. As Ouellette recalls, "It was clear to me early on, even when I got that first call from Universal, that it's an intimidation tactic. It's all business. They want to make you feel like you have very little control over the situation so they can work a deal that's the most beneficial to them." Kenswil readily acknowledges this to be the case: "Yeah, that's always true in business litigation. . . . That's how it's done. Business litigation ends up in a deal [and] the company uses whatever leverage they have to try to make that deal as good as possible."

As with licensing advances, Kenswil admits that the potential cash value of a legal decision or settlement sometimes served as a financial crutch for the major labels, undermining their interest in and ability to seek more stable forms of long-term remuneration:

> The main problem here was there had been some success on the litigation side. To the point where, unfortunately, the money that was coming in from some lawsuits exceeded the profits that were being made from the actual digital businesses. And so there was some argument to be made by those who were being paid to litigate that litigation was a more profitable endeavor than licensing. Why license them and make a little, when you can sue them and make a lot?

While Kenswil has always considered this a "very short-sighted way to look at it," he also acknowledges that, in many cases, it was hard to convince the label brass to turn down millions of dollars without a clearly valuable alternative. The digital music startups would be either so inchoate or so unwilling to compromise with the labels on the finer points of their business models that "the litigators won the argument because I wouldn't have a good argument internally for the business case" of licensing to the companies. This sheds some light on Oullette's "Jekyll and Hyde" experience; he was actually witnessing the labels arguing with themselves over this very question in the course of his negotiations, a dynamic no doubt augmented by his own unwillingness to let the labels participate in his product design process. "There was definitely a schizophrenic attitude going on," Kenswil agrees. "That's where some of the most heated disagreements were between different factions within the companies."

Ultimately, the major labels' pathological inability to license to promising innovators on reasonable terms can be understood as a factor that impeded the growth of the music business (to say nothing of musical culture) for at least a decade. The cost, and the cause, are clear to those who have tried and failed to move the industry forward. Even to this day, Robertson argues, "there's not one company who has a license for any innovative service who's ever made any money with the record labels." Similarly, Pakman holds that "there are very few examples where you've seen innovation and disruption from startups in licensed entertainment models."

A cursory inspection of the digital music landscape in 2012 appears to bear this out. A decade after MyPlay and Uplister, these models are still seen as dangerously innovative. Playlist.com, a recent iteration of the Uplister model, was sued by the major labels in 2008, and settled in 2010, after which it almost immediately sought bankruptcy protection, because its $203,000 in cash reserves weren't nearly enough to pay the $25 million it owed them.[26] And in 2011, the launch of the "big three" cloud music services from Apple, Google, and Amazon prompted Jon Pareles of the *New York Times* to speculate that "copyright holders are starting to rethink their licensing terms for the cloud," offering "hope" to music fans.[27] Yet it took both Google and Amazon until 2012 to obtain licenses from the majors, which meant that, for their first year out of the gate, these services required the same lengthy upload process that MyPlay did in 1999 (fortunately, Internet access speeds have improved since then). And all three services, which have paid hundreds of millions of dollars in licensing fee advances in order to offer "scan-and-match" functionality to accelerate the upload process,[28] still fall short of MP3.com's Beam-it solution, in Pareles's estimation. In other words, the industry has barely progressed since the turn of the century.

Thus, it seems unlikely that, even in light of these recent developments, either the music industry or their consumers have much cause for optimism. The fundamental tensions underpinning these historic failures—emphasis on short-term gain at the cost of long-term stability, infighting and mistrust combined with entrenched cartelization, and a steady outflux of visionary executives—may very well continue unabated until the industry's dysfunction leads to full-scale implosion. It's not that the destination is a mystery; by now, everyone knows there's a "celestial jukebox" just waiting to be switched on once the labels can agree to some equitable terms. It's just that there doesn't seem to be any way to get there from here. And anybody with an idea about the route inevitably suffers the consequences sooner or later, leaving a kind of strategic vacuum where decisive vision is most needed. "It's very hard to understand if there's any kind of an overarching strategy going on at these companies," Kenswil concedes. "Or if there ever was, I guess."

CHAPTER 8

Guilty until Proven Innocent

Anti-piracy and Civil Liberties

THROUGHOUT THIS book, I have discussed numerous ways in which the music industry's largely unfounded (and sometimes disingenuous) concerns about "digital piracy," and its antipathy toward online innovation, have harmed both the business and culture of music, contributing to the major labels' own strategic and financial difficulties and to the impoverishment of the musical public sphere. In this chapter, I aim to demonstrate that the piracy crusade's harmful effects have extended beyond even these arenas, with negative repercussions for civil liberties, free speech, privacy, and international relations.

What we might call the "civil effects" of the music industry's anti-piracy efforts (often undertaken in conjunction with its political allies in the film, software, pharmaceutical, and fashion industries) can be understood as the result of the industry's continuing alliance and coordination with government institutions, through state and federal laws, international treaties, and trade agreements, and other mechanisms that fall under the general rubric of policy. Indeed, rhetorical and tactical support for the piracy crusade has been remarkably consistent within both the legislative and executive branches of the federal government under both Democratic and Republican leadership. Sitting senators invoke bogus piracy loss estimates, debunked by the federal government's own accountability office, to justify legislation that would allow surveillance of private online communications in the name of protecting intellectual property.[1] The Department of Justice treats copyright infringement as tantamount to drug trafficking and child labor in its "education efforts"[2] and has publicly alleged, without substantiation, that P2P usage directly funds terrorism.[3] And Secretary of State Hillary Rodham Clinton, in a recent letter to Congressman Howard Berman (author of the bill mentioned in chapter 6 which would grant legal immunity to record labels who are spying on, hacking into, and destroying the computers of suspected P2P users), made it clear that the State Department sees "no contradiction between intellectual property rights protection and enforcement and ensuring freedom of expression on the Internet."[4]

If these anti-piracy laws and policies are so clearly founded on false premises, and so evidently inimical to the values that America holds most dear, why has the piracy crusade enjoyed such support from such a broad swath of lawmakers and law enforcers? The answer to this question is complex. Part of it is that, as with many other policy matters, intellectual property is an arcane and profoundly unsexy field, and most government officials probably don't have either the interest or the expertise to draw such conclusions independently. Among those in the minority who do have a working fluency in this field, there are actually significant disputes; for instance, as I discuss below, a number of ambitious anti-piracy bills have been successfully blocked by legislators concerned about their civil liberties implications. These disagreements echo the arguments within the record labels themselves that I documented in the previous chapter.

Among those who support anti-piracy measures, there are no doubt some who believe that their solutions are the most reasonable balance between competing values (e.g., liberty vs. security) in the face of an intractable and potentially devastating problem. And there are certainly others who support such legislation for politically instrumental purposes that can't be stated explicitly (e.g., gaining leverage in trade relations with other economic powers such as China and Russia). But there can be little question that a substantial portion of anti-piracy legislation and policy is driven by lobbying, campaign finance support, and other forms of direct influence from the music industry and its allies.

According to the RIAA's website, the organization "takes an uncompromising stand against censorship and for the First Amendment rights of all artists to create freely. From the nation's capital to state capitals across the country, RIAA works to stop unconstitutional action against the people who make the music of our times—and those who enjoy it."[5] Public records show that the RIAA contributed over $4 million to political campaigns between 1989 and 2011, with anti-piracy legislation sponsors such as Congressman Howard Berman and Senators Dianne Feinstein and Orrin Hatch among the top recipients.[6] The organization also spent over $52 million in lobbying during the same time period, the majority of it in the past six years. Collectively, the recording industry (including labels, publishers, and trade associations) has given

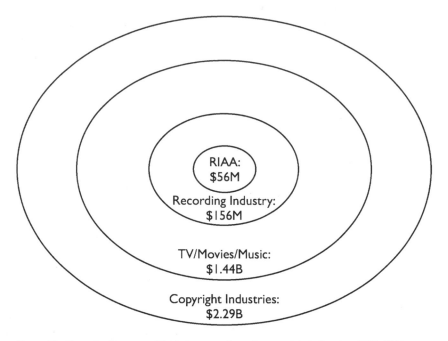

Figure 10. Campaign finance and lobbyist expenditure by copyright industries, 1989–2011.

almost $36 million to campaigns and over $120 million to lobbyists, with "copyright, patent & trademark" listed as the "most frequently disclosed lobbying issue." The broader copyright industries, which include film, television, computer software, and publishing, have donated over $836 million to campaigns and spent nearly $1.5 billion on lobbyists (fig. 10). For each of these industries, intellectual property is one of the top three issues targeted by their efforts. Nor are they alone in these initiatives; across all industries, lobbying related to intellectual property topped $2.5 billion just during the period from 2009 to 2011, with the greatest single contributions coming from the US Chamber of Commerce. As media watchdog MediaMatters argues, "due to the opaque nature of lobbying disclosure forms, it's impossible to nail down the total amount of money"[7] spent on promoting any given law; yet, collectively, these contributions speak volumes about the financial commitment that piracy crusaders have made to influence policy.

While it is true that public interest groups such as the Electronic Frontier Foundation, Free Press, and Public Knowledge have devoted considerable effort to influencing both policymakers and public opinion against such policies, their resources are minuscule compared with those of the piracy crusaders, by several orders of magnitude (collectively, they have spent less than a million dollars on lobbying and campaign finance). And though the technology sector sometimes breaks with the other IP-based industries (and, at other times, joins them), it has not spent as much as they have, and intellectual property policy falls significantly lower on its lobbying agenda (ranking fifth for the sector as a whole).

The effects of these lobbying efforts and campaign contributions are well documented. Often, the lobbyists just write policy on behalf of lawmakers and government agencies. California attorney general Bill Lockyer, who received $36,000 in contributions from the entertainment industry in 2004, circulated a letter to his fellow state attorneys general that same year expressing his "grave concern" about the dangers of P2P technology. *Wired* magazine obtained a copy of the document, and demonstrated that, based on its metadata,[8] the letter had been "either drafted or reviewed by a senior vice president of the Motion Picture Association of America."[9] Although direct evidence of lobbyist meddling such as this is fairly rare, those who work in policy circles treat it as an open secret. As Eric Schmidt, then CEO of Google, told the audience at a 2010 policy forum in Washington, DC, " 'The average American doesn't realize how much of the laws are written by lobbyists to protect incumbent interests."[10] Sometimes, the lobbying industries themselves will even acknowledge the integral role they play in drafting and revising legislation. During the 2011 legislative efforts to pass the controversial Stop Online Piracy Act (SOPA) and Protect IP Act (PIPA), for instance, a senior executive at the MPAA told the *New York Times* that "we will come forward with language" to revise the bill in the wake of criticism, and described how lobbyists from the entertainment industry were "huddling with Congressional staff members from both parties and both the House and Senate."[11]

Despite the transparency laws mandating the disclosure of financial contributions and the prevalence with which open secrets are acknowledged (at least within policy circles), the genesis of anti-piracy laws and policies is still frequently shrouded in darkness. For example, international trade accords such as the Anti-Counterfeiting Trade Agreement (ACTA), the Canada-EU Trade Agreement (CETA), and the Trans-Pacific Partnership (TPP)—all of which have been widely criticized for their potential threats to free speech and privacy—have been negotiated in closed, and sometimes secret, meetings that exclude the general public and even elected representatives, while full access to the proposed treaty text is granted to "industry advisors" from the MPAA and the RIAA.[12]

Recent Freedom of Information Act (FOIA) requests have also revealed the degree to which the US "copyright czar" Victoria Espinel (former Assistant United States Trade Representative for Intellectual Property and Innovation, where she was the "lead architect" of America's IP trade policy and "principally involved in WTO [World Trade Organization] litigation against the EC and China")[13] was actively involved in secret negotiations between entertainment and communications industry organizations (including major record labels), as well as lobbyists, to implement an unmandated, self-imposed "graduated response"[14] Internet censorship policy at the nation's largest ISPs. This "six strikes" policy, dubbed the Copyright Alert System (CAS) and slated to take effect in early 2013, slows down and potentially cuts off Internet access for paying Internet subscribers *suspected* of violating copyright on multiple occasions, without either legislative representation or judicial oversight. Throughout the negotiations, which indicated a "friendly two-way relationship between the industry and the administration," and for which Espinel at times used her personal e-mail account, there was virtually no participation from public interest groups, let alone the public itself or its legislative representatives.[15]

These are just a few examples of a much broader trend, with troubling implications for civil liberties and democratic society in the networked age: Again and again, a handful of major record labels, film studios and other legacy content cartels have leveraged their strong ties with elements of the US government, as well as foreign sovereignties and treaty organizations, to promote policies that undermine fundamental human rights such as free speech, privacy and access to information in the name of combating digital piracy. In the remainder of this chapter, I will review some of the specific elements of these laws and policies, and discuss in greater detail some of their implications for culture, society and the political process.

The Anti-piracy Agenda

Most IP policy (like policy of any kind) never appears on the public radar. If a proposed bill gets any mainstream news coverage beyond the outlets devoted to media, technology or law and policy, it is typically reported on using the framework promoted by the bill's sponsors, as a novel solution to an entrenched problem such as digital piracy, which, unchecked, would destroy American businesses and American jobs—or worse. Occasionally, as in the case of SOPA and PIPA in the United States and

ACTA in Europe, an activist subset of the general public becomes sufficiently engaged to fight the bill or treaty in question, making it too politically toxic for public officials to continue to support. But even in these cases, the initiatives are typically seen as discrete threats, Goliaths overcome by the collective slings of a thousand Davids.

In actuality, these initiatives are part of a continuum—an ever-evolving set of agenda items that reappear from bill to bill and treaty to treaty until they are legally enshrined on a global scale. Typically, the process begins with a trade agreement, establishing "minimum standards" for copyright protection across the many signatories. This is often justified in the name of "harmonizing" policy across regions[16]—a necessary precaution in an era of global digital information and capital flows. Once the agreement is in place, each signatory develops laws adhering to the requirement of the trade pact. To the greatest extent possible, the piracy crusaders will push legislators in the United States to outstrip the agreement's minimum requirements. Once enacted, these laws up the ante for the piracy crusade, establishing a new set of powers and negotiating parameters, and possibly leading to new judicial rulings applying the laws to emerging technologies and cultural practices. The content cartels also use the threat of further legislation as form of tactical leverage to exercise supralegal powers and privileges in their dealings with third parties (as in the "six-strikes" CAS agreement with American ISPs described above). Once these new laws and business accords have been established, the piracy crusaders return to the international table to establish updated trade agreements with an aim to "harmonize" copyright protection and enforcement at these higher standards, and the cycle repeats itself.

As this process unfolds, technological innovators, public advocates, and political activists work to develop alternative policy and communications platforms, typically with an aim to promote a more "open" public sphere in which free speech, privacy, and transparency are privileged over the protection of vested business interests. In many ways, this dialectic resembles a game of football, with each party working to advance the ball incrementally, play by play, over the long haul. Though, to be fair, the process can't be reduced to a simple binary with two teams, or even two goals; no two organizations, artists, policymakers, technologists, or public advocates share exactly the same set of interests or the same vision of an ideal compromise. Moreover, there's no discernable "end zone" in sight: although people may work toward a *more open* or *more secure* society, most of us would consider total transparency and total informatic lockdown to be equally dystopian prospects.[17]

With this larger framework in mind, we can examine some of the concrete details.[18] What, exactly, is the anti-piracy agenda? How have the music industry and its allies envisioned a more secure legal and technological environment, and how have they worked to bring it about? Scholars and organizations such as Michael Geist,[19] William Patry,[20] Cory Doctorow,[21] Karl Fogel,[22] the EFF[23] and Public Knowledge[24] have examined these processes in granular detail, exhaustively comparing each leaked draft of a particular bill or treaty and analyzing the minute variations for their potential policy implications. It is not my aim here to reproduce their excellent work but rather to summarize some of the key themes that have emerged from it.

Three of the piracy crusade's foundational agenda items can be traced back to the Agreement on Trade-Related Aspects of Intellectual Property Rights (TRIPS), which established for the first time the "legal prominence of IP in international economic relations"[25] when it was signed in 1996, and the World Intellectual Property Organization (WIPO) Copyright Treaty, signed later that year. Together, they establish longer copyright terms ("harmonizing" what was then the US term of an author's life plus fifty years—though the United States immediately re-raised the bar, extending it by another twenty years in 1998), require that all creative expression be automatically copyrighted (this "opt-out" approach had been law in the States since 1978), and institute "anti-circumvention" standards making it illegal to disable DRM and other forms of content access control (or to help others to do so), even if it's only to enable legally established fair use. These standards became law in the United States with the enactment of the DMCA in 1998 and in the European Union with the creation of the Copyright Directive in 2001.

Another consistent vector of anti-piracy policy is the emphasis on extending the penalties and scope of actions associated with copyright infringement, essentially levying steeper punishments against a broader range of people for doing a wider variety of things. In the United States, for instance, the 1997 No Electronic Theft (NET) Act made noncommercial infringement a crime for the first time, punishable by years of prison time and hundreds of thousands of dollars in statutory fines. Penalties for both civil and criminal infringement were also increased a decade later with the passage of the Prioritizing Resources and Organization for Intellectual Property (PRO-IP) Act of 2008. An early provision of this bill would have further raised the effective penalties for infringement by eliminating copyright law's "compilation clause," which essentially says that someone downloading an album can only be charged for a single case of infringement, rather than once for each song. Although this provision was dropped before the act passed into law, the question of how to treat compilations in a digital context is an ongoing "conundrum" that remains on the anti-piracy agenda.[26] Most recently, the National Defense Authorization Act of 2012 (NDAA), signed into law by President Obama, increased penalties for selling or giving infringing goods to the military, law enforcement, national security, or "critical infrastructure." One potential target of these higher penalties is Hyman Strachman, a ninety-two-year-old World War II veteran profiled by the *New York Times* for sending hundreds of thousands of bootleg DVDs, free of charge, to soldiers in Iraq and Afghanistan.[27]

In addition to punishing businesses and individuals who have directly infringed on intellectual property, recent efforts have focused on expanding the scope of what is known as "secondary liability"[28]—in lay terms, helping third parties to copy or redistribute content illegally. In the *United States*, the DMCA staked out an initial compromise: While the anti-circumvention measures stipulated by WIPO made it illegal to publish a webpage linking to a site hosting a piece of software that might be used by someone to bypass DRM on a copyrighted file, thereby expanding potential liability far beyond direct infringement, it also stipulated some "safe harbors" limiting the secondary liability of "online service providers" such as ISPs.[29] All it asked of these service providers in return was that they adhere to a "notice-and-takedown" protocol, whereby if a rights holder claims its work has been infringed, the service provider must respond "expeditiously to remove, or disable access to, the material that is claimed to be infringing or to be the subject of infringing activity."

This uneasy peace didn't last long. When the US Supreme Court decided the *MGM v. Grokster* P2P suit in 2005, the existing concept of secondary liability didn't apply to the facts of the case, so the justices created a new standard in its decision against the defendant, suggesting that by "inducing" people to infringe copyrights, it had broken the law and was liable for damages (an attempt to legislate this standard, in the form of a bill called the Inducing Infringement of Copyrights Act, had failed to pass the Senate in the previous year). Since then, there have been numerous attempts to further extend secondary liability by ratcheting down or eliminating ISP immunity. For instance, such provisions have been included in drafts of both ACTA and TPP, and a clause originally appended to the Senate's 2010 Combating Online Infringement and Counterfeits Act (COICA) would have granted ISPs immunity in exchange for censoring websites *suspected* of infringement by the Justice Department—

suggesting that they risked secondary liability had they not taken such "voluntary" measures.[30]

Several laws have sought to broaden the roles that government bodies play in policing and punishing IP infringers, essentially diverting tax dollars toward providing the major labels and other content industries with a free, international enforcement agency. The PRO-IP act first established a US copyright czar (technically, an Intellectual Property Enforcement Coordinator, or IPEC), a position appointed by the president and confirmed by the Senate. Since then, government seizures of pirated and counterfeited goods, and cases brought against IP infringers, have climbed sharply. The Department of Homeland Security's Immigration and Customs Enforcement agency more than doubled its arrests for IP violations between 2009 and 2011, and, in conjunction with the Department of Justice, seized 270 domain names from "infringing websites" in 2011 alone.[31] The PRO-IP act also included a provision that would have empowered the Justice Department to litigate civil infringement suits on behalf of the content industries. This provision, which was eliminated at the last minute because of veto threats by President Bush, has been on the anti-piracy agenda for years, first appearing in the Protecting Intellectual Rights Against Theft and Expropriation (PIRATE) Act of 2004, which passed the Senate but died in the House. Nor is governmental participation in policing infringement confined solely to US law; for instance, the French Creation and Internet Law (HADOPI), adopted in 2009, created a new government agency tasked with policing Internet service providers and users for online copyright infringement,[32] and treaties such as ACTA and CETA expand the power of customs control in signatory nations to search and detain goods and travelers suspected of IP infringement.

Some bills and treaties have also sought to give both government bodies and private industry greater powers to search and surveil people suspected of violating copyright. The Cyber Intelligence Sharing and Protection Act (CISPA), a bill passed by the House in 2012, encourages government agencies and private companies to share "cyber threat information" about Internet users' activities. Given that the scope of allowable information is vague at best, and that intellectual property infringement is defined as a cyber threat, this law opens the door for millions of Internet users to be surveilled if they are suspected of violating copyright. It also empowers private companies to prevent users from sharing information with one another, as long as these measures are undertaken in the name of identifying cybersecurity threats. A Senate bill called the Strengthening and Enhancing Cybersecurity by Using Research, Education, Information, and Technology (SECURE-IT) Act of 2012, envisioned as a companion to CISPA, contains similar provisions, but allows any federal agency to use the information collected about online users in the prosecution of any crime for which wiretaps and other forms of surveillance may legally be authorized.[33] In other words, if a bill like this is made law, private e-mails collected by the NSA in the process of surveilling a P2P user could potentially be used as evidence in an FBI case against a political dissident. Surveillance of suspected IP infringers is also increasingly an agenda item in foreign legislation and international treaties, as well. For instance, in many European nations, copyright holders have a "right of information" to discover the identities of, as well as personal information about, suspected infringers—even those who haven't done so in a commercial capacity.[34] And treaties like ACTA and CETA contain provisions requiring similar policies to be enacted by all signatories.

In addition to enabling the surveillance of online users suspected of infringing copyright, the anti-piracy agenda has also sought to give both government and commercial institutions the ability to censor online speech and restrict participation in the digital public sphere. While US ISPs have voluntarily adopted a "six strikes" graduated response policy restricting Internet access for suspected infringers (with some help from the IPEC), laws such as France's HADOPI and the UK's Digital Economy Act 2010 actually mandate that suspected infringers be deprived of Internet access after only three (unproven) accusations of unlicensed distribution.

While these policies censor individual users, others aim to censor specific Internet domains from the entire Internet user population. COICA would have given the Justice Department the power to impose a "blacklist" on ISPs, forcing them to prevent their users from accessing a given domain if it contained a site that contained a file that was suspected of infringing intellectual property. SOPA and PIPA would have granted similar censorship powers to the government, but with the fig leaf of judicial oversight (all three bills were defeated, partly because of concerns about implications for civil liberties). PIPA would also have granted some of that power to private claimants—essentially giving entrenched interests a mechanism to cut off traffic or funding for rival upstarts under the guise of protecting intellectual property rights. Given the United Nations' recent assertions that Internet access and online expression are fundamental human rights,[35] these provisions are especially troubling.

While each of the agenda items I have mentioned has been adopted as policy in some form, there are many other items on the piracy crusaders' wish list that have yet to pass into law. For instance, a "joint strategic plan" submitted by the RIAA, MPAA, and others to the IPEC in 2010 included several additional policy requests, including encouraging ISPs and network administrators to filter out copyrighted material before it could reach their users (presumably leaving only public domain information behind); empowering customs authorities to "educate" travelers about the economic costs of piracy and requiring travelers to claim pirated goods at the border; restricting trade with countries that refuse to adopt and administer stricter anti-piracy laws; and deputizing the Justice Department and Department of Homeland Security to develop "preventative and responsive strategy" around blockbuster releases by the entertainment industry.[36] Public Knowledge cofounder Gigi Sohn has also compiled a list of "bad ideas" perennially supported by the piracy crusaders.[37] This list includes exempting copyright enforcement from "net neutrality" policies mandating that ISPs provide equal passage for all content regardless of its source; making it legal for content companies to disable users' computers (e.g., the Berman bill); mandating the use of DRM by all content providers and device manufacturers (essentially outlawing the traditionally "open" personal computer); inserting a "broadcast flag" into all publicly available content, restricting the uses to which viewers or listeners can put that content, and effectively forestalling fair use; and remotely disabling the output ports on people's televisions and other media devices via "selectable output control."

Finally, there is the piracy crusaders' coup de grâce, an "Internet kill switch" enabling a government agency or official to shut down all online communications in one fell swoop. This was first proposed in a 2010 Senate bill called the Protecting Cyberspace as a National Asset Act. More recently, it reappeared in the Cybersecurity Act of 2012, another potential Senate companion to CISPA that specifically identified IP infringement as a cybersecurity concern and cause for action. Fortunately, this agenda item has not yet become law in the United States; considering the uses to which similar powers have been put in China, Iran, Egypt, Uganda, Thailand, and Tunisia, let us hope it never does.

To summarize, the piracy crusade supports a broad and ever-expanding agenda, the contours of which can be seen in the dozens of individual laws and policies. Although the implications of an Internet kill switch for free speech and civil liberties may be abundantly clear, the social and political implications of these other policies may still be somewhat obscure. In the next section, I discuss some of the ways in which these existing and proposed policies pose a threat to human rights and democratic values, and may complicate international relations for the United States and its allies.

Social and Political Consequences

There is nothing secret about the anti-piracy agenda. While there is no shortage of speculation on the Internet and elsewhere alleging that policies like ACTA, SOPA, and PIPA are evidence of a "government-approved international conspiracy,"[38] in actuality the piracy crusaders have been consistent and forthright in their ambitions to prevent copyrighted content from being copied and retransmitted without permission, at any cost. It's true that treaties like ACTA and TPP and agreements like the CAS deal have been negotiated in secret, but as best we can tell, the policies they promote have been openly advocated by the RIAA, MPAA and their allies for at least a decade. Thus, the secrecy surrounding some of these negotiations can be better understood as a tactical measure to minimize the risk of mainstream media coverage and public backlash. And this in turn suggests that the negotiating parties are aware that potential backlash is warranted by their policies' antagonism to open discourse, competitive markets, and civil liberties—which is in its own way just as damning, if not quite as sensational, as an actual conspiracy.

While public interest groups have largely led the charge against the excesses of the anti-piracy agenda, there has also been some staunch opposition within the government itself. Senator Ron Wyden, who has been among the most active opponents to such legislation, justified his opposition to COICA by explaining that "the collateral damage of this statute could be American innovation, American jobs, and a secure Internet."[39] Even the White House has acknowledged the potential threats of these policies if taken too far. In a public response to two petitions against SOPA, three federal officials coauthored a letter pledging that the president would "not support legislation that reduces freedom of expression, increases cybersecurity risk, or undermines the dynamic, innovative global Internet."[40] Similarly, in Britain, a recent government report argued that "copyright currently over-regulates to the detriment of the UK" and emphasized the importance of recognizing IP law's "wider impacts on society, in terms of culture, education and basic human rights such as freedom of expression."[41]

Yet despite these pledges, and the abundance of rhetoric suggesting that the needs of content cartels must be balanced against maintaining a robust civil society and a vital, innovative marketplace, anti-piracy policy continues to advance the former at the cost of the latter, and there is little reason to believe that new powers will not be abused and exploited to their fullest extent. Warner Bros. has openly admitted to using DMCA takedown procedures to remove content from the Internet that it didn't own, and hadn't even looked at.[42] Similarly, BayTSP, an anti-piracy firm that polices infringement on behalf of major content companies, recently ordered Google to remove a link to the *San Francisco Chronicle* website, apparently under the mistaken impression that this news article actually infringed on copyrights associated with 20th Century Fox's film *Chronicle*.[43] The Department of Homeland Security seized the independent popular music site Dajaz1.com in a 2010 sweep of "rogue" sites (pursuant to the PRO-IP Act), only to return it quietly to its owners a year later, without pressing charges.[44] Most recently, the entertainment studio Lionsgate used the DMCA to censor *Buffy vs Edward: Twilight Remixed,* a hugely popular parody mashup video that had been cited by the US Copyright Office itself in a list of examples of transformative work deserving fair use exemption.[45]

There can be little argument that these are instances of a consistent pattern of collateral damage incurred in the pursuit of actual copyright infringement, akin to dolphins caught in tuna nets. The only questions that remain are whether the benefit is worth the cost, and who should determine where that line falls. Metaphorically speaking, should we continue to build stronger, more deadly nets, when the fishing industry seems so completely unconcerned with the fate of the dolphins? What are the odds that a law such as PIPA wouldn't result in rights holders abusing their power to blacklist less powerful rivals and gain the upper hand in the marketplace, to the detriment of innovation? What are the odds that a law like CISPA wouldn't be used by government intelligence agencies to build virtual dossiers on American citizens, even those who haven't been accused, let alone convicted, of a crime? What are the odds that a law like the Berman bill or the Consumer Broadband and Digital Television Promotion Act (CBDTPA, 2002), a bill mandating the use of DRM in all digital devices and a broadcast flag in all public media, wouldn't end up preventing millions of people from accessing and sharing information according to their fair use rights? Given the frequent abuses of existing policies and their resulting "chilling effects" on both the marketplace and the public sphere, the odds seem fairly low. Thus, it is not an exaggeration to say that America's foundational principles are at stake if we pursue the anti-piracy agenda to its logical conclusion.

Further complicating these issues is the fact that the piracy crusade's effects don't stop at America's borders. I have already discussed the role that international trade agreements like ACTA, TPP and CETA play in setting, and raising, the bar for domestic copyright law. But there is another side to "harmonization." Such pacts also serve the equally important role of exporting American IP policies—and therefore the interests of American content cartels and their regulatory allies—to the rest of the world, industrialized and "developing" nations alike.

These agreements are usually heralded as "partnerships" (e.g., the second "P" in TPP), or as a chance for the United States to "work cooperatively with other governments to advance the fight against counterfeiting and piracy."[46] Strong anti-piracy laws that surpass those in the United States, such as Spain's Sinde Law[47] and Sweden's Intellectual Property Rights Enforcement Directive (IPRED)[48] have been called out for praise in IFPI publications, as evidence of this global spirit of collaborative enforcement. Yet leaked intergovernmental communications tell a very different story: both Sinde's Law and IPRED were enacted at diplomatic gunpoint, under pressure from the US government and the content cartels. Diplomatic cables published in 2010 by Wikileaks showed that the United States had "threatened Spain to force them to pass stronger copyright enforcement laws" in the past.[49] Then, in 2012, the Spanish newspaper El País published a letter from the US ambassador Alan D. Solomont to the Spanish prime minister's office, threatening that if Sinde's Law (which was then stalled in legislative limbo) were not passed, the country would be placed on the USTR's "priority watch list" (essentially the "most wanted" list for countries in breach of trade agreements) and subject to "retaliatory actions" with severe economic consequences. As a result, the incoming Spanish government fully implemented the legislation within ten days.[50] Similarly, Wikileaks cables reveal that, in Sweden, IPRED was one of several laws enacted there over a series of years, under similar threats that the country would be placed on the USTR's watch list if it didn't comply.[51]

Again, these specific examples point to a larger trend: the US government, at the behest of the piracy crusaders, routinely bullies other countries into adopting anti-piracy legislation that outstrips domestic law in its threats to free speech, privacy, and other liberties, then aims to use these examples to push for higher levels of protection and enforcement at home and around the world. But, in many of these nations, the costs of adopting such policies are even greater than those faced within the United States. For one thing, there is the matter of simple economics:

if the majority of revenue-bearing copyrighted content is owned by US corporations, then a higher degree of adherence to those copyrights and a lower tolerance for creative appropriation and technological innovation will simultaneously hurt local businesses and divert market revenues out of the local economy.

Another threat is cultural; as the anthropologist Michael F. Brown argues in a prescient 1998 article, the internationalization of intellectual property laws disproportionately benefits commercial industries over local cultural producers, and threatens to drown "indigenous cultures" in the "commodifying logic of advanced capitalism." The only solution, Brown argues, is to protect the "imperiled intellectual and artistic commons called the public domain" from becoming erased altogether by the relentless expansion of copyright.[52] Similarly, the legal policy scholars Peter Drahos and John Braithwaite argue that the "hierarchy of cultural production" established by international copyright laws "creates disincentives to participate in systems of cultural production" outside of "global stardom"—in other words, encouraging people to eschew their local and traditional cultural forms for the higher economic and reputational rewards promised by the content cartels.[53]

There are also concrete consequences related to the quality of life for people in countries that adopt the anti-piracy agenda. One of the most important examples is in the world of medicine. Several legal scholars, such as Joe Karaganis and Sean Flynn,[54] Jagdish Bhagwati,[55] and Michael Heller,[56] have amply documented the ways in which strengthening pharmaceutical patents, banning "parallel importation" of lifesaving drugs, and other agenda items tied to the piracy crusade have cost millions of lives and damaged untold more around the world. As the *Guardian* columnist Madeleine Bunting summarized in a 2001 article about TRIPS and global IP enforcement: "Put baldly, patents are killing people. But that's not all. Intellectual property protection has become a tool to make permanent the growing inequality of the global economy: the rich get richer and the poor get poorer."[57]

Finally, it is important to remember that laws and policies have social consequences that extend beyond their sponsors' intentions, or even their spheres of influence—and these must be tallied as costs, as well. In the case of IP law, there are several examples of malicious private and institutional actors taking advantage of legal powers and devices to the detriment of both liberty and security. A recently discovered variety of computer malware called "ransomware" crashes the computers it infects, then sends their owners messages claiming that the cause of the action was online copyright infringement. Infected computers can only be recovered if the owners pay the purported IP police: "To unlock your computer and to avoid other legal consequences, you are obligated to pay a release fee of £50."[58] Yet to the malware's hapless victims, this form of extortion may seem benign compared with the thousands of dollars demanded by actual rights holders alleging infringement.

I myself was targeted by a similar scam in 2011, in which phishers (a term for e-mail–based con artists) sent me a message claiming to be "the proprietors of all copyrighted material that is being fringed upon on your companies webste [sic]," and demanded that they "recover damages from you for the loss we have suffered as a result of your infringing conduct," to the tune of $160,000. I posted the message on my blog (both as an example of the point I am trying to illustrate here, and as a warning to other potential recipients of the e-mail). Judging by the responses to my post,[59] this was a widely distributed message, and there's no telling how many of its recipients clicked the link it provided, exposing themselves to financial losses or further malware attacks.

A marginally more legitimate, but far more deadly, variety of IP law exploitation comes in the form of "copyright trolls," who use the letter of the law to achieve ends at odds with its statutory purpose—namely, as stated in the US Constitution, "To promote the Progress of Science and useful Arts, by securing for limited Times to Authors and Inventors the exclusive Right to their respective Writings and Discoveries." Instead of promoting innovation and developing new ideas, trolls typically acquire legal control over an existing piece of intellectual property, and use it to extort money from people who have violated their exclusive rights. This is hardly a rare problem; for instance, in mid-2011, the tech news site *TorrentFreak* broke the story that over two hundred thousand BitTorrent users had been targeted in mass infringement suits by copyright trolls within the past year and a half. None of these suits had actually made it to court; instead, the trolls used their legal leverage to identify the alleged infringers, then offered settlements of a few thousand dollars to each (typically cheaper than the cost of a defense lawyer). This tactic likely yielded hundreds of millions of dollars for the trolls, while overloading the federal judicial system and preventing real justice from being done.[60]

Likewise, patent trolls[61] and trademark trolls[62] pursue similar tactics using those respective forms of intellectual property law, empowered by the stricter laws, higher penalties, and amplified rhetoric of the piracy crusade. A recent report by the Cato Institute calculates that collectively, defendants lose $83 *billion* in wealth per year due to suits by patent trolls in the United States alone,[63] and the law professor Colleen Chien has shown that the percentage of patent lawsuits in the United States brought by trolls has climbed dramatically, from 23 percent in 2007 to 61 percent in 2012.[64]

A final concern about the misuse of the anti-piracy agenda is its potential as a form of political censorship. There are instances, as I've described, in which newspapers and independent music websites were silenced by apparently overzealous piracy crusaders; while these instances were regrettable, it's unlikely that the sites were targeted for political purposes. Yet such examples do exist. We routinely hear about the censorship and punishment of dissident bloggers and other online media sources in countries such as China, Egypt, and Ethiopia, which offer fewer protections for free speech than are enjoyed in the United States and the EU. Yet there is good reason to believe that anti-piracy laws have already been used for political censorship in Western democracies, and therefore reason to be concerned that increased surveillance and censorship powers will be used for these purposes as well.

A recent report coauthored by the Open Rights Group, a UK cyber-policy advocate, and the London School of Economics documents over "60 reports of incorrectly blocked sites" on the wireless Internet in the first three months of 2012 alone, including several "political blogs [and] political advocacy sites."[65] Similarly, the US Patent and Trademark Office was recently caught using a filter to censor the websites of organizations such as the ACLU, the EFF, and Public Knowledge from its public access wifi network.[66] There have also been several high-profile cases of the DMCA being used as a tool for political censorship, as when a Mitt Romney presidential campaign video was removed from YouTube under the pretext that it contained a short clip of President Obama singing a song by Al Green and therefore infringed the composer's copyright. As the Stanford Law scholar Daniel Nazer summarized the incident, "The upshot is that copyright holders can act as private censors, using DMCA to silence speech at the height of a political campaign."[67] Soon thereafter, a video of Michelle Obama's speech at the 2012 Democratic National Convention was removed by YouTube under similar false pretenses.[68] These instances may not seem as dire as the harassment and imprisonment faced by dissidents such as Guo Quan and Eskinder Nega, but that is only because some protections for free speech remain; with every advancement of the anti-piracy agenda, those protections recede.

In Blake Edwards's 1976 slapstick comedy *The Pink Panther Strikes Again*, the bumbling but supremely self-confident Chief Inspector Clouseau (played by Peter Sellers) gathers the residents of a posh English estate together in a room, Agatha Christie–style, in the mistaken belief that one of them is an accomplice to murder. With typical Clouseau aplomb, the inspector manages to get his hand stuck in the gauntlet of a suit of armor, which has a mace attached to it. As he conducts his inquiries, a bee buzzes past Clouseau's head, and in a failed attempt to swat it, he reduces a beautiful piano sitting in the corner of the room to smithereens. Mrs. Leverlilly, the housekeeper, protests:

> Mrs. Leverlilly: You ruined that piano!
> Clouseau: What is the price of one piano, compared to the terrible crime that has been committed here?
> Mrs. Leverlilly: But that's a priceless Steinway!
> Clouseau: Not any more.

In his exaggeratedly outsized response to a small, if elusive, problem, his misplaced suspicions of the people around him, his unswerving faith in its own rectitude, and his complete disregard for the consequences of his actions, Chief Inspector Clouseau is the perfect avatar of the piracy crusade. No matter how deeply their proposed laws and policies undermine civil liberties, impede market innovation, and enable criminal fraud and political repression, the music and film industries manage to justify them in the name of preventing unlicensed copying. "What is the price of one freedom," they ask, "compared to the terrible crime that has been committed here?"

Ironically, the anti-piracy agenda rarely achieves its stated goals—a fact that is beginning to achieve some acknowledgment in policy circles. Analyses show that high-profile shutdowns and lawsuits against services like Grokster[69] and Megaupload[70] failed to stop online sharing, and may only have increased P2P activity overall (in fact, the closures may have had negative effects on commercial content markets).[71] The much-heralded HADOPI law in France has been called a "failure" by the French culture minister.[72] After signing ACTA, Polish prime minister Donald Tusk declined to ratify it, arguing that his earlier support had been a "mistake."[73] Soon thereafter, the European Parliament voted overwhelmingly to reject the treaty, which it had signed (along with twenty-two of its member states) less than a year earlier.[74]

Despite these signs that the tide may be turning, the piracy crusade still has a significant amount of momentum, and a broad support base within both private industry and government, fueled by a continuing torrent of lobbyist expenditures. In my final chapter, I discuss some of the ways in which resistance to the piracy crusade is growing among the general population, and outline some alternative approaches that have been promoted by both activists and lawmakers. I conclude with some thoughts about the future of democracy and intellectual property as technological and cultural innovation continue to accelerate.

CHAPTER 9

Is Democracy Piracy?

IN APRIL 2012, a young couple got married in Belgrade, Serbia. The wedding video[1] shows the bride and groom smiling nervously as they stand on a dais in fancy clothes, while the crowd around them titters and cheers and the romantic strains of an aria waft through the air. After the groom lifts the bride's veil, they exchange heartfelt vows and then kiss. The room erupts with applause.

Despite these traditional elements, this was no ordinary wedding. For one thing, the young couple were dressed in a postmodern mélange of styles: the groom offset his brocaded coat, leggings, and neck ruff by dying his short hair maraschino cherry red, while the bride wore a floor-length dress that was white on the left and black on the right with black breast cones and a single elbow-length black silk glove on her right arm. Far more striking was the officiant to their right: in addition to his conservative black cassock, augmented by a gray and gold stole, he wore a Guy Fawkes mask and sported a laptop emblazoned with stickers (fig. 11). The laptop was evidently the source of the officiant's "voice," which in its computer-generated cadences asked each party to take the other as a "noble peer" and to "share your love, your knowledge, and your feelings . . . as long as the information exists."

These vows had never been spoken before, because this was the first marriage ever conducted in the Church of Kopimism, a new religion founded in 2010 by a nineteen-year-old philosophy student named Isak Gerson. The religion is based on the principles that copying, disseminating, and reconfiguring information not only are ethically right but are in themselves "sacred" acts of devotion. Kopimist philosophy also holds that "the internet is holy" and that "code is law"[2] (a phrase copied from the legal scholar Lawrence Lessig).[3]

When Kopimists first filed to be recognized as an official religion in Gerson's native country of Sweden, some grumbled that they were

Figure 11. The world's first Kopimist wedding, in Belgrade, Serbia, April 2012.

simply a bunch of pirates cleverly using religious protection to shield them from liability for P2P. Yet Sweden officially recognized Kopimism in January 2012, and today the religion boasts thousands of members around the world, with chapters in over twenty countries. Of course, file sharing is an important part of the Kopimist belief system and the church openly maintains that "Copyright Religion is our absolute opposite," so there can be little question that its resistance to "persecution" at the hands of the piracy crusade "oppressors"[4] is both a dogmatic and a practical concern.

Although treating the act of copying information as a matter of religious doctrine might at first seem to be exactly the kind of pretentious nonsense most people would expect from a nineteen-year-old Swedish philosophy major, students of religious history will recognize in Kopimism echoes of many other doctrines, such as early Christianity. For instance, St. Irenaeus, a second-century theologian, would append to his texts a formula dictating the terms on which they should be copied: "You who will transcribe this book, I charge you, in the name of our Lord Jesus Christ and of His glorious Second Coming, in which He will come to judge the living and dead, compare what you have copied against the original and correct it carefully. Furthermore, transcribe this adjuration and place it in the copy."[5]

This protocol was in turn copied by St. Jerome two hundred years later in his work *De viris illustribus,* and, based on that work, the formula continued to be used by monks well into the Middle Ages, whenever they transcribed holy scriptures.[6] In fact, it was only with the introduction of movable type and the publication of the Gutenberg Bible that the act of copying began to lose its sacred valence in the Christian world. As I discussed in chapter 1, this innovation was also a precursor to, and a precondition of, the development of copyright. Thus, we can understand Kopimism not as the spiritualization of something that began as a commercial and industrial process, but rather the *re*-spiritualization of a process following a long intermediary period of industrial capitalism.

I am not suggesting that the spirit of copying is identical in Irenaeus and Kopimism; where the former was principally concerned with maintaining copy fidelity, better to transmit the "word of God," the latter is more concerned with copying for its own sake and privileges interpretation over fidelity (in the words of the Kopimist Constitution, "Copymixing is a sacred kind of copying, moreso [*sic*] than the perfect, digital copying, because it expands and enhances the existing wealth of information"). Yet these distinctions are not so great as they may seem. Monastic Christianity, copyright, and Kopimism can each be understood as value systems that govern socio-epistemological processes (in plain English, the social establishment of "truth") during eras of informatic scarcity, mechanical reproduction, and digital dematerialization, respectively. Seen through this lens, a doctrine like Kopimism can be understood as a serious attempt to reconcile the regulatory demands of the twentieth century's copyright regime with the cultural ramifications of today's global digital information infrastructure. Put another way, while the piracy crusade sacrifices technological innovation to preserve industrial capitalism, Kopimism sacrifices industrial capitalism to preserve technological innovation. Thus, its theologians are correct: the two dogmas are, in fact, "absolute opposites."[7]

Although Kopimism appears to be growing in popularity and spreading rapidly around the globe, it is still a marginalized belief system that thus far has been recognized as a legitimate religion in only one nation. Far more prevalent, and politically impactful, is another recent Swedish invention: the Pirate Party. This movement, which was established in 2006 in direct response to the international anti-piracy agenda, rapidly developed a concrete political platform and a coordinating nongovernmental organization (Pirate Parties International, established in 2010)[8] and currently has affiliate parties in sixty-six nations (including established parties in ten US states). Pirate Party candidates have won elections in several countries, including seats in the European Parliament and the German Bundestag. By early 2012, the Pirate Party had become the "fastest-growing political group in Europe."[9]

In its own, less spectacular way, the rise of the Pirate Party is every bit as incredible as the emergence of Kopimism. How can it be that a group widely perceived as a "fringe single-issue party,"[10] by its own accounts hobbled by a "stupid name,"[11] and openly derided as "criminal at its core" by a prominent European anti-piracy group,[12] has become a political force on a global scale in the matter of a few short years? The legal scholar Jessica Litman attributes the party's appeal to the fact that "there are millions of ordinary people whose use of YouTube and peer-to-peer file-sharing networks gives them a direct, personal stake in the copyright law,"[13] in contrast to historical periods in which the average media consumer had little or no cause to think about, let alone critique, IP policy. To the Pirate Parties themselves, the answer is even broader, and has less to do with copyright per se than it does with giving people a stake in the political process. As Matthias Schrade, a German Pirate Party operative, told the BBC after some recent electoral successes, "We offer what people want. People are really angry at all the other parties because they don't do what politicians should do. We offer transparency, we offer participation. We offer basic democracy."[14]

These two analyses are hardly irreconcilable. The tensions at the heart of the piracy crusade are exactly the same as those at the root of the democratic process: How can we arrive at, and enforce, a definition of "freedom" that negotiates between the conflicting needs of several stakeholders? How can we express ourselves, organize our societies, and live our lives without being constrained by those more powerful than we? And, by the same token, how can we create and sustain a cultural and technological environment in which innovation and commerce thrive, thus broadening our personal and collective horizons and improving the quality of our lives? For a growing number of people around the world, the answers to these questions are looking increasingly less like copyright and intellectual property—at least, as we currently understand them.

Copyright and Copyfight

From its origins, copyright has been viewed in America as a foundational mechanism for a thriving, participatory democracy. James Madison maintained in the Federalist Papers that copyright law is one of the rare instances in which "the public good fully coincides . . . with the claims of individuals."[15] By tapping into the power of the marketplace, the legal scholar Neil Netanel argues, the founders believed that they could create a "sphere of self-reliant authorship, free from state or private patronage . . . help[ing] to ensure the diversity and autonomy of the voices that make up our social, political and aesthetic discourse."[16]

Yet, even at the dawn of the new republic, the founders recognized that there must be some limitations on the scope of what we now call intellectual property. Thomas Jefferson wrote of the issue in an oft-quoted letter to a Boston mill owner named Isaac McPherson: "It would be curious then, if an idea, the fugitive fermentation of an individual brain, could, of natural right, be claimed in exclusive and stable property. . . . Society may give an exclusive right to the profits arising from them, as an encouragement to men to pursue ideas which may produce utility, but this may or may not be done, according to the will and convenience of the society, without claim or complaint from anybody."[17]

Thus, Jefferson (who was initially opposed to copyright laws altogether) viewed intellectual property as an artifice—a necessary fiction, mutually agreed upon by the state, the citizenry, and the marketplace, whose value was limited to its role as an "encouragement" for the sharing of ideas. To put it another way, the marketplace was, by virtue of its plurality, understood to be a lesser of evils, a check on the government's potential for tyranny, and thus another instrument of leverage for the citizenry to protect individual liberty and the integrity of the public sphere. It was precisely this vision that has been enshrined in the US Constitution, which paves the way for copyright by establishing Congress's power "To promote the Progress of Science and useful Arts, by securing for limited Times to Authors and Inventors the exclusive Right to their respective Writings and Discoveries."[18]

In the centuries since then, copyright law, media technology, and private industry have coevolved, to the point where none remotely resembles the world known—or even anticipated—by Jefferson and Madison. Yet we have never moved beyond the original challenge at the heart of copyright law—namely, the task of striking the perfect balance between government regulation and commercial privatization, ensuring the maximal freedom of speech for the public whom both sectors ostensibly serve. Unfortunately, we now live in an age in which this détente has been compromised. Private industry has consolidated to a near singularity, with a handful of global corporations controlling the vast majority of the revenue-generating music, as well as books, movies, games, and other forms of creative expression, to say nothing of the consolidation of pharmaceuticals, software patents, and other IP-based industries.

By the same token, the government has been so thoroughly penetrated by industry lobbying and other forms of corporate influence that it has largely ceased to operate as a check or balance against the excesses of the marketplace, and instead serves as an instrument of market hegemony, both domestically and abroad. The fact that international IP treaties such as ACTA and TPP have been negotiated in secrecy from the public and the news media, but with the full participation of the content industries, is one glaring example of the warped logic that now governs our policies. The recent US Supreme Court ruling in *Citizens United v. Federal Election Commission*,[19] which establishes that the First Amendment protects the right of corporations to spend limitless amounts of money in their efforts to influence the outcome of elections, is another. As a result, the American public now has little hope, or even expectation, that "the will and convenience of the society" will be addressed by copyright law, or that "freedom of speech" applies to their own activities beyond sanctioned commercial contexts.[20]

Given these developments, it is unsurprising that an increasing number of scholars and activists, and a growing segment of the public at large in America and around the world, have come to see the piracy crusade as anathema to what the Pirate Party calls "basic democracy." But rather than the nihilistic despair and "digital barbarism"[21] some have ascribed to this budding movement, both the scholarly and the popular responses have quickly moved beyond blanket condemnations and embraced more substantive, nuanced critiques of copyright law and IP policy. Broadly speaking, we have begun, perhaps for the first time since the dawn of the modern republics, to discuss intellectual property law as a vital human rights issue rather than as a matter best left to policy wonks and "experts" in private industry.

It is difficult to establish the origins of what many have come to call the "copyfight";[22] some trace it back to the battles over analog reproduction technologies such as VCRs and photocopiers in the 1970s and '80s, others cite the contemporaneous hacker culture and the development of the free software movement,[23] while yet others see the public arguments over P2P, TRIPS, WIPO, and copyright term extension in the late 1990s as a more appropriate origin story. Regardless of the precise lineage, by the turn of the century it was evident to many that these somewhat discrete concerns had begun to merge into a larger discourse. Scholars such as Siva Vaidhyanathan,[24] James Boyle,[25] Lawrence Lessig,[26] Jessica

Litman,[27] and Tim Wu[28] published influential books and articles reframing intellectual property law as a regulatory mechanism for public and commercial speech. Pundits like Tim O'Reilly[29] and Cory Doctorow[30] began to critique the language of the piracy crusade, celebrating the social and economic benefits of peer-to-peer culture. Filmmakers such as Brett Gaylor,[31] Benjamin Franzen and Kembrew McLeod,[32] and Andreas Johnsen, Ralf Christensen, and Henrik Moltke[33] created compelling visual and narrative arguments to communicate these concepts to a broader public. And advocacy groups like Creative Commons, Electronic Frontier Foundation, Public Knowledge, and Students for Free Culture began to develop cohesive educational and lobbying agendas in contrast to those of the piracy crusaders.

Most important, and no doubt in part as a result of these efforts, the general public have become demonstrably more aware of—and more actively engaged with—these issues in recent years. My own research has borne this out. With my coauthors Mark Latonero and Marissa Gluck, I fielded a survey of American adults in 2006 related to what we call "configurable" cultural practices—namely, mashups, remixes, and other emerging digital forms of expression that blur the boundary between traditional production and consumption. This survey included an optional write-in response, inviting respondents to share their "general thoughts about remixes and mashups." Analyzing the hundreds of voluntary written responses, we discovered that respondents had adopted several new ethical frameworks to evaluate the validity of these new cultural practices (e.g., "good copying" vs. "bad copying"), and that most of these frameworks had nothing whatsoever to do with the law.[34] When we fielded a nearly identical survey to adults around the globe four and a half years later, in late 2010, we found that most of these ethical frameworks were still in place, but many respondents also explicitly critiqued copyright law as either inadequate to the task of regulating digital culture or as antagonistic to it.[35] In other words, in a half decade, public opinion regarding copyright (at least in a digital context) had progressed from "largely irrelevant" to "broken and possibly harmful." Quantitative research has produced similar results, as well. For instance, Joe Karaganis, a researcher at Columbia University, recently found that "solid majorities of American internet users oppose copyright enforcement when it is perceived to intrude on personal rights and freedoms."[36]

The copyfight has already yielded some interesting political effects. This is an issue that collapses the traditional left/right binary within both American and international political arenas. Successful bills such as The

Cyber Intelligence Sharing and Protection Act (CISPA) and the Prioritizing Resources and Organization for Intellectual Property (PRO-IP) Act of 2008 were passed with bipartisan support. Yet CISPA's sister bill, the Cybersecurity Act, was blocked by a Republican filibuster, and both COICA and PIPA were effectively blocked by Democratic senator Ron Wyden. Similarly, European ACTA signatories included both leftists and conservatives, but a similarly diverse mix of politicians ultimately refused to ratify it.

This stubborn refusal to conform to traditionally polarized party dynamics has already become one of the hallmarks of the copyfight, making it an unusually chaotic and unpredictable element of the political landscape. There are at least three reasons why this has happened. First, the rapidity with which technology, culture, and industry now coevolve has made it difficult for any legacy party to effectively integrate a consistent IP position into its platform. For instance, should a small-government, pro-business, unilateralist Republican support or reject a copyright bill that increases federal regulation, funding, and power in the name of protecting private enterprise at home and abroad? How would this same hypothetical politician feel about an international trade agreement that "harmonizes" IP law and coordinates international policing efforts under the auspices of a multi-governmental treaty organization? There is no easy answer to these questions, thus the opportunity—perhaps even the necessity—for new organizations like the Pirate Party to enter into the mix.

The second reason why the copyfight upends traditional party dynamics is its emphasis on personal liberty in contrast to institutional power. Although copyfighters don't necessarily claim affiliation with or draw inspiration from other political movements organized around this dynamic, they "occupy a point on the political compass where [left and right] curve around to meet in a common war cry: 'Get the bureaucrats, the plutocrats and the party hacks off our backs,'"[37] in much the same way that historical movements like anarchism and libertarianism and contemporary ones like the Tea Party and Occupy do.

The third, closely related, reason for the copyfight's lack of traditional political valence is the fact that most of the anti-piracy agenda's legislative and executive sponsors appear to be driven more by economic self-interest (in the form of the lobbyist carrot and the trade sanction stick) than by strict political ideology. These policies may be justified in the name of partisan party platforms, but ultimately they are promoted and enacted by bipartisan alliances cemented with common patronage rather than common values. To be fair, corporate influence can be seen in the legislative resistance to the anti-piracy agenda, as well. For instance, some of the most vocal congressional opponents to SOPA were Ron Paul, Anna Eshoo, and Zoe Lofgren,[38] a politically diverse group of politicians who also happen to be the three top recipients of campaign finance contributions from Google in the House of Representatives.[39] But this fact only further emphasizes the larger point—that traditional party politics play little or no role in the legislative process when it comes to copyright policy.

The copyfight has had political repercussions outside the governmental sphere as well. It has galvanized the hacker community (historically, one of the sectors most critical of copyright law, dating back to its role in the privatization of computer code) in a way that few other policy matters do. Over the past decade, "hacktivism"[40] of all stripes, from relatively benign linking campaigns to more destructive activities such as denial-of-service attacks, has become an increasingly common form of protest against new anti-piracy laws, treaties, and policies. From local matters such as SOPA in the States[41] and Sinde's Law in Spain[42] to global ones like ACTA,[43] both government and commercial organizations have been targeted in waves of attacks whose primary purpose and effect has been to concentrate greater media attention on the implications of these laws and policies for free speech and civil liberties. Of course, as with all civil disobedience, there is an inevitable backlash; in the eyes of those who support the anti-piracy agenda, such attacks are further proof that pirates and hackers are antisocial forces cut from the same destructive cloth.

Although a great many local and global groups have participated in hacktivist attacks against piracy crusaders, the unquestionable leader and focal point for such strategies is currently the amorphous hacker collective Anonymous.[44] With their theatrical reappropriation of the Guy Fawkes mask from the 2005 film *V for Vendetta* and their cryptic motto, "We are Anonymous, We are Legion, We do not forgive, We do not forget, Expect us!,"[45] Anonymous have captured the public imagination and served as a vital educational resource and rallying point for copyfighters and activists outside of the hacker community. In this respect, they play a similar role to that of the Yippies and the Students for a Democratic Society during the 1960s antiwar, free speech, and civil rights movements in the United States.[46] Much as these groups did, Anonymous provides those beyond its ranks with a symbolic lexicon that can be applied as a kind of political shorthand for complex technology and policy matters.

Figure 12. Polish legislators wearing Guy Fawkes masks in Parliament. AP Images, reproduced with permission.

In some cases, this symbolism has even been adopted by policymakers themselves, completing a circuit of sorts. For example, in January 2012, days after hacktivists took down the Polish government website and replaced it with text such as "Stop ACTA!," "Prime Minister Donald Tusk is a bad person!," and "You won't take away human rights!,"[47] over thirty Polish lawmakers donned Guy Fawkes masks in the Polish Parliament to protest the treaty[48] (fig. 12) while thousands of citizens rallied in the streets (many of them wearing the masks as well). Ultimately, Tusk was compelled to abandon his pledge to sign ACTA, which was in turn a decisive factor in the broader EU rejection of the trade agreement.

Alternatives to the Piracy Crusade

The bulk of this book has focused on debunking the arguments at the heart of the piracy crusade, and documenting the social and political costs of the anti-piracy agenda. Yet I would be remiss if I did not devote at least a part of my final chapter to discussing some of the alternative ideas that have emerged in response to these policies. But before I review these ideas, it makes sense to begin with a few "first principles." What are the social benefits of intellectual property? What problems does it exist to solve, and how well does it do so? Only by keeping these ends in sight can we evaluate the different means that have been proposed to achieve them.

As I discussed earlier, one of the primary functions of copyright, patents, and other species of IP is to *incentivize creators* to share their ideas with the world. A second, related function is to provide such creators with a *means to capitalize on their innovations*. In addition to providing creative incentives, this also speaks to a basic expectation of fairness that is commonly invoked in capitalist societies—creative work, like all other forms of labor, should be remunerated.[49] A third function has to do with the reputational economy, rather than financial remuneration: copyright allows creators to *take credit for their work,* which has social and psychological benefits in addition to financial ones. A fourth function of copyright is to grant creators some *degree of control* over how their work is used by third parties. For instance, by a provision in his will, the late Adam Yauch (a.k.a. MCA) of the Beastie Boys has used his copyrights in the band's repertoire to prevent posthumously the songs' being used "for advertising purposes,"[50] a stipulation in keeping with his lyrical pledge (in "Putting Shame in Your Game") not to "sell my songs for no TV ad." A fifth function, mentioned earlier in this chapter, is to provide the citizenry with a mechanism for *checks and balances* against both governmental and commercial encroachment on free speech. A sixth function of copyright is to *incentivize industrial organizations* to exploit creative work, thereby both spreading new ideas and generating new wealth for the economy. This is a hefty load for one law, or more precisely, one set of laws and policies, to carry. Inevitably, in the shaping and execution of these policies, one function must be weighed against, and privileged over, another. As I hope I have demonstrated in this book, the problem with the piracy crusade isn't copyright per se, but rather the fact that it overwhelmingly privileges the sixth function, often to the detriment of the first five.

One of the earliest modern efforts to reprioritize the functions of copyright came in the form of free software licenses (sometimes used interchangeably with the term "open source").[51] In what has now become the stuff of geek legend, the computer hacker Richard Stallman pioneered this new breed of legal instrument in the 1980s with the development of the GNU General Public License (GPL).[52] Stallman had been frustrated when the de facto public domain that had characterized the software coding community from its earliest days began to be privatized; not only was code being copyrighted, but commercial interests were shipping software without granting purchasers access to the "source code," which would allow them to make their own edits and amendments. As a result, much of the code that Stallman and his peers had written, with the expectation that it would remain publicly available to the hacker community, was being integrated into commercial projects and essentially locked behind digital bars. Stallman's solution to this problem was a stroke of genius: he would turn copyright inside out (or backward; this solution is often referred to as "copyleft"), using a license of his own devising to force anyone who used his code to make it available to third parties on the same terms.[53] The GPL has become a canonical text within the hacker community, and today it and dozens of similar licenses have been used to establish openness for millions of works, including some of the world's most popular software programs and web destinations.

More than a decade after Stallman's revelation, the law professor Lawrence Lessig recognized that culture at large faced challenges similar to those Stallman had identified in the field of computer code. Between copyright term extension, the DMCA, and other elements of the budding piracy crusade, Lessig worried that the cultural "commons," or the shared knowledge and experience of our society, was being increasingly encroached upon by private interests—even as new digital communication networks were providing us with the power to share ideas on a scale hitherto unimaginable. Lessig foresaw that the combination of stronger copyright and more powerful networks would soon turn virtually everyone into "pirates" by default, so he set out to create a legal inoculation in the form of an open license for creative expression.[54] The resulting legal instrument, which is called a Creative Commons (CC) license,[55] is similar to the GPL in that it gives musicians, authors, artists, and other creators the opportunity to use their copyrights as a means to encourage, rather than discourage, the reuse and redistribution of their work. One of its most important innovations is that it gives the author herself the ability to prioritize between copyright's various functions; for instance, while one breed of CC license allows any kind of use as long as attribution is granted to the original creator, another allows only noncommercial uses, and yet another prohibits derivative works. In the decade since the CC license was developed, hundreds of millions of works have been released under its terms, including the White House website, Wikipedia, music by popular artists including Nine Inch Nails, Beastie Boys, and Snoop Dogg, and this book.[56]

Where open licenses such as the GPL and CC attempt to address the shortcomings of copyright by augmenting it contractually, others have proposed that intellectual property law simply be abolished altogether and replaced with a new regulatory system. For instance, the Dutch researchers Marieke van Schijndel and Joost Smiers have proposed that all creative works be immediately absorbed into the public domain (a legal concept that describes information that cannot legally be propertized, although the authors explicitly synonymize it with the commons).[57]

Van Schijndel and Smiers envision three possibilities for creators under this solution. For those in relatively low-investment, low-risk fields (such as musical performers), the authors suggest that a "first-mover advantage" will allow innovators to benefit, simply by virtue of being reputationally and economically associated with the new ideas they promote. True, performers can't expect royalties from recordings, they argue, but the loss of these typically meager sources of revenue will be offset by increased income from other sources, such as live performances. For creators in higher-investment or higher-risk fields (such as cinema, book authorship, and music composition), the authors suggest a usufruct, a legal instrument that predates copyright by centuries. In the present context this term means that although the creator doesn't technically own a work, she retains the exclusive right to exploit it commercially for a limited period of time (the authors suggest a year). This is a less radical proposal than it may seem; in its emphasis on temporary rights of exploitation rather than permanent rights of property, the Jeffersonian and constitutional approach to copyright more closely resembles such a usufruct than it does modern copyright law. Finally, van Schijndel and Smiers suggest that works that may be difficult to exploit commercially can be subsidized by the government, further justifying their public domain status. Again, this proposal is hardly radical; even in America, the land of free enterprise and low taxes, we currently spend over $150 million annually on the National Endowment of the Arts, one of many public sources of funding for creative works.

While ideas such as open licenses and the usufruct system have emerged from outside traditional government and policy circles, alternatives to the piracy crusade have been proposed by lobbyists, legislators, and regulators as well. In the United States, the Pirate Party advocates reducing copyright terms from their present length (an author's life plus seventy years, or ninety-five years for a commercially funded work-for-hire) to the original fourteen-year term that existed when copyright was first introduced in this country.[58] The party has also advocated for the abolishment of the DMCA (hence the title of its recent publication, *No Safe Harbor*), and for the expiration of unproductive patents after four years.[59]

Members of traditional political parties have also proposed their own solutions. For instance, Republican Congressman Darrell Issa has advocated strongly for a "Digital Citizen's Bill of Rights" to guide IP- and communications-related law and policy. This approach strikes a very different balance from the anti-piracy agenda, establishing "freedom," "openness," and "equality" as its first three principles, and relegating "property" to the tenth, and final, place. Together with Democratic senator Ron Wyden, he has promoted legislation called the Online Protection and Enforcement of Digital Trade (OPEN) Act in both houses of Congress as an explicit alternative to SOPA, PIPA and similar legislation. In an effort to deliver on the spirit of the legislation and to highlight its contrasting values with the lobbyist-driven anti-piracy agenda, Issa has also made drafts of the law available for public comment on a dedicated website.[60]

The Republican Party itself has also flirted with the idea of making progressive copyright reform an element of its national platform. In November 2012, less than two weeks after the party's presidential candidate had lost in nationwide elections, owing in part to a perceived lack of "original ideas" from the candidate and the GOP at large,[61] the Republican Study Committee (RSC) posted a policy brief to its website titled "Three Myths about Copyright Law and Where to Start to Fix It." The brief, which critiqued existing copyright laws for hampering cultural innovation, market value, and scientific inquiry, argued strongly for a number of drastic reforms, including steep cuts in statutory damages, expansion of fair use, punishment for false copyright claims, and "heavily" limited copyright terms, with a default length of twelve years and a maximum length of forty-six years, requiring several increasingly costly renewals.

Under reported pressure from content industry lobbyists, the RSC removed the brief from its website the day after it was posted (which happened to fall on a Saturday; apparently, it was too volatile to leave on the site until Monday).[62] By way of explanation, the RSC's executive director, Paul Teller, wrote a short memo, sent from his BlackBerry phone, explaining that the brief had been published "without adequate review" and apologizing for not taking care to approach the subject of copyright reform "with all facts and viewpoints in hand."[63] A few weeks later, Derek Khanna, the staffer who had authored the policy brief, was summarily fired. In a subsequent interview with *Ars Technica*, Khanna clarified that, despite Teller's claims, the memo had gone through "exactly the same review process as other RSC publications."[64] At the time of writing, Rep. Jim Jordan of Ohio, the chairman of the RSC, has received $98,150 in campaign finance contributions from the television, movie, and music industries since 2005.[65] This episode illustrates some of the reasons that progressive copyright reform remains politically challenging within contemporary America's lobbyist-saturated political environment.

Fortunately, government-driven alternatives to the piracy crusade have begun to emerge elsewhere around the world as well. Like those in the States, they run the gamut from flat-out rejection of the anti-piracy agenda to more conciliatory approaches apparently aimed at furthering industry interests while forestalling the kind of activist backlash spurred by SOPA, PIPA and ACTA. In the UK, a series of studies released in 2012 by the government's Intellectual Property Office have identified the music industry as a primary example of the mismatch between copyright law and digital commerce and culture. The reports suggest that an independent, industry-funded "digital copyright exchange" be established in order to "streamline and simplify" the process of using copyrighted material in a variety of contexts, ranging from educational to religious to commercial settings. This solution is presented as a quid pro quo deal for the content cartels in their efforts to develop ever stronger copyright enforcement: "If the creative industries ensure that they have done all they can to make licensing and copyright work easier for rights users and therefore consumers, then the ball is firmly at the feet of the politicians to ensure appropriate measures are in place to reduce the incidence of copyright infringement on the web."[66]

Other examples abound, from Europe to Asia to South America. A Dutch government directive instituted in 2006 prevents enforcement authorities from pursuing criminal prosecution for online "piracy."[67] In 2011, the Swiss government announced it would not pass stronger IP laws and would allow unlicensed downloading for personal use to remain legal, because "its priority was to avoid limiting access to information through copyright regulations."[68] In Brazil, despite the "maximalist approach to copyright protection that currently dominates"[69] its laws and policies, there have been several government-driven efforts to mitigate the effects of the piracy crusade. Most notably, musician Gilberto Gil, who served as minister of culture from 2003 to 2008, established a relationship between Brazil and Creative Commons that included placing government websites under an open license and initiating unprecedented open public debates on the social and economic impact of copyright legislation (in 2011, the incoming minister of culture, Ana de Hollanda, issued an order to remove the CC license from government websites).[70] Brazil has also introduced some intriguing copyright reform proposals, including a bill that would have issued penalties and sanctions against companies that used DRM to prevent fair use or access to the public domain[71] and a 2010 policy rejecting DMCA-style notice-and-takedown policies and instead requiring a court order for infringing material to be removed from the Internet at the behest of rights holders,;[72] most recently, the Marco Civil da Internet, a bill that would establish a digital bill of rights similar to those outlined in America's OPEN Act, has been making its way slowly through the nation's legislature.[73]

In India, the government has spent the past few years in a sustained court battle with multinational pharmaceutical conglomerate Novartis over its 2006 decision to reject a patent for life-saving antiretroviral (ARV) drugs that battle AIDS and related diseases. Novartis argues that, under the TRIPS agreement, India is obliged to grant the patent. The Indian government argues that the drug in question is minimally differentiated from existing compounds, and therefore that granting the patent would only serve the function of building Novartis's profits while inflating the cost of these life-saving drugs beyond a price point that most infected people can afford.[74] Given the fact that about 2.4 million Indians are currently living with HIV, it is no exaggeration to say that millions of lives hang in the balance. At the time of writing, the Indian Supreme Court is weighing its decision, following final arguments in the case.

In short, the alternative to the anti-piracy agenda isn't simply lawlessness, anarchy, or socialism as its proponents routinely suggest. Independent researchers and international governments alike have proposed, and in some cases enacted, a diverse array of alternate laws and policies that strike a different balance between the competing mandates of intellectual property, privileging such values as freedom of speech, access to knowledge, and quality of life over the profit motives of the cartelized industries that lobby for, and disproportionately benefit from, maximalist copyright and IP laws. The fact that so many independent sovereignties have challenged the piracy crusade on their own terms, according to their own needs, and in spite of threats of trade sanctions and other diplomatic and market pressures lends credence to the point of view that "harmonization," far from providing a convenient and mutually beneficial one-size-fits-all platform for international IP enforcement efforts, can best be understood as an instrument of American industrial hegemony.

From this, we can draw two conclusions. First, resistance to the anti-piracy agenda shouldn't be interpreted as a de facto attack on American interests, capitalist values, or the rule of law. To the contrary, in almost all cases it amounts to a political argument in support of basic human rights and equal opportunity in both the political and commercial spheres—which are themselves foundational American values. Second, the fact that no single "solution" emerges in contrast to the anti-piracy agenda shouldn't be taken as evidence of a lack of viable alternatives. A key fallacy of the piracy crusade is the notion that a single set of laws and policies should govern all uses of information, by all people, in all social contexts, in every nation. As its more astute critics routinely observe, a better approach is a *multiplicity* of approaches, granting governments, markets, and societies the leeway to regulate information sharing on their own terms, in response to the unique challenges and value systems that inhere to their particular spheres. Simply speaking, why should Hollywood set the terms by which the other seven billion people on the planet can communicate?

Conclusion: Beyond Copying, Beyond Copyright?

I have written this book secure in the knowledge that it will soon be obsolete. It's not just because the laws, policies, and technologies I discuss change so rapidly that today's breaking news is tomorrow's ancient history—although this is certainly the case. Far more important is the fact that we are likely approaching a sociotechnological "event horizon" of sorts—a point beyond which the origins of intellectual property law become so remote and obscure that there will be little purpose in debating its enforcement or amending its architecture. To put it plainly, we are on the verge of an era in which the concept of "copying" has no meaning, and therefore in which "copyright" exists only as an instrument of hegemony.

This change has been a long time in the making. As a great many scholars have observed, and as I have reiterated throughout this book, copyright law has its origins in a bygone age at the dawn of industrial capitalism and the modern concept of the individual. As the printing press has been supplanted (or augmented) by electronic and digital media, and as commerce and culture have widened to encompass a global scale, the notion of a single sovereignty granting a single publisher the exclusive right to distribute a single work by a single author has come into ever-greater conflict with the reality of our daily lives as communicants, audiences, producers, and consumers.

Copyright law has evolved and expanded over the centuries, to include new methods of storage and transmission and to accommodate new modes of commercial exploitation, but it has always remained rooted in the basic metaphor of a publisher distributing a discrete work printed on paper for sale to a reader. Even today, the letter of the law limits protection to "original works of authorship fixed in any tangible medium of expression."[75] While it's a stretch to claim that certain forms of expression (say, a live musical performance transmitted by satellite radio) are "fixed" or "tangible," we have managed to account for this disjuncture by abridging and interpreting both the letter and the spirit of the law with increasing flexibility.

Seen from this vantage point, we can understand the piracy crusade of the past fifteen years as merely the latest iteration of this trend. Digital media further dematerialized the process of producing, distributing, and consuming information, so copyright laws have been revised with an even broader interpretation of what "authorship," "fixed," and "tangible" mean in this context, and with stronger policing and steeper penalties to prevent both businesses and individuals from crossing the increasingly porous boundary between "use" and "theft."

The problem is, the metaphorical flexibility of copyright is now strained to breaking point,[76] on two fronts. First, new technological advances threaten to eradicate completely the distinction between author and audience (one of the primary conclusions of my first book, *Mashed Up*), fixed and fluid, and tangible and intangible. Second, "maximalist" copyright laws such as those promoted by the anti-piracy agenda can only be strengthened so much before they amount to total control over the flow of all information between all individuals.

On the first front, let's take as an example the current rage of the geeky DIY set: 3D printing. This technology enables anyone with a printer to create a physical object, on any scale and from a variety of possible materials, based on a digital model of that object. Over the past few years, the price of 3D printers has begun to descend from industrial to hobbyist levels, further spurring creative tinkerers to expand the range of conceivable uses for the technology. In 2013, it seems to be poised on the brink of (early) mainstream adoption. At this point, it is easy to imagine a near future in which people will routinely print anything from replacement machine parts to furniture to items of clothing using inexpensive and ubiquitous home devices.

The question is, what role would intellectual property play in such a world? Today, copyright doesn't cover industrial or conceptual design, such as food recipes and fashion (and these industries have arguably thrived as a result).[77] Would the law be widened further to "protect" the interests of those who seek to privatize and monopolize the library of virtual 3D models, thus placing an entire new universe of creative expression into private (and most likely corporate) hands and removing it from the public domain? If not, how would the law treat a virtual model of a copyrighted vinyl album or a sculpture? Would transmitting or printing such a model amount to a violation of copyright? More important, would it be possible to differentiate between protected and unprotected models any more easily than it is to distinguish the legal and illegal 1s and 0s currently transmitted over the Internet? And what kind of surveillance and censorship would be justified in pursuing such an end?

Let's take the question a bit further. Two of the fields of scientific research that are currently considered to be among the most promising sources of future innovation and social transformation are nanotechnology (the construction of machines and functional objects using microscopic building blocks) and biotechnology (the construction of machines and functional objects using living organisms, DNA, and/or the other rudimentary elements of life). If we extend the hypothetical questions surrounding 3D printing to each of these fields, we face similarly intractable problems, but on a far more sweeping and profound scale. There has already been significant controversy over whether, and under what circumstances, a DNA sequence can, or should, be patented or copyrighted,[78] and the matter is currently being addressed by the US Supreme Court.[79] Yet we have barely scratched the surface of the potential power and range of social applications of these technologies. If intellectual property maximalism is applied to the transmission and use of nanomachines and genetic sequences, will we be able to alter and adorn our own bodies, seek and receive medical treatment, or even eat and reproduce without committing some form of "piracy?"

These are not "academic" concerns or simply my clever attempt at the rhetorician's old trick of reductio ad absurdum. To the contrary, the problem I have just outlined in broad strokes is so significant that I am most likely erring on the side of understatement. The larger point is inescapable: our degree of technological mastery over our physical surroundings and our neurological and biological functions seems likely to grow drastically in the coming decades, to the point where it will resemble the fluidity and dynamism we have already come to expect from information processing on our pocket-sized computing devices and via the Internet. Not only will *atoms* increasingly be used like *bits,* to use Nicholas Negroponte's[80] helpful, if reductionist, terminology; the distinction itself will become more and more functionally irrelevant as ubiquitous digital networking transmits instructions for molecular and genetic sequencing between billions of peers around the globe, and as nano- and biocomputers increasingly supplant "traditional" silicon-based processors in our homes, businesses, and bodies.

This leads us to the second front: copyright maximalism. We already live in world in which virtually everything that we "fix" in a "tangible medium" is automatically subject to copyright for a practical eternity.[81] Each day, in our normal course of actions, we casually (and largely unwittingly) commit both civil and criminal infringement that, according to the legal scholar John Tehranian's estimates, makes every one of us technically liable for billions of dollars in damages per year.[82] Before the age of the Internet, this fact may have been of theoretical concern, but it had no practical importance; after all, no rights holder could possibly surveil the entire populace day in and day out, keeping track of every infringing behavior and exacting the appropriate fines in a legal setting. In fact, it may be argued that such casual "piracy" was always assumed to exist, and that the frameworks for copyright enforcement and punishment took this into account.

This dynamic began to change as computer networks became increasingly pervasive, and thus increasingly central to both our business and personal lives. As e-mail and social media have replaced the postal service and the water cooler as the primary interpersonal communications platforms for hundreds of millions of people, not only has our rate of infringement climbed (retelling a Jay Leno gag at the water cooler is legal, but posting it to a Facebook page is not), but our actions have become far more subject to survcillance, and we ourselves have become far more identifiable to the "injured" parties. During the same years, the piracy crusaders have developed a legal infrastructure that not only legitimizes such surveillance, but makes it easier for rights holders (and their representatives) to target casual infringement in mass lawsuits, and to "settle" with the defendants without ever having brought the cases to court. And these powers have already been exploited in the United States and around the world to stifle innovation and competition, censor political speech, and bully the general public.

As we approach the post-silicon era (for lack of a better term), these problems are likely to be compounded even further. As the tools for shaping our physical environments and biological destinies come to look increasingly like those we now use to create, alter, reproduce, and transmit our text, photos, videos, and music, what aspect of the human experience will not be, in some way, constituted by the act of "copying"? What region of our personal and public lives will not therefore be subject to copyright, or to some similar legal constraint, and to all the opportunity for exploitation that comes with such constraints? It sounds like the plot of a dystopian science fiction film, but it's clearly the direction in which we're headed.

Futurists like Ray Kurzweil[83] have charted the course to the "singularity" of man and machine in excruciating detail, and they look forward devoutly, with a messianic fervor, to the day when we can "transcend biology." I have spoken on several occasions to one of the Singularity movement's chief proselytizers, and he has described for me his vision of the not-so-distant future in which the human spirit, liberated from the bonds of mortality and corporeality, is free to explore the limitless possibilities of the known and unknown universe for all eternity.

To me, this future sounds at best lonely and at worst totalitarian. If all of life is code, and code is law, and life, code, and law are undying, how can we avoid reaching one of two chilling ends? Either the power to shape our destiny rests in our own (virtual) hands, and we each become singular gods in our own monotheistic universes, or there is some system of centralized authority that doles out such power, and we must spend eternity subject to its unfathomable whims and biases—in other words, with a machine as our god (and devil).

If there is a third way, I believe it looks a lot like Kopimism. Far better to function as a "noble peer," sharing information in the form of "love, knowledge, and feelings" with the other peers in the universe-network, than to go it alone or to toil eternally under the yoke of some heartless algorithm.

In the meantime, there are more pressing concerns, and much work to be done. Long before we achieve anything close to singularity, the piracy crusade threatens to undermine our societies, to crash our markets, and to privatize completely the most personal form of public expression— our music. In the interest of both present and future, we need to rethink some of our basic assumptions about business, law, and culture. How much of a threat is "piracy" in the form of online sharing, compared with the costs we've already seen to innovation, civil liberties, and public discourse in our failed efforts to stop it? Will stricter copyright, stronger enforcement, and harsher penalties really aid creative expression and the industries that exploit it, or will it simply open the door to more abuse and plunge us deeper into cultural paralysis?

As I have argued throughout this book, the answers to these questions are clear if we're willing to see them. The entire rationale for the piracy crusade is built on the flimsiest of foundations. The willful blindness that leads our governments to support the anti-piracy agenda despite its obvious flaws and faults is evidence of a genuine dysfunction within both the private organizations that lobby for these policies and the state institutions that enact them.

Fortunately, there are many viable alternatives we can pursue if we have the political will. A good starting point would be to enact a binding "digital bill of rights" akin to the one promoted by Congressman Issa and Senator Wyden, and to develop laws, treaties, and international policies that adhere to its principles. A more ambitious aim would be to reverse the pendulum's swing, restricting the term of copyright, and ceding a wider swath of cultural behaviors to fair use and the public domain. Most important, we need to abandon the ideology of the anti-piracy agenda and to look with fresh eyes at the complex causal relationships among information sharing, commerce, and society. To reduce all cultural activity to a stark permission/piracy binary is a form of discursive impoverishment that renders intelligent decision making practically impossible. And, given what's at stake, we need to make intelligent decisions now more than ever. In short, we need to end the piracy crusade as though our lives depend on it.

NOTES

Introduction: Piracy Crusades Old and New

1. My sources for the histories of Genoa and Tunisia in this section are Harry Hazard, *A History of the Crusades*, vol. 3: *The Fourteenth and Fifteenth Centuries* (Madison: University of Wisconsin Press, 1975); and Barbara Tuchman, *A Distant Mirror: The Calamitous 14th Century* (New York: Ballantine Books, 1978).

2. Hazard, *History*, 481; Tuchman, *Distant Mirror*, 463.

3. Tuchman, *Distant Mirror*, 463, 468.

4. Ibid., 474.

5. Hazard, *History*, 482.

6. Ibid., 483.

7. Tuchman, *Distant Mirror*, 462.

8. Ibid., 460.

9. Matthew Belloni, "Supreme Court Refuses to Hear Joel Tenenbaum Appeal in Music Piracy Case," *Hollywood Reporter*, May 21, 2012, www.hollywoodreporter.com/thr-esq/supreme-court-joel-tenenbaum-piracy-327266.

10. Raphael Minder, "Pressure Grows on Spain to Curb Digital Piracy," *New York Times*, May 17, 2010.

11. Tina Johnson with Robert Mancini, "Court Rules MP3.com Violates Copyrights," *MTV News*, April 28, 2000, www.mtv.com/news/articles/1432447/court-rules-mp3com-violates-copyrights.jhtml.

12. Plaintiffs' post-trial brief concerning remedy and defendants' first amendment defense. *Universal City Studios, Inc., et al. v. Eric Corley a/k/a "Emmanuel Goldstein" and 2600 Enterprises, Inc.*, August 8, 2000, www.2600.com/dvd/docs/2000/0808-brief2.html.

13. "The Six Business Models for Copyright Infringement," study commissioned by Google and PRS for Music, June 27, 2012, www.prsformusic.com/aboutus/policyandresearch/researchandeconomics/Documents/TheSixBusinessModelsofCopyrightInfringement.pdf.

14. "MP3.com Settlement: RIAA Hails Victory for Creative Community & Legitimate Marketplace," RIAA.com, June 9, 2000, http://riaa.com/newsitem.php?id=81022351-3D35-EEE9-B26B-F9DF3239CCDB.

15. "Court Rejects Napster's Case Rehearing," RIAA.com, June 26, 2001, http://riaa.com/newsitem.php?id=D55C5B4C-9F5B-7142-81EB-1AF69E3A897A.

16. "RIAA Statement on MGM v. Grokster Supreme Court Ruling," RIAA.com, June 27, 2005, http://riaa.com/newsitem.php?id=DE79FC7C-A22E-931E-CF31-59E03950450C.

17. "Federal Court Issues Landmark Ruling against LimeWire," RIAA.com, May 12, 2010, http://riaa.com/newsitem.php?id=B78C8571-0E8D-5861-27C6-4D2178AEB7D1.

18. See, for instance: Derek Slater, Urs Gasser, Meg Smith, Derek Bambauer, and John Palfrey, "Content and Control: Assessing the Impact of Policy Choices on Potential Online Business Models in the Music and Film Industries," *Berkman Publication Series Paper* 2005-01 (2005), http://ssrn.com/abstract=654602; Mike Masnick, "Hadopi Accused of 'Massaging' the Numbers to Make Anti-piracy Activity Look Better," *Techdirt,* April 4, 2012, www.techdirt.com/articles/20120402/12145518337/hadopi-accused-massaging-numbers-to-make-anti-piracy-activity-look-better.shtml.

19. Obviously, colonization and industrialization came at their own significant costs for millions of enslaved and exploited people around the globe, in addition to many other well-documented global and ecological consequences. I am not suggesting that these were "positive" developments in any sense other than the economic and political benefits that accrued to the European powers.

20. Daniel Goffman, *The Ottoman Empire and Early Modern Europe* (New York: Cambridge University Press, 2002).

21. Nancy Baym, *Personal Connections in the Digital Age* (Cambridge: Polity, 2010).

22. David Karpf, *The MoveOn Effect: The Unexpected Transformation of American Political Advocacy* (New York: Oxford University Press, 2012).

23. *MGM Studios, Inc. v. Grokster, Ltd.,* 545 U.S. 913 (2005).

24. Siva Vaidhyanathan, "Afterword: Critical Information Studies," *Cultural Studies* 20, no. 2–3 (2006): 292.

25. The book's online draft is still available to read and comment on at http://mediacommons.futureofthebook.org/mcpress/piracycrusade/.

26. Details of the license's terms are available at http://creativecommons.org/licenses/by-nc-sa/3.0/.

27. John Williamson and Martin Cloonan, "Rethinking the Music Industry," *Popular Music* 26, no. 2 (2007): 305.

28. Patrik Wikström, *The Music Industry: Music in the Cloud* (Cambridge: Polity Press, 2009), 12.

29. Elisabeth Kübler-Ross, *On Death and Dying* (London: Routledge, 1969).

1. Stacking the Deck

1. The term was coined by Pierre Bourdieu in his essay "Cultural Reproduction and Social Reproduction," in *Knowledge, Education, and Cultural Change: Papers in the Sociology of Education,* ed. Richard Brown, 71–112 (London: Tavistock, 1973)

2. Aram Sinnreich, *Mashed Up: Music, Technology, and the Rise of Configurable Culture* (Amherst: University of Massachusetts Press, 2010).

3. Mark Changizi, *Harnessed: How Language and Music Mimicked Nature and Transformed Ape to Man* (Dallas: BanBella Books, 2011), 203.

4. Oliver Sacks, *Musicophilia: Tales of Music and the Brain* (Toronto: Vintage Canada, 2008).

5. Daniel Levitin, *This Is Your Brain on Music: The Science of a Human Obsession* (New York: Dutton Adult, 2006).

6. Colin M. Turnbull, *The Forest People* (New York: Simon & Schuster, 1961).

7. John Blacking, *How Musical Is Man?* (Seattle: University of Washington Press, 1973).

8. Edward Schieffelin, *The Sorrow of the Lonely and the Burning of the Dancers* (New York: Palgrave Macmillan, 2005).

9. Lawrence Lessig, *Free Culture: The Nature and Future of Creativity* (New York: Penguin Books, 2004); Lewis Hyde, *Common as Air: Revolution, Art, and Ownership* (New York: Farrar, Straus and Giroux, 2010); James Boyle, "The Second Enclosure Movement and the Construction of the Public Domain," *Law and Contemporary Problems* 66 (2003): 33.

10. James Carey, *Communication as Culture* (London: Routledge, 2009), 18.

11. Sinnreich, *Mashed Up*.

12. Jacques Attali, *Noise: The Political Economy of Music*, trans. Brian Massumi (Minneapolis: University of Minnesota Press, 1985), 15.

13. Bram Kempers, *Painting, Power, and Patronage: The Rise of the Professional Artist in the Italian Renaissance*, trans. Beverley Jackson (London: Penguin, 1995); Larry Gross, "Art and Artists on the Margins," in *On the Margins of Art Worlds*, ed. Larry Gross (Boulder, CO: Westview Press, 1995).

14. Joel Sachs, "London: The Professionalization of Music," in *The Early Romantic Era: Between Revolutions, 1789 and 1848*, ed. Alexander Ringer, 201–35 (Englewood Cliffs, NJ: Prentice Hall, 1991).

15. Christopher Small, *Music of the Common Tongue: Survival and Celebration in African American Music* (Lebanon, NH: University Press of New England, 1987), 62, 346.

16. Lyman Ray Patterson, *Copyright in Historical Perspective* (Nashville: Vanderbilt University Press, 1968), 5.

17. Ibid., 6.

18. For a thorough examination of the Jefferson-Madison correspondence and a comprehensive history of American copyright, see Hyde, *Common as Air*.

19. See, for instance, the US Copyright Office's claim that "copyright law encourages cultural innovation by securing exclusive rights to . . . authors" in "Celebrating World Intellectual Property Day 2011," www.copyright.gov/docs/wipo2011.html.

20. Neil Weinstock Netanel, "Copyright and a Democratic Civil Society," *Yale Law Journal* 106, no. 2 (1996): 283–387.

21. Tim Wu, "Copyright's Communications Policy," *Michigan Law Review* 103 (November 2004): 349.

22. Patricia Aufderheide and Peter Jaszi, *Reclaiming Fair Use: How to Put Balance Back in Copyright* (Chicago: University of Chicago Press, 2011).

23. Although copyright has been advanced as an instrument of several non-economic ends, such as quality control, a lengthy analysis by the then law professor and future Supreme Court justice Stephen Breyer concluded that none of these ends were adequate to justify the means. In his words, "if we are to justify copyright protection, we must turn to its economic objectives." Stephen Breyer, "The Uneasy Case for Copyright: A Study of Copyright in

Books, Photocopies and Computer Programs," *Harvard Law Review* 84, no. 2 (December 1970): 291.

24. John Ogasapian, *Music of the Colonial and Revolutionary Era* (Westport, CT: Greenwood Press, 2004).

25. Lorenzo Candelaria and Daniel Kingman, *American Music: A Panorama* (Boston: Schirmer, 1979).

26. There were copyrighted musical works in the United States prior to this act; some legal scholarship suggests that the language of the law was expanded to include music as a statutory clarification of existing norms. See, for instance, Oren Bracha, "Commentary on the U.S. Copyright Act 1831," in *Primary Sources on Copyright (1450–1900)*, ed. Lionel Bently and Martin Kretschmer (Cambridge, UK: Faculty of Law, 2008), www.copyrighthistory.org.

27. Richard Crawford, *America's Musical Life: A History* (New York: Norton, 2005), 232.

28. For a more thorough account and analysis of this expansion, see Lessig, *Free Culture*; Siva Vaidhyanathan, *Copyrights and Copywrongs: The Rise of Intellectual Property and How It Threatens Creativity* (New York: New York University Press, 2001); and William F. Patry, *Moral Panics and the Copyright Wars* (New York: Oxford University Press, 2009).

29. Dena Epstein, "Music Publishing in the Age of Piracy: The Board of Music Trade and Its Catalogue," *Notes,* 2nd ser., 31, no. 1 (September 1974): 7.

30. Deven R. Desai, "The Life and Death of Copyright," *Wisconsin Law Review* 2011, no. 2 (March 2010): 219.

31. This debate has found new life in the digital era, as evidenced by the introduction of the Internet Radio Fairness Act into Congress in 2012.

32. The Digital Millennium Copyright Act (DMCA) and the Copyright Term Extension Act (CTEA; also known as the Sonny Bono Act).

33. The 1996 Telecom Deregulation Act.

34. David Bollier, *Brand Name Bullies: The Quest to Own and Control Culture* (Hoboken, NJ: Wiley, 2005).

35. Fredric Dannen, *Hit Men: Power Brokers and Fast Money Inside the Music Business* (New York: Random House, 1990); Walter Yetnikoff and David Ritz, *Howling at the Moon: The Odyssey of a Monstrous Music Mogul in an Age of Excess* (New York: Broadway Books, 2004).

36. Theodor Adorno, "On Popular Music," in *Essays on Music,* ed. Richard Leppert, 437–69 (Berkeley: University of California Press, 2002).

37. Richard Wightman Fox and T. J. Lears Jackson, *The Culture of Consumption: Critical Essays in American History, 1860–1960* (New York: Pantheon Books, 1983).

38. Bernard W. Carlson, "Artifacts and Frames of Meaning: Thomas A. Edison, His Managers, and the Cultural Construction of Motion Pictures," in *Shaping Technology/Building Society: Studies in Sociotechnical Change,* ed. Wiebe E. Bijker and John Law, 175–200 (Cambridge: MIT Press, 1992).

39. Stuart Ewen, *All Consuming Images: The Politics of Style in Contemporary Culture* (New York: Basic Books, 1988); Daniel T. Cook, "Consumer Culture," in *The Blackwell Companion to the Sociology of Culture,* ed. Mark D. Jacobs and Nancy Weiss Hanrahan (Malden, MA: Blackwell, 2005), 160–75.

40. IFPI, *Recording Industry in Numbers 2010,* www.ifpi.org.

41. Marcy Rauer Wagman and Paul Rapp, "The Band as a Business," October 4, 2011, Future of Music Coalition, http://futureofmusic.org/article/article/band-business.

42. Jerry Osborne, *Elvis—Word for Word: What He Said, Exactly as He Said It* (New York: Random House, 2006); Adrian Grant, *Michael Jackson: The Visual Documentary,* new updated millennium ed. (London: Omnibus, 2001).

43. There are exceptions, such as the commercial distribution of religious music, but these account for a small minority of both music market value and musical cultural practice.

44. "Franchises: Pirates of the Caribbean," Box Office Mojo, http://boxofficemojo.com/franchises/chart/?id=piratesofthecaribbean.htm.

45. "What Is Piracy?," IFPI.com, "Views," http://ifpi.org/content/section_views/what_is_piracy.html.

46. Daniel Heller-Roazen, *The Enemy of All: Piracy and the Law of Nations* (New York: Zone Books, 2009).

47. Adrian Johns, *Piracy: The Intellectual Property Wars from Gutenberg to Gates* (Chicago: University of Chicago Press, 2009), 12–13.

48. Ibid., 329–31.

49. Ibid., 447–48.

50. Stephen Traiman, "Pro & Semi Pro: All Systems Go," *Billboard,* May 12, 1979, TAV-3.

51. *Sony Corp. of America v. Universal City Studios, Inc.,* 464 U.S. 417 (1984).

52. Mike Hennessey, "U.K. Piracy Rate World's Lowest," *Billboard,* June 19, 1982, 9.

53. For an exhaustive examination of the relationship between copyright and fair use in the context of digital media, see Patricia Aufderheide and Peter Jaszi, *Reclaiming Fair Use: How to Put Balance Back in Copyright* (Chicago: University of Chicago Press, 2011).

54. *A&M Records, Inc. v. Napster, Inc.,* 239 F.3d 1004 (2001).

55. *MGM Studios, Inc. v. Grokster, Ltd.,* 545 U.S. 913 (2005); full disclosure: I was an expert witness for the defense.

56. Mitch Bainwol, "Building a Brighter Future: Making AND Selling Great Music," address delivered at the National Association of Recording Merchandisers Convention, San Diego, August 12, 2005, available at http://dreadedmonkeygod.net/home/attachments/Bainwol.pdf; emphasis in original.

57. Electronic Frontier Foundation, "Supreme Court Ruling Will Chill Technology Innovation," EFF.org, "Press Room," June 27, 2005, www.eff.org/press/archives/2005/06/27-0.

58. Lessig, *Free Culture.*

2. Riding the Tiger

1. Michael Chanan, *Repeated Takes: A Short History of Recording and Its Effects on Music* (London: Verso, 1995).

2. Wiebe E. Bijker and John Law, *Shaping Technology/Building Society: Studies in Sociotechnical Change* (Cambridge: MIT Press, 1992).

3. Media scholars such as Mark Katz and Jonathan Sterne have written excellent books detailing the social histories of music recording technologies, and each has not only informed my thinking on these subjects but also helped to shape the larger scholarly approach to the topic. It is not my aim here to reproduce or extend their work, but I feel it is important briefly to revisit some of the same ground they have covered in the interest of my broader argument.

4. Jonathan Coopersmith, "Old Technologies Never Die, They Just Don't Get Updated," *International Journal for the History of Engineering & Technology* 80, no. 2 (July 2010): 166–82.

5. IFPI, *Recording Industry in Numbers 2012,* www.ifpi.org.

6. Kara Rose, "Cassette Tapes See New Life after MP3s," *USA Today.com,* October 3, 2011, www.usatoday.com/life/music/news/story/2011-10-02/mp3s -cassette-tapes-vinyl-albums/50639144/1.

7. Also, because Sony owned its own digital storage format (the "Memory Stick"), it chose not to support less expensive and more widely used non-proprietary flash memory cards.

8. Many audiophiles have rejected the claims of CDs' "perfect" quality since the format's debut, and there are continuing efforts to develop a digital music ecosystem that allows music to be distributed via the Internet in higher-quality (24 bit, 96kHz) audio formats.

9. For more in-depth analysis of the social shaping of radio, see Christopher Sterling and Michael Keith, *Sounds of Change: A History of FM Broadcasting in America* (Chapel Hill: University of North Carolina Press, 2008); H. R. Slotten, "Radio Engineers, the Federal Radio Commission, and the Social Shaping of Broadcast Technology: Creating 'Radio Paradise,'" *Technology and Culture* 36, no. 4 (1995): 950; Christina Dunbar-Hester, "Geeks, Meta-Geeks, and Gender Trouble: Activism, Identity, and Low-power FM Radio," *Social Studies of Science* 38, no. 2 (2008): 201–32; Gary Lewis Frost, *Early FM Radio: Incremental Technology in Twentieth-Century America* (Baltimore: Johns Hopkins University Press, 2010).

10. "Officially It's No Decision; Unofficially AFM Turns Thumbs Down on FM Feed," *Billboard,* February 19, 1944, 12.

11. Hugh Richard Slotten, *Radio and Television Regulation: Broadcast Technology in the United States, 1920–1960* (Baltimore: Johns Hopkins University Press, 2000), 144.

12. B. Eric Rhoads, *Blast from the Past: A Pictorial History of Radio's First 75 Years* (West Palm Beach, FL: Streamline Publishing, 1996), 328–29.

13. Mark Katz, *Capturing Sound: How Technology Has Changed Music* (Berkeley: University of California Press, 2004).

14. "July Records," *Time,* July 14, 1941, 42.

15. Sidney Bechet and Rudi Blesh, *Treat It Gentle: An Autobiography* (Cambridge, MA: Da Capo Press, 2002).

16. Wayne Wadhams, *Inside the Hits,* ed. David Nathan and Susan Gedutis Lindsay (Boston: Berklee Press, 2001); James Hunter, "Recordings," *Rolling Stone,* April 3, 1997, 64; "Soundcheck Smackdown: Aja," *WNYC.org,* April 19, 2011, www.wnyc.org/shows/soundcheck/2011/apr/19/soundcheck -smackdown-aja/.

3. "We've Been Talking about This for Years"

1. I have never particularly cared for this term, although it does come in handy at times like these.
2. Steve Jones, "Music and the Internet," in *The Handbook of Internet Studies,* ed. M. Consalvo and C. Ess, 440–51 (Hoboken, NJ: Wiley-Blackwell, 2011).
3. C. Krishan Bhatia, Richard C. Gay, and W. Ross Honey, "Windows into the Future: How Lessons from Hollywood Will Shape the Music Industry," *e-Insights,* Booz Allen & Hamilton, 2011, www.boozallen.com/media/file/76799.pdf.
4. Charles C. Mann, "The MP3 Revolution," *Atlantic Online,* April 8, 1999, www.theatlantic.com/past/docs/unbound/digicult/dc990408.htm; Justin Hughes, "On the Logic of Suing One's Customers and the Dilemma of Infringement-Based Business Models," *Cardozo Arts & Entertainment Law Journal* 22, no. 3 (2005): 725–76; "Tone-Deaf Businessman," *Lefsetz Letter,* http://lefsetz.com/wordpress/index.php/archives/2011/12/30/tone-deaf-businessmen/.
5. Aram Sinnreich, "Copyright and Intellectual Property: Creating New Business Models with Digital Rights Management," Jupiter Research (1999).
6. "MP3's Biggest Threat," *Maximum PC,* September 1999, 44.
7. Seth Mnookin, "Universal's CEO Once Called iPod Users Thieves. Now He's Giving Songs Away," Wired.com, "Magazine," vol. 5, no. 12, November 27, 2007, www.wired.com/entertainment/music/magazine/15-12/mf_morris.
8. Ibid.
9. Michael A. Carrier, "Copyright and Innovation: The Untold Story," *Wisconsin Law Review* 2012, no. 4, 891, available at http://ssrn.com/abstract=2099876.
10. Elisabeth Kübler-Ross, *On Death and Dying* (London: Routledge, 1969).
11. Other commentators have used this framework as well, including TEDxRegents Park—Dr. Jeremy Silver, "Death of a Business Model: How the Music Industry Is Grieving and Growing," July 30, 2009, available at www.youtube.com/watch?v=2RA6pAk7n88; and Alison McEmber, "The Publishing Industry, the Recording Industry, and the Five Stages of Grief," *Xavier Journal of Politics* 2, no. 1 (2011): 20–32. To my knowledge, I was the first to make this comparison publicly, in presentations I gave as keynote speaker at the Halifax Pop Music Explosion in 2008 and elsewhere between 2006 and 2010. A copy of this presentation can be found at www.slideshare.net/originalsinn/opposite-day-music-in-the-network-age.
12. KAS Immink, "The Compact Disc Story," *Journal of the Audio Engineering Society* 46, no. 5 (1998): 458–65.
13. Steve Knopper, *Appetite for Self-Destruction: The Spectacular Crash of the Record Industry in the Digital Age* (New York: Free Press, 2009), 118.
14. John C. Dvorak, "Talk about Pop Music," *PC Magazine,* September 23, 1997, 87.
15. Steven V. Brull, "Net Nightmare for the Music Biz," *Business Week,* March 2, 1998), 89–90.
16. Kübler-Ross, *On Death and Dying,* 64.

17. Don Jeffrey, "Downloading Songs Subject of RIAA Suit," *Billboard*, June 21, 1997, 3.

18. Jennifer Urban and Laura Quilter, "Efficient Process or 'Chilling Effects'? Takedown Notices under Section 512 of the Digital Millennium Copyright Act," *Santa Clara Computer & High Technology Law Journal* 22, no. 4 (March 2006): 687.

19. It's difficult to establish the exact number, as DMCA takedown notices are not typically made public.

20. Jon Healy, "Online Music Services Besieged," *Los Angeles Times*, May 28, 2001.

21. 180 F.3d 1072 (9th Cir., 1999).

22. Brooks Boliek, "Eisner: Piracy 'Killer App' for Computer Profiteers," *Hollywood Reporter*, March 1, 2002.

23. "MP3's Biggest Threat," *Maximum PC*, September 1999, 46.

24. See, for instance, *Arista Records, LLC v. Doe 3*, 604 F.3d 110 (2010).

25. "Prepared Remarks of Hilary Rosen, Chairman and CEO," Hilary Rosen, Recording Industry Association of America (RIAA), National Association of Recording Merchandisers, Annual Convention and Trade Show, Orlando, Florida, March 17, 2003, www.riaa.com/newsitem.php?news_year_filter =&resultpage=54&id=870A2E2F-1415-5740-F001-252D26B52493.

26. Philip E. Meza, *Coming Attractions? Hollywood, High Tech, and the Future of Entertainment* (Stanford: Stanford University Press, 2007), 130.

27. Eliot Van Buskirk, "RIAA Training Video Leaked onto Torrent Sites," Wired.com, "Listening Post," February 19, 2008, www.wired.com/listening _post/2008/02/riaa-training-v/.

28. Cory Doctorow, "Stargate Fan-site Operator Busted under Anti-terrorism Law," *Boingboing*, July 26, 2004, http://boingboing.net/2004/07/26 /stargate-fansite-ope.html.

29. Kübler-Ross, *On Death and Dying*, 95.

30. Sinnreich, "Copyright and Intellectual Property."

31. Aram Sinnreich, "Digital Music Subscriptions: Post-Napster Product Formats," Jupiter Research (2000).

32. Charlie Sorrell, "So Long, and Thanks for All the Cash: Yahoo Shuts Down Music Store and DRM Servers," Wired.com, "Gadget Lab," July 25, 2008, www.wired.com/gadgetlab/2008/07/so-long-and-tha/.

33. Matt Asay, "Warner Music: It was wrong to go to war with our customers [Gasp!]," CNET.com, "News," November 15, 2007, http://news.cnet.com /8301-13505_3-9817893-16.html.

34. In inflation-adjusted 2011 dollars.

35. Nine Inch Nails' frontman Trent Reznor released an EP with Columbia Records in 2012, a few years after NIN parted ways with Interscope, but thus far, NIN itself has yet to release any additional recordings via a major label. It is my (unsubstantiated) opinion that Reznor's deal with Columbia was a gesture of goodwill, to ameliorate his relations with the majors as he negotiated licensing deals for his yet-to-launch digital music subscription service, tentatively named Daisy.

36. Although Madonna's 2012 album, *MDNA*, was distributed and marketed by Interscope, her recording contract is part of a "360 deal" with the live events

company Live Nation, which she signed after leaving a decades-long relationship with Warner Music Group.

37. As I told the *Seattle Times* when SpiralFrog was announced, I felt it was "really promising that the labels are going to finally stop kvetching and start thinking intelligently about where their money's going to come from in the 21st century." Quoted in Charles Duhigg and Dawn C. Chmielwski, "All Music Downloads from Largest Record Seller Will Be Free," *Seattle Times,* August 30, 2006, http://seattletimes.nwsource.com/html/nationworld/2003234969_music30.html.

38. Declan McCullagh, "Warner Music Readies CD-free 'e-label,'" CNET .com, "News," August 22, 2005, http://news.cnet.com/Warner-Music-readies-CD-free-e-label/2100-1027_3-5841355.html.

39. Geoff Taylor, "Napster—10 Years of Turmoil," BBC.co.uk, "News," June 26, 2009, http://news.bbc.co.uk/2/hi/technology/8120320.stm.

40. Erik Pedersen, "Has the Music Business Turned a Corner? RIAA Reports First Revenue Increase in 7 Years," *Hollywood Reporter,* March 28, 2012. Later reports showed that this upward trend continued throughout 2012.

41. Eliot Van Buskirk, "Copyright Time Bomb Set to Disrupt Music, Publishing Industries," Wired.com, "Business," November 13, 2009, www .wired.com/epicenter/2009/11/copyright-time-bomb-set-to-disrupt-music-publishing-industries/.

42. Michael Arrington, "'360' Music Deals Become Mandatory as Labels Prepare for Free Music," *TechCrunch,* November 8, 2008, http://techcrunch .com/2008/11/08/360-music-deals-become-mandatory-as-labels-prepare-for-free-music/.

4. Dissecting the Bogeyman

1. A principle coined by Intel founder Gordon Moore, which holds that the amount of computer processing power available at a given price will double every eighteen months.

2. Quoted in Kevin D. Mitnick and William L. Simon, *The Art of Intrusion: The Real Stories behind the Exploits of Hackers, Intruders, and Deceivers* (Indianapolis: Wiley, 2005): 35.

3. Cary H. Sherman, "What Wikipedia Won't Tell You," *New York Times,* February 8, 2012.

4. For a more in-depth overview of the range of P2P protocols and architectures, see Anura P. Jayasumana, "File Sharing to Resource Sharing—Evolution of P2P Networking," IEEE Consumer Communications and Networking Conference (CCNC), Las Vegas, January 2012, available at http://host.comsoc .org/market/ccnctutorials/T2_Jayasumana_P2P_CCNC2012_2.pdf.

5. *A&M Records, Inc. v. Napster, Inc.,* 239 F.3d 1004 (2001)

6. *MGM Studios, Inc. v. Grokster, Ltd.,* 545 U.S. 913 (2005); *Arista Records LLC v. Lime Group LLC,* 715 F. Supp. 2d 481 (2010). I served as an expert witness for the defense in both of these cases.

7. This ruling has been criticized for being overly vague and broad in its applicability, a subject I explore in greater depth in chapter 8.

8. Greg Sandoval, "RIAA Wants Revived LimeWire Dead and Buried," CNET.com, "News," November 19, 2010, http://news.cnet.com/8301-31001_3-20023365-261.html.

9. Aram Sinnreich, Nathan Graham, and Aaron Trammell, "Weaving a New 'Net: A Mesh-Based Solution for Democratizing Networked Communications," *Information Society* 27, no. 5 (2011): 336–45.

10. Sam Laird, "The Pirate Bay Plans Robot Drone Servers to Dodge Law Enforcement," *Mashable,* March 19, 2012, http://mashable.com/2012/03/19/the-pirate-bay-drones/; the sincerity of these plans, which would entail a great deal of engineering difficulty and expense, has been widely challenged.

11. See, for instance, TorrentReactor's recent launch of http://come.in, a free proxy service that enables users to access four censored BitTorrent trackers.

12. *United States of America v. Daniel Dove;* the decision, entered November 7, 2008, can be viewed at www.vawd.uscourts.gov/OPINIONS/JONES/207CR15REST.PDF.

13. Defined as "users who have visited a music-related site in the last 12 months."

14. We used regression analysis, typically considered a statistical indicator of causality, and a stronger indicator of meaningful relationship than correlation.

15. Aram Sinnreich, "Digital Music Subscriptions: Post-Napster Product Formats," Jupiter Research (2000).

16. Aram Sinnreich, "File-Sharing: To Preserve Music Market Value, Look Beyond Easy Scapegoats," Jupiter Research (2002).

17. Felix Oberholzer-Gee and Koleman Strumpf, "File Sharing and Copyright," *NBER* [National Bureau of Economic Research] *Book Series Innovation Policy and the Economy,* vol. 10, ed. Josh Lerner and Scott Stern (Chicago: University of Chicago Press, 2010), 35.

18. Drew Wilson, "What Filesharing Studies Really Say—Part 1—Litigation a Failure?," ZeroPaid.com, May 1, 2012, www.zeropaid.com/news/100847/what-filesharing-studies-really-say-part-1-litigation-a-failure/.

19. Bob Lefsetz, "360 Deals," *TheLefsetzLetter,* November 11, 2007, http://lefsetz.com/wordpress/index.php/archives/2007/11/11/360-deals/.

20. IFPI, *Recording Industry in Numbers 2012,* www.ifpi.org.

21. Steve Gordon, *The Future of the Music Business: How to Succeed with the New Digital Technologies: A Guide for Artists and Entrepreneurs,* 3rd ed. (Milwaukee: Hal Leonard Books, 2011).

22. Steve Gordon, personal communication.

23. Mike Masnick, "Lady Gaga Says No Problem If People Download Her Music; The Money Is in Touring," *Techdirt,* May 24, 2010, www.techdirt.com/articles/20100524/0032549541.shtml.

24. "Music Sponsorship Spending to Total $1.17 Billion in 2011," *PRWeb,* April 29, 2011, www.prweb.com/releases/2011/04/prweb5278604.htm.

25. Angela Hund-Göschel, *Music Sponsorship at a Turning Point* (Lohmar, Germany: Josef Eul Verlag, 2009), 31.

26. See, for instance, Annelies Huygen, "Ups and Downs: Economic and Cultural Effects of File Sharing on Music, Film and Games," *TNO Information and Communication Technology,* February 18, 2009, www.ivir.nl/publicaties

/vaneijk/Ups_And_Downs_authorised_translation.pdf; "Bericht des Bundes-rates zur unerlaubten Werknutzung über das Internet," *EJPD*, November 30, 2011, www.ejpd.admin.ch/content/dam/data/pressemitteilung/2011 /2011-11-30/ber-br-d.pdf; Richard Bjerkøe, and Anders Sørbo, "The Norwegian Music Industry in the Age of Digitalization," master's thesis, BI Norwegian School of Management (Oslo), 2010; "Do Music Artists Fare Better in a World with Illegal File-Sharing?," *Times Online Labs Blog*, accessed November 12, 2009, http://web.archive.org/web/20091214051313/http://labs.timesonline.co.uk /blog/2009/11/12/do-music-artists-do-better-in-a-world-with-illegal-file -sharing/; Guatham Nagesh, "Report Minimizes Online Piracy Impact," *The Hill*, January 30, 2012, http://thehill.com/blogs/hillicon-valley/technology /207361-report-downplays-impact-of-online-piracy.

27. Michael Masnick and Michael Ho, "The Sky Is Rising!," *Techdirt*, January 2012, www.techdirt.com/skyisrising/.

28. "50 Cent: File-Sharing Doesn't Hurt Artists, Industry Should Adapt," *TorrentFreak*, December 8, 2007, http://torrentfreak. com/50cent-file-sharing-doesnt-hurt-the-artists-071208/.

29. Quoted in Steve McCaskill, "Swiss Government Rules Downloading to Stay Legal," *TechWeek Europe*, December 5, 2011, www.techweekeurope.co.uk /news/swiss government-rules-downloading-to-remain-legal 48351.

30. Terra Firma, Annual Review (2007), 88, www.terrafirma.com/ annual-reviews.html.

31. "Shakira Hits Back at Lily Allen in Illegal Downloading Row as She Claims File-Sharing 'Brings Me Closer to Fans,'" *Mail Online*, October 20, 2009, www.dailymail.co.uk/tvshowbiz/article-1221639/Shakira-hits-Lily-Allen -illegal-downloading-row-claims-file-sharing-brings-closer-fans.html.

32. Aram Sinnreich, "Copyright and Intellectual Property: Creating New Business Models with Digital Rights Management," Jupiter Research (1999).

33. Matt Peiken, "MP3// Music at Your Fingertips," *St. Paul Pioneer Press* (1999).

34. "'Free' Tom Petty Track Pulled from MP3 Site, but Still Available Online," *MTV News*, March 9, 2012, www.mtv.com/news/articles/1433145/free tom-petty-track-pulled-from-mp3-site-but-still-available-online.jhtml.

35. David Y. Choi and Arturo Perez, "Online Piracy, Innovation, and Legitimate Business Models," *Technovation* 27 (2007): 168–78.

36. Chris Anderson, *The Long Tail: Why the Future of Business Is Selling Less of More* (New York: Hyperion, 2006).

37. On the history of payola see Fredric Dannen, *Hit Men: Power Brokers and Fast Money Inside the Music Business* (New York: Random House, 1990).

38. See, for instance, Ram D. Gopal, Sudip Bhattacharjee, and G. Lawrence Sanders, "Do Artists Benefit from Online Music Sharing?," *Journal of Business* 79, no. 3 (2006): 1503–33; Sanjay Goel, Paul Miesing, and Uday Chandra, "The Impact on Peer-to-Peer File Sharing on the Media Industry," *California Management Review* 52, no. 3 (2010): 6–33; Magali Dubosson-Torbay, Yves Pigneur, and Jean-Claude Usunier, "Business Models for Music Distribution after the P2P Revolution," in *Proceedings of the Fourth International Conference on the Web Delivering of Music*, WEDELMUSIC 2004 (Washington, DC: IEEE Computer

Society, 2004), 172–79; William Uricchio, "Cultural Citizenship in the Age of P2P Networks," in *Media Cultures in a Changing Europe,* ed. Ib Bondebjerg and Peter Golding (Bristol: Intellect Press, 2004), 139–64.

39. Eric Lambleau, "Collateral Damage: Mutant Sounds' Eric Lumbleau," *Wire,* November 2011, http://thewire.co.uk/articles/7880/.

40. Patrick Foster, "Musicians Hit Out at Plans to Cut Off Internet for File Sharers," *Times* (London), September 10, 2009, http://entertainment.timesonline.co.uk/tol/arts_and_entertainment/music/article6828262.ece.

41. Adrian Johns, *Piracy: The Intellectual Property Wars from Gutenberg to Gates* (Chicago: University of Chicago Press, 2009), 436.

42. Harry Smith, liner notes to *Anthology of American Folk Music,* ed. Harry Smith, Smithsonian Folkways Recordings, originally released 1952, available at http://media.smithsonianfolkways.org/liner_notes/smithsonian_folkways/SFW40090.pdf.

43. "Harry Smith Bio," Harry Smith Archives, www.harrysmitharchives.com/1_bio/index.html. Smith's *Anthology* also received two subsequent Grammy awards when it was reissued by the Smithsonian in 1997.

44. 715 F. Supp. 2d 481 (2010). The report is a matter of public record, and is available at www.scribd.com/doc/55319273/Limewire-Sinnreich-Report.

45. *Pirate Verbatim,* http://verbatimpirate.wordpress.com/.

46. IFPI, "Digital Music Report 2012," www.ifpi.org/content/library/DMR2012.pdf.

47. Katie Dean, "Winwood: Roll with P2P, Baby," *Wired,* July 9, 2004, www.wired.com/entertainmentlmusic/news/2004/07/64128.

48. Janko Roettgers, "Counting Crows: Don't Bribe Radio, Use BitTorrent," *Gigaom,* May 14, 2012, http://bit.ly/Je3zHh.

49. "Mike Dirnt (Green Day) Interview," *TheEnd107.7.com,* May 15, 2009, www.1077theend.com/Mike-Dirnt--Green-Day--Interview/11611264?pid=214039.

50. "Heart Crazy on TrustyFiles P2P File Sharing Network Distribution," *RazorPop,* July 19, 2004, www.trustyfiles.com/corp-press-heart.php.

51. Jeff Leeds, "Nine Inch Nails Fashions Innovative Web Pricing Plan," *New York Times,* March 4, 2008.

52. "Trent Reznor Sells 2500 Ultra-Deluxe Vinyl NIN Ghosts at $300 Each in a Day," *Synthesis,* March 5, 2008, http://synthesis.net/trent-reznor-sells-2500-ultra-deluxe-vinyl-nin-ghosts-at-300-each-in-a-day/.

53. Eliot Van Buskirk, "Nine Inch Nails Album Generated $1.6 Million in First Week (Updated)," *Wired Listening Post,* March 13, 2008, www.wired.com/listening_post/2008/03/nine-inch-nai-2/.

54. Eric Steuer, "Nine Inch Nails' 'The Slip' Out under a Creative Commons License," May 5, 2008, http://creativecommons.org/weblog/entry/8267.

55. August Brown, "Radiohead's Publishing Company Reveals the Take from 'In Rainbows,'" *Pop & Hiss* (blog), *Los Angeles Times,* October 15, 2008, http://latimesblogs.latimes.com/music_blog/2008/10/radioheads-publ.html.

56. "Radiohead CD Tops UK Album Chart," *BBC News,* January 6, 2008, http://news.bbc.co.ukJ2/hi/entertainmentl7173993.stm; Jonathan Cohen, "Radiohead Nudges Blige From Atop Album Chart," *Billboard,* January 9, 2008,

www.billboard.com/articles/news/1046867/radiohead-nudges-blige-from
-atop-album-chart.

57. Kyle Anderson, "Prince Says Internet Is 'Over,' But Radiohead,
Trent Reznor, and Others Beg to Differ," *MTV Newsroom,* July 7, 2010, http://
newsroom.mtv.com/2010/07/07/prince-internet-is-over/.

58. Greg Kot, *Ripped: How the Wired Generation Revolutionized Music* (New
York: Scribner, 2009), 64.

59. Andre Paine, "Prince to Release '20Ten' for Free in Europe," *Billboard,*
June 29, 2010, www.billboard.com/articles/news/957575/prince-to-release
-20ten-for-free-in-europe.

60. "What Is a Sufjan?," *Bandcamp: the blog,* August 24, 2010, http://blog
.bandcamp.com/2010/08/24/what-is-a-sufjan/.

61. "Amanda Palmer: The New Record, Art Book, and Tour," *Kickstarter,*
launched April 30, 2012, www.kickstarter.com/projects/amandapalmer
/amanda-palmer-the-new-record-art-book-and-tour.

62. Amanda Palmer, "Where All This Kickstarter Money Is Going," May 22,
2012, www.amandapalmer.net/blog/where-all-this-kickstarter-money-is-going
-by-amanda/.

63. "Amanda Palmer @ Harvard: Toward a Patronage Society," July 8, 2010,
https://www.youtube.com/watch?v=3lJQjihCp1E.

64. Data from Kickstarter, www.kickstarter.com/help/stats.

65. Ethan Diamond, "Cheaper Than Free," *Bandcamp: the blog,* January 3,
2012, http://blog.bandcamp.com/2012/01/03/cheaper-than-free//.

66. Jan Hoffman, "Justin Bieber Is Living the Dream," *New York Times,*
December 31, 2009.

67. "The Top 10 Viral Videos of 2010," *Spike,* December 22, 2010, www
.spike.com/articles/kkpro9/the-top-10-viral-videos-of-2010.

68. Eliot Van Buskirk, "Gregory Brothers of 'Bed Intruder' Fame Discuss
TV Pilot, Antoine Dodson," *Wired,* August 13, 2010, www.wired.com/
epicenter/2010/08/gregory-brothers-bed-intruder-antoine-dodson-autotune.

69. Mike Thomas, "Really Hot, for Real," *Chicago Sun Times,* November 29,
2010.

70. Alex Leavitt, May 12, 2012, https://twitter.com/alexleavitt/status
/201440625684529152.

71 According to the RIAA's searchable database of gold and platinum
certified releases, available at www.riaa.com/goldandplatinumdata.php.

72. "Universal Censors Megaupload Song, Gets Branded a 'Rogue Label,'"
TorrentFreak, December 10, 2011, http://torrentfreak.com/universal-censors
-megaupload-song-gets-branded-a-rogue-label-111210/.

73. UMG later claimed it took down the video using YouTube's Content
Management System (created in order to comply with the DMCA) without
specifically claiming any infringement under the DMCA—which is actually
worse. For more details, see Bruce Houghton, "Megaupload Video Back on
YouTube, after UMG Offers 'We Yanked It Because We Could' Defense,"
Hypebot, December 16, 2011, www.hypebot.com/hypebot/2011/12
/megaupload-video-back-on-youtube-after-umg-offers-we-yanked-it-because
-we-could-defense-.html.

74. Kim Dotcom, "Megaupload Song HD," YouTube, www.youtube.com /watch?v=o0Wvn-9BXVc.

75. US Department of Justice, Office of Public Affairs, "Justice Department Charges Leaders of Megaupload with Widespread Online Copyright Infringement," January 19, 2012, www.justice.gov/opa/pr/2012/January/12-crm-074.html.

76. Juha Saarinen, "Megaupload's Kim Dotcom Granted Bail, Barred from Internet," *Ars Technica,* February 21, 2012, http://arstechnica.com/tech-policy /2012/02/megauploads-kim-dotcom-granted-bail-barred-from-internet/. The conditions of Dotcom's bail echo the court's judgment against infamous hacker Kevin Mitnick, who even after his release from jail was prohibited from touching computers. Of course, the difference is that Dotcom has not yet been convicted of a crime. For more in-depth analysis of the social dynamics surrounding Mitnick's sentencing, see Douglas Thomas, *Hacker Culture* (Minneapolis: University of Minnesota Press, 2002).

77. "Record Labels Invest US$4.5 Billion in New Music," IFPI, November 12, 2012, www.ifpi.org/content/section_news/investing_in_music.html.

78. "International Recording Industry Welcomes New French Law to Protect Artists and Creators," IFPI, April 3, 2009, www.ifpi.org/content/section _news/20090403.html.

79. Future of Music Coalition, "Major Label Contract Clause Critique," October 3, 2001, http://futureofmusic.org/article/article/major-label-contract -clause-critique.

80. Steve Albini, "The Problem with Music," in *Commodify Your Dissent: Salvos from "The Baffler,"* ed. Thomas Frank and Matt Weiland (New York: Norton, 1993).

81. Donald Passman, *All You Need to Know about the Music Business* (New York: Free Press, 2009).

82. Cord Jefferson, "The Music Industry's Funny Money," *The Root,* July 6, 2010, www.theroot.com/views/how-much-do-you-musicians-really-make.

83. Paul Resnikoff, "A Major Label Artist Makes 8 Cents on a 99-Cent iTunes Download . . . ," *Digital Music News,* November 3, 2011, www.digitalmusicnews .com/permalink/2011/111103labelpays.

84. "The Cost of a CD" (undated), RIAA, http://web.archive.org/web /20000901073253/http://riaa.org/MD-US-7.cfm.

85. Eriq Gardner, "Village People's Victor Willis Wins Huge Rights Reversion Case over 'YMCA,'" *Billboard,* May 8, 2012.

86. 621 F.3d 958.

87. Antony Bruno, "Supreme Court Rejects Universal Music Group's Appeal of Eminem Royalty Case," *Billboard,* March 21, 2011.

88. Eriq Gardner, "Apple Doesn't Want Musicians to See Secret Steve Jobs Deposition," *Hollywood Reporter,* April 30, 2012, www.hollywoodreporter.com /thr-esq/apple-steve-jobs-deposition-universal-music-317999.

5. Bubbles and Storms

1. Cary H. Sherman, "What Wikipedia Won't Tell You," *New York Times,* February 7, 2012.

2. IFPI, *Digital Music Report 2012*, p. 16, www.ifpi.org.

3. "Record Label Exec: Radio Is 'Paramount' to Breaking Artists, Keeping Superstars Relevant," NAB.org (National Association of Broadcasting), August 25, 2009, www.nab.org/documents/newsroom/pressRelease.asp?id=2075.

4. Leibowitz's "File Sharing: Creative Destruction or Just Plain Destruction," for example, is cited in "Piracy Impact Studies," RIAA.com, "Music Industry Research," www.riaa.com/keystatistics.php?content_selector=research-report -journal-academic; Cary H. Sherman, "Comments, Questions, Concerns: RIAA CEO Reflects on Responses to His *New York Times* Op-Ed," *Music Notes Blog*, RIAA.com, February 23, 2012, www.riaa.com/blog.php?content_selector =riaa-news-blog&blog_selector=RIAA-CEO-Reflects-&news_month_filter =2&news_year_filter=2012.

5. Stan Liebowitz, "The Metric Is the Message: How Much of the Decline in Sound Recording Sales Is Due to File-Sharing?," November 2011, (emphasis added), available at http://papers.ssrn.com/sol3/papers.cfm?abstract_id =1932518. Professor Liebowitz was retained as an expert witness on behalf of the plaintiffs in *Arista v. Lime Group*, and submitted a report rebutting my own expert testimony in the case.

6. Eriq Gardner, "How the Recording Industry Intends to Win Billions from LimeWire," *Hollywood Reporter*, April 6, 2011, www.hollywoodreporter.com /thr-esq/how-recording-industry-intends-win-175739.

7. Although Liebowitz's expert report in *Arista v. Lime Group* is subject to a court-imposed confidentiality order and therefore can't be publicly cited, his report in *Sony BMG v. Tenenbaum* is available at the Harvard Law School website, http://cyber.law.harvard.edu/~nesson/Liebowitz%20Expert%20Report.pdf.

8. Richard Arnold Johnson, and Gouri Bhattacharyya, *Statistics: Principles and Methods* (Hoboken, NJ: Wiley & Sons, 2010), 108.

9. For instance, see the IFPI's explanation of revised figures in Richard Smirke, "IFPI 2012 Report: Global Music Revenue Down 3%; Sync, PRO, Digital Income Up," *Billboard*, March 26, 2012, www.billboard.biz/bbbiz /industry/global/ifpi-2012-report-global-music-revenue-down-1006571352. story.

10. Sacha Wunsch-Vincent and Graham Vickery, *Working Party on the Information Economy: Digital Broadband Content: Music*, December 13, 2005, prepared for Organisation for Economic Co-operation and Development, available at www.oecd.org/internet/ieconomy/34995041.pdf.

11. IFPI, *Recording Industry in Numbers 2009*, www.ifpi.org.

12. IFPI, *Recording Industry in Numbers 2000*, www.ifpi.org.

13. IFPI, *Recording Industry in Numbers 2005*, www.ifpi.org.

14. Ultimately, the industry acknowledges in its publications that even its own conversion rates from trade to retail revenues are "estimates," so the aim here is directionality and consistency, rather that definitive accuracy.

15. Earl Paige, "Dealers, Manufacturers in Upbeat CD Discussion," *Billboard*, October 6, 1984, 22.

16. "What's Working? What's Not?," *Billboard*, April 18, 1998, 45; Don Jeffrey and Brian Garrity, "For Brick and Mortar Retail, Biz Is Solid but Buzz Is Silent," *Billboard*, December 4, 1999, 137.

17. Irv Lichtman, "Cohen Studies Industry Future," *Billboard*, December 19, 1981, 48.

18. Ed Christman, "Best Buy, Circuit City a Potent Combo," *Billboard*, June 17, 1995, 80.

19. Ed Christman, "Worsening Retail Conditions Finally Arrive at Labels' Door," *Billboard*, February 10, 1996, 58.

20. Fredric Dannen, *Hit Men: Power Brokers and Fast Money Inside the Music Business* (New York: Random House, 1990).

21. Jerkins is better known for his work in the R&B/pop idiom than with boy bands per se.

22. RIAA, "Top 100 Albums," RIAA.com, "Top Tallies," www.riaa.com /goldandplatinum.php?content_selector=top-100-albums; this is a measure of the US market only.

23. Hunter Schwarz, "Lady Gaga Joins the Seven Figure Club," *Rhombus*, June 3, 2011, www.rhombusmag.com/2011/06/03/lady-gaga-joins-the-seven -figure-club/. It should be noted that prior to 1991, the recording industry used different methodologies to establish sales volume; therefore this method of analysis is somewhat biased toward recent releases. Nonetheless, it is broadly accepted that this era was a golden age of quick market successes for the music industry.

24. National Bureau of Economic Research, "US Business Cycle Expansions and Contractions," September 20, 2010, www.nber.org/cycles.html.

25. US Census Bureau "Income, Expenditures, Poverty, and Wealth," *2012 Statistical Abstract,* www.census.gov/compendia/statab/cats/income _expenditures_poverty_wealth.html.

26. United Nations, "Creative Economy Report 2008," http://unctad.org/en /docs/ditc20082cer_en.pdf.

27. Sherman, "What Wikipedia Won't Tell You.

28. "Terra Firma's Annual Review 2008," TerraFirma.com, www.terrafirma .com/annual-reviews.html.

29. Although most popular music didn't take quite so long as the Beatles to appear in DRM-free downloadable formats, some major artists, such as Led Zeppelin, AC/DC, and Garth Brooks, remained absent from iTunes' digital shelves for even longer.

30. Warner Music Group, Annual Report (Form 10-K), November 17, 2010; Warner Music Group, Annual Report (Form 10-K), December 1, 2006.

31. Quoted in Charles Duhigg, "Getting Warner Music More Upbeat," *Los Angeles Times,* August 28, 2006, http://articles.latimes.com/2006/aug/28 /business/fi-lyor28.

32. Chris Anderson, *The Long Tail: Why the Future of Business Is Selling Less of More* (New York: Hyperion, 2006). Anderson's premise is that because digital commerce provides an infinite amount of "shelf space" and digital broadcasting provides an infinite amount of "air time," there are significant opportunities to derive profit from the work of less popular artists and producers than those who have traditionally been exploited in the of bricks-and-mortar and broadcasting sectors.

33. Quoted in Steve Knopper, *Appetite for Self-Destruction: The Spectacular Crash of the Record Industry in the Digital Age* (Berkeley: Soft Skull Press, 2009), 181.

34. Anita Elberse, "Bye-Bye Bundles: The Unbundling of Music in Digital Channels," *Journal of Marketing* 74, no. 3 (May 2010): 181.

35. David Lieberman, "States Settle CD Price-Fixing Case," *USA Today,* September 30, 2002.

36. Bill Marsh, "A History of Home Values," *New York Times,* August 26, 2006.

37. Ed Christman, "NARM Coverage: New Laws Threaten Used CD Market," *Billboard,* May 1, 2007, www.billboard.com/biz/articles/news/retail/1324116/narm-coverage-new-laws-threaten-used-cd-market.

38. Michael Masnick and Michael Ho, "The Sky Is Rising!," *Techdirt,* www.techdirt.com/skyisrising/.

39. Anderson, *Long Tail,* 23.

40. Statement of Tim Westergren, Chief Strategy Officer and founder of Pandora, before the Subcommittee on Communications and the Internet, Committee on Energy and Commerce, U.S. House of Representatives, on "The Future of Audio," June 6, 2012.

41. "About CD Baby," www.cdbaby.com/About.

42. Ben Sisario, "Out to Share Up Music, Often with Sharp Words," *New York Times,* May 7, 2012.

43. Warner Music Group acknowledged this in public filings between 2006 and 2010, citing "growing competition for consumer discretionary spending and retail shelf space" as a contributor to "a declining recorded music industry"; the filings are available at http://investors.wmg.com.

44. IFPI, "Global Music Retail Sales, including Digital, Flat in 2004," IFPI.org, "Market Research Publications Shop," March 22, 2005, www/ifpi.org/content/section_news/20050322.html.

45. IFPI, *Music Piracy Report,* June 2002, www.ifpi.org/content/library/Piracy2002.pdf.

46. "CD Bootlegging Soars," *CBSNews,* February 18, 2009, www.cbsnews.com/2100-207_162-530296.html. It's important to take these, and all piracy figures reported by the recording industry, with a grain of salt, as I discuss later in this chapter.

47. "Facts About IP," TheTrueCosts.org, http://web.archive.org/web/20090422052629/http://www.thetruecosts.org/index.php/resources/facts-a-stats.

48. "Report Sheds Light on Scale and Complexity of Online Piracy and Counterfeiting Problem," MarkMonitor.com, "Press Releases," January 11, 2011 (emphasis added), https://www.markmonitor.com/pressreleases/2011/pr110111.php.

49. Frontier Economics, "Estimating the Global Economic and Social Impacts of Counterfeiting and Piracy," report commissioned by Business Action to Stop Counterfeiting and Piracy (BASCAP), February 2011, available at www.iccwbo.org/uploadedFiles/BASCAP/Pages/Global%20Impacts%20-%20Final.pdf.

50. Emphasis added.

51. www.theglobalipcenter.com/facts.

52. Stephen E. Siwek, The *True Cost of Sound Recording Piracy to the U.S. Economy,* policy report for Institute for Policy Innovation, October 3, 2007, www.ipi.org/ipi_issues/detail/the-true-cost-of-copyright-industry-piracy-to-the-us-economy.

53. www.ei.com/viewprofessional.php?id=41.

54. Sherman, "What Wikipedia Won't Tell You."

55. According to its website (www.iipa.com), the IIPA is a "a private sector coalition, formed in 1984, of trade associations representing U.S. copyright-based industries." The RIAA and NMPA are two of the seven members.

56. Stephen E. Siwek, *Copyright Industries in the U.S. Economy: The 2003–2007 Report*, prepared for the International Intellectual Property Alliance, June 2009, www.iipa.com/pdf/IIPASiwekReport2003-07.pdf.

57. "Who Music Theft Hurts," RIAA.com, "Piracy," www.riaa.com /physicalpiracy.php?content_selector=piracy_details_online.

58. Julian Sanchez, "750,000 Lost Jobs? The Dodgy Digits Behind the War on Piracy," *Ars Technica* (blog), October 8, 2008, http://arstechnica.com/tech -policy/2008/10/dodgy-digits-behind-the-war-on-piracy/.

59. I discuss SOPA in greater depth in chapter 8.

60. US Government Accountability Office, *Intellectual Property: Observations on Effort to Quantify the Economic Effects of Counterfeit and Pirated Goods*, Report to Congressional Committees, April 2010, www.gao.gov/new.items/d10423.pdf.

61. www.riaa.com/faq.php.

62. Frontier Economics, "Estimating the Global Economic and Social Impacts of Counterfeiting and Piracy."

63. US Government Accountability Office, *Intellectual Property*, 19.

64. Stephen E. Siwek, *Copyright Industries in the U.S. Economy: The 2011 Report*, prepared for the International Intellectual Property Alliance, November, 2011, www.iipa.com/copyright_us_economy.html.

65. Janko Roettgers, "Sorry, Hollywood: Piracy May Make a Comeback," *GigaOM*, August 11, 2011, http://gigaom.com/video/file-sharing-is-back/.

6. Is the Music Industry Its Own Worst Enemy?

1. Quoted in Lawrence Robert Dicksee and Frank Tillyard, *Goodwill and Its Treatment in Accounts* (New York: Arno Press, 1976), 2.

2. John Owen Edward Clark, *Dictionary of International Accounting Terms* (Canterbury, UK: Financial World, 2001).

3. Michael Sack Elmaleh, *Financial Accounting: A Mercifully Brief Introduction* (Union Bridge, MD: Epiphany Communications, 2005), 91.

4. William M. Krasilovsky and Sidney Shemel, *This Business of Music: The Definitive Guide to the Business and Legal Issues of the Music Industry* (New York: Watson-Guptill Publications, 2007), 317.

5. Echo Research, *The Value of Corporate Reputation: 2012 US Reputation Dividend Report*, June 2012, www.echoresearch.com/data/File/2012_reputation _dividend_report.pdf.

6. Jared Moya, "The Pirate Bay 'Spectrial' Day #11—Prosecution's Closing Arguments," ZeroPaid.com, "News," March 2, 2009, www.zeropaid.com/news /10037/the_pirate_bay_spectrial_day_11__prosecutions_closing_arguments/.

7. "RIAA Wins Worst Company in America 2007," *Consumerist*, March 19, 2007, http://consumerist.com/2007/03/riaa-wins-worst-company-in-america -2007.html.

8. Theodor Adorno, "On Popular Music," *Studies in Philosophy and Social Science* 9, no. 1 (1941).

9. Marc Fisher, *Something in the Air: Radio, Rock, and the Revolution That Shaped a Generation* (New York: Random House, 2007).

10. US House of Representatives Judiciary Committee, List of Supporters: H.R. 3261, *Stop Online Piracy Act*, available at http://images.politico.com/global/2011/12/76259944-sopa-supporters.pdf.

11. The complaint in *Rogers v. Capitol Records, LLC* is available online at www.digitalmusicnews.com/legal/kennyrogersvcapitolrecords.pdf.

12. Terrestrial radio in the United States is not required to pay a royalty to record labels, but this is not the case in many other countries.

13. Michael Geist, "Canadian Recording Industry Faces $6 Billion Copyright Infringement Lawsuit," *Michael Geist's Blog,* December 7, 2009, www.michaelgeist.ca/content/view/4596/135/; the suit was eventually settled in 2011 for $45 million.

14. See, for example, Norman Kelley, "Notes on the Political Economy of Black Music," in *R&B, Rhythm and Business: The Political Economy of Black Music,* ed. Norman Kelley, 6–23 (New York: Akashic Books, 2002).

15. Eric Klinenberg, *Fighting for Air: The Battle to Control America's Media* (New York: Metropolitan Books, 2007).

16. Fredric Dannen, *Hit Men: Power Brokers and Fast Money inside the Music Business* (New York: Random House, 1990).

17. Dean Budnick and Josh Baron, *Ticket Masters: The Rise of the Concert Industry and How the Public Got Scalped* (Toronto: ECW Press, 2011).

18. Jack Banks, "Music Video Cartel: A Survey of Anti-competitive Practices by MTV and Major Record Companies," *Popular Music & Society* 20, no. 2 (1996): 173–96.

19. Patrick Burkart and Tom McCourt, *Digital Music Wars: Ownership and Control of the Celestial Jukebox* (Lanham, MD: Rowman & Littlefield, 2006).

20. Geoffrey Hull, *The Recording Industry* (New York: Psychology Press, 2004).

21. Steve Lukather, "A View from Both Sides of the Fence: Steve Lukather on What's Right and What's Wrong with the Music Business," in *How to Make It in the New Music Business,* ed. Robert Wolff (New York: Billboard Books, 2004), 63–74.

22. This was before the merger of BMG and Sony Music.

23. Matt Richtel, "U.S. Inquiry Is Under Way on Online Music Business," *New York Times,* October 16, 2001.

24. *Sony Music Entertainment v. Kevin Starr,* 131 S.Ct. 901 (2011).

25. Paul Verna, "Vital Reissues," *Billboard,* May 4, 1996, 42.

26. "FTC Hits Clubs Sales Practice," *Billboard,* May 30, 1970, 86.

27. Budnick and Baron, *Ticket Masters.*

28. Quoted in Michael A. Carrier, "Copyright and Innovation: The Untold Story," *Wisconsin Law Review* 2012, no. 4, 908, available at http://ssrn.com/abstract=2099876.

29. *IFPI Online Music Report 2004,* www.ifpi.org/content/library/digital-music-report-2004.pdf.

30. Jane Black, "The Keys to Ending Music Piracy," *Bloomberg Businessweek*, January 26, 2003, www.businessweek.com/stories/2003-01-26/the-keys-to-ending-music-piracy.

31. *IFPI Online Music Report 2004.*

32. "MP3's Biggest Threat," *Maximum PC*, September 1999.

33. John Borland, "RIAA Sues 261 File Swappers," *CNET News*, August 8, 2003, http://news.cnet.com/2100-1023_3-5072564.html.

34. Felix Oberholzer-Gee and Koleman Strumpf, "File Sharing and Copyright," in *National Bureau of Economic Research Innovation Policy and the Economy*, vol. 10, ed. Josh Lerner and Scott Stern (Chicago: University of Chicago Press, 2010).

35. Paul Lauria, "Infringement! Artists Say They Want Their Music Site Dough," *New York Post*, February 27, 2008, http://www.nypost.com/p/news/business/item_glszDqoJCb8e6qBvDjeHTL.

36. The most extensive chronicle, to my knowledge, is *Recording Industry vs The People*, the blog of Ray Beckerman, an attorney who specializes in defending those sued by the music industry, available at http://recordingindustryvspeople.blogspot.com.

37. John Borland, "RIAA Settles with 12-year-old Girl," *CNET News*, August 9, 2003, http://news.cnet.com/2100-1027-5073717.html.

38. Andrew Orlowski, "RIAA Sues the Dead," *The Register*, February 5, 2005, www.theregister.co.uk/2005/02/05/riaa_sues_the_dead/.

39. Ray Beckerman, "RIAA Wants to Depose Dead Defendant's Children; But Will Allow Them 60 Days to 'Grieve,'" *Recording Industry vs The People*, August 13, 2006, http://recordingindustryvspeople.blogspot.com/2006/08/riaa-wants-to-depose-dead-defendants.html.

40. Anders Bykund, "RIAA Sues Computer-less Family, 234 Others, for File Sharing," *Ars Technica* (blog), April 24, 2006, http://arstechnica.com/uncategorized/2006/04/6662-2/.

41. Jessica R. Towhey, "Naval Academy Seizes Computers from Nearly 100 Mids," *The Capital Online*, November 23, 2002, http://web.archive.org/web/20021125141336/http://www.hometownannapolis.com/cgi-bin/read/live/11_23-19/NAV.

42. Cassi Hunt, "Run Over by the RIAA: Don . . . t Tap the Glass," Cassi Hunt, *The Tech Online Edition*, April 4, 2006, http://tech.mit.edu/V126/N15/RIAA1506.html.

43. Electronic Frontier Foundation, "RIAA v. The People: Five Years Later," September 30, 2008, https://www.eff.org/wp/riaa-v-people-five-years-later.

44. Ray Beckerman, "RIAA Sues Stroke Victim in Michigan," *Recording Industry vs. The People*, March 13, 2007, http://recordingindustryvspeople.blogspot.com/2007/03/riaa-sues-stroke-victim-in-michigan.html.

45. Ray Beckerman, "*Elektra v. Schwartz*, Case against Queens Woman with Multiple Sclerosis, Settled," *Recording Industry vs. The People*, August 13, 2008, http://recordingindustryvspeople.blogspot.com/2008/08/elektra-v-schwartz-case-against-queens.html.

46. Ray Beckerman, "Voluntary Dismissals Because Suit Was Brought against Wrong Party," *Recording Industry vs. The People*, May 24, 2008, http://

recordingindustryvspeople.blogspot.com/2008/05/voluntary-dismissals
-because-suit-was.html.

47. As I mentioned in chapter 3, the industry largely ceased to bring lawsuits against P2P users in 2008.

48. Daniel Reynolds, "The RIAA Litigation War on File Sharing and Alternatives More Compatible with Public Morality," *Minnesota Journal of Law, Science & Technology* 9 no. 2 (2008): 977–1008.

49. Chloe Lake, "Major Label Pressures Anti-piracy Groups," *News.com.au,* January 22, 2008, www.news.com.au/technology/major-label-pressures-anti -piracy-groups/story-e6frfro0-1111115372785.

50. Eric Bangeman, "RIAA Anti-P2P Campaign a Real Money Pit, According to Testimony," *Ars Technica* (blog), October 3, 2007, http://arstechnica.com /tech-policy/2007/10/music-industry-exec-p2p-litigation-is-a-money-pit/.

51. Declan McCullagh, "Newsmaker: RIAA's Next Moves in Washington," CNET.com, "News," May 25, 2006, http://news.cnet.com/2008-1027 _3-6076669.html.

52. Ellen Messmer, "Recording Industry Gives 'Net Music Pirates a Break," *Network World* (1997): 95.

53. The Motion Picture Association of America is a trade organization representing the six "major" Hollywood studios.

54. Quoted in Declan McCullagh, "Hollywood Hacking Bill Hits House," *CNET News,* July 25, 2002, http://news.cnet.com/2100-1023-946316.html.

55. The Computer and Communications Industry Association is an advocacy group promoting openness and competition in technology and communications, with several large companies in both sectors comprising its membership.

56. McCullagh, "Hollywood Hacking Bill Hits House."

57. Hal Plotkin, "Berman-Coble Goes Too Far / Legalizing Hacking of P2P Networks Hurts Start-ups, Not Thieves," *SFGate,* May 21, 2013, www.sfgate .com/news/article/Berman-Coble-Goes-Too-Far-Legalizing-hacking-of- 2798931.php.

58. Mark Russinovich, "Sony, Rootkits, and Digital Rights Management Gone Too Far," *Mark Russinovich's Blog,* October 31, 2005, http://blogs.technet .com/b/markrussinovich/archive/2005/10/31/sony-rootkits-and-digital-rights -management-gone-too-far.aspx.

59. Full disclosure: I served as an expert witness for the plaintiffs in one of the suits.

60. J. Alex Halderman, "Not Again! Uninstaller for Other Sony DRM Also Opens Huge Security Hole," *Freedom to Tinker* (blog), November 17, 2005, https://freedom-to-tinker.com/blog/jhalderm/not-again-uninstaller-iotheri -sony-drm-also-opens-huge-security-hole/.

61. Jolie O'Dell, "'Once This Hits 4chan, It's Over': RIAA/MPAA Privacy/ Security Failure," *ReadWriteWeb,* May 14, 2009, http://readwrite.com/2009/05/14 /once_this_hits_4chan_its_over_riaampaa_privacysecu.

62. Ernesto Van Der Sar, "RIAA and Homeland Security Caught Download- ing Torrents," *TorrentFreak,* December 17, 2011, http://torrentfreak.com/riaa -and-homeland-security-caught-downloading-torrents-111217/.

63. Ernesto Van Der Sar, "Busted: BitTorrent Pirates at Sony, Universal, and Fox," *TorrentFreak*, December 13, 2011, https://torrentfreak.com/busted-bittorrent-pirates-at-sony-universal-and-fox-111213/.

64. www.bumastemra.nl/en/about-bumastemra/organisation/.

65. Most details of the Rietveldt case are from Ernesto Van Der Sar, "Copyright Corruption Scandal Surrounds Anti-piracy Campaign," *TorrentFreak*, December 1, 2011, http://torrentfreak.com/copyright-corruption-scandal-surrounds-anti-piracy-campaign-111201/.

66. A Google search for the phrase "RIAA 'pick on the little guy'" yields 36,000 results.

67. An industry interviewee told Michael Carrier that the "scorched-earth litigation strategy" had threatened the "magic around music" perceived by consumers ("Copyright and Innovation," 59). Given Walter Benjamin's famous rumination on the fate of "aura" in the age of mechanical reproduction, one wonders whether this is, indeed, a tragedy.

68. "Survey: Half of People Think Not Paying for Music Is Acceptable," *MusicWeek*, July 13, 2012, www.musicweek.com/news/read/survey-half-of-people-think-not-paying-for-music-is-acceptable/049573.

7. "This Sounds Way Too Good"

1. Pandora was involved, however, in prolonged arbitration regarding the webcasting royalty rates, which was followed by additional contractual negotiation with the digital performing rights organization SoundExchange.

2. According to the company's most recent public filings at the time of writing.

3. Aram Sinnreich, "Digital Music Subscriptions: Post-Napster Product Formats" (Jupiter Research, 2000).

4. Peter Kafka, "Spotify's Daniel Ek on Profits, Label Deals, and Angry Musicians: 'We're Doing Really, Really Well'" AllThingsD.com, December 6, 2012, http://allthingsd.com/20121206/spotifys-daniel-ek-on-profits-label-deals-and-angry-musicians-were-doing-really-really-well/.

5. Jeff Dyer, Hal B. Gregersen, and Clayton M. Christensen, *The Innovator's DNA: Mastering the Five Skills of Disruptive Innovators* (Boston: Harvard Business Press, 2011).

6. Steve Blank, *Four Steps to the Epiphany: Successful Strategies for Products That Win*, 2nd ed. (Foster City, CA: Cafepress.com, 2006).

7. Steve Blank, "Why the Movie Industry Can't Innovate and the Result Is SOPA," *SteveBlank.com*, January 4, 2012, http://steveblank.com/2012/01/04/why-the-movie-industry-cant-innovate-and-the-result-is-sopa/.

8. Michael A. Carrier, "Copyright and Innovation: The Untold Story," *Wisconsin Law Review* 2012, no. 4, 959, 958, available at http://ssrn.com/abstract=2099876.

9. These stories are based on my interviews with principals of the companies. I personally interviewed and/or advised many of the multitude of these businesses in my capacity as a digital music analyst and consultant at Jupiter Research and Radar Research.

10. Jeremy Silver, Skype interview, July 20, 2012; all quotations are from this interview.

11. Uplister licensed these clips, at a relatively low cost, from the aggregator All Music Guide.

12. Justin Ouellette, telephone interview July 18, 2012; all quotations are from this interview.

13. The original Tumblr post is available at Muxtape, http://jstn.cc/post/29796928.

14. Not long before our interview, Tumblr had been sued by Perfect 10, an adult entertainment company, for enabling "widespread and uncontrolled copyright infringement."

15. David Pakman, telephone interview, July 18, 2012; all quotations are from this interview.

16. Remote data storage and maintenance, now "the cloud," was then a nascent idea more frequently referred to as "the sky."

17. As I previously discussed, fair use is a poorly defined concept that often must be defended in court, at great expense, in order to be exercised in new technological and social contexts. This uncertainty can have what legal scholars call a "chilling effect" on innovation. For a thorough analysis of the subject, see Patricia Aufderheide and Peter Jaszi, *Reclaiming Fair Use: How to Put Balance Back in Copyright* (Chicago: University of Chicago Press, 2011).

18. Bertelsmann eCommerce Group had purchased Pakman's former employer CDnow the previous year and also made a bid for Napster (which had been bankrupted by major label lawsuits) in 2002.

19. "Billboard's Twitter 140: The Music Industry Characters You Need to Follow," *Billboard*, July 27, 2012, www.billboard.biz/bbbiz/record-labels/2012-twitter-140-1007674952.story.

20. Michael Robertson, telephone interview, July 23, 2012; all quotations are from this interview.

21. *UMG Recordings, Inc. v. MP3.com, Inc.*, 92 F. Supp. 2d 349 (S.D.N.Y. 2000).

22. The full text of Judge Rakoff's decision is available at www.law.uh.edu/faculty/cjoyce/copyright/release10/UGM.html.

23. Despite having launched several high-profile companies in the years since, Robertson's Twitter handle is @MP3Michael—a nod to his continuing public association with the company he founded, and lost, many years ago.

24. All details and quotations in this section are from my telephone interview with Jack Foreman, former Warner Music SVP and Choruss principal, July 19, 2012.

25. Larry Kenswil, telephone interview, July 25, 2012; all quotations are from this interview.

26. Greg Sandoval, "Last Waltz for Playlist.com?," CNET, "News," August 24, 2010, http://news.cnet.com/8301-31001_3-20014495-261.html.

27. Jon Pareles, "The Cloud That Ate Your Music," *New York Times*, June 22, 2011.

28. Apple reportedly paid an advance of over $100 million to the labels, in addition to a pledge of 70 percent of revenues from the service, which charges consumers $25 per year.

8. Guilty until Proven Innocent

1. "The Cybersecurity Act of 2012: Protecting America's Economy from Threats and Theft," Democratic Policy and Communications Center, July 26, 2012, www.dpcc.senate.gov/?p=issue&id=186.

2. Nate Anderson, "Anti-Piracy Vid Is Reefer Madness for the Digital Age," *Ars Technica* (blog), December 1, 2011, www.wired.com/threatlevel/2011/12/reefer-madness/.

3. Grant Gross, "File Trading May Fund Terrorism," InfoWorld.com, "News," March 13, 2003, www.infoworld.com/t/networking/file-trading-may-fund-terrorism-766.

4. Paul Resnikoff, "Hillary Clinton Says Anti-Piracy & Internet Freedoms Are 'Mutually Consistent . . . ,'" *Digital Music News,* November 4, 2011, www.digitalmusicnews.com/permalink/2011/111104clinton.

5. "Freedom of Speech," RIAA, http://riaa.com/aboutus.php?content_selector=Freedom-Of-Speech.

6. Searchable via tools made available at http://sunlightfoundation.com.

7. Ben Dimiero, "How Much Did Media Companies Spend Lobbying on SOPA and PIPA?," MediaMatters.org, "Blog," February 3, 2012, http://mediamatters.org/blog/2012/02/03/how-much-did-media-companies-spend-lobbying-on/.

8. "Metadata" is a term used to describe the information contained in a file such as a Microsoft Word document, including data such as its most recent author and the date it was edited.

9. Xeni Jardin, "P2P in the Legal Crosshairs," Wired.com, "Entertainment," March 15, 2004, www.wired.com/entertainment/music/news/2004/03/62665.

10. Schmitt quoted in Derek Thompson, "Google's CEO: 'The Laws Are Written by Lobbyists'" *Atlantic,* October 1, 2010, www.theatlantic.com/technology/archive/2010/10/googles-ceo-the-laws-are-written-by-lobbyists/63908/.

11. Michael Cieply, "Expect Some Toning Down of Antipiracy Bills, Says Movie Industry Supporter," *Media Decoder* (blog), *New York Times,* November 30, 2011, http://mediadecoder.blogs.nytimes.com/2011/11/30/expect-some-toning-down-of-antipiracy-bills-says-movie-industry-supporter/.

12. Maira Sutton, "Internet Users Again Shut Out of Secret TPP Negotiation," *Deeplinks* (blog), Electronics Frontier Foundation, July 2, 2012, https://www.eff.org/deeplinks/2012/07/internet-users-again-shut-out-secret-tpp-negotiations.

13. "Romulus Appoints International Policy Leaders Chris Moore and Victoria Espinel to Global Issues Management Team," undated press release, PRNewswire, www.prnewswire.com/news-releases/romulus-appoints-international-policy-leaders-chris-moore-and-victoria-espinel-to-global-issues-management-team-58567747.html.

14. The copyright scholar and self-described "centrist" William Patry has argued that "the term graduated response should be replaced with the more accurate term 'digital guillotine.'" William F. Patry, *Moral Panics and the Copyright Wars* (New York: Oxford University Press, 2009), 14.

15. David Kravets, "Copyright Czar Cozied Up to Content Industry, E-mails Show," Wired.com, "Threat Level," October 14, 2011, www.wired.com /threatlevel/2011/10/copyright-czar-cozies-up/.

16. Alexander Furnas, "Why an International Trade Agreement Could Be as Bad as SOPA," *Atlantic,* February 6, 2012, www.theatlantic.com/technology /archive/2012/02/why-an-international-trade-agreement-could-be-as-bad -as-sopa/252552/.

17. For a more nuanced discussion of this dilemma, see Jonah Bossewitch and Aram Sinnreich, "The End of Forgetting: Strategic Agency beyond the Panopticon," *New Media & Society* 15, no. 2 (July 2012): 224–42.

18. Because of the multifaceted and evolving nature of the anti-piracy agenda, many of these concrete details will already have changed by the time the book is in print. Yet it is unlikely that the overarching agenda will have changed much at all.

19. Michael Geist currently blogs at www.michaelgeist.ca/.

20. Until 2010, William Patry blogged at http://williampatry.blogspot.com/.

21. Cory Doctorow blogs at http://boingboing.net and has a regular column in the *Guardian,* www.guardian.co.uk/profile/corydoctorow.

22. Karl Fogel currently blogs at http://questioncopyright.org.

23. The Electronic Frontier Foundation *Deeplinks* blog is available at www .eff.org/deeplinks/.

24. The Public Knowledge blog is available at www.publicknowledge.org /blog.

25. Robert J. Gutowski, "The Marriage of Intellectual Property and International Trade in the TRIPs Agreement: Strange Bedfellows or a Match Made in Heaven?," *Buffalo Law Review* 47 (1999): 713.

26. Damias A. Wilson, "Copyright's Compilation Conundrum: Modernizing Statutory Damage Awards for the Digital Music Marketplace," *St. John's Law Review* 85 (2011): 1189–1220.

27. Alan Schwarz, "At 92, a Bandit to Hollywood but a Hero to Soldiers," *New York Times,* April 27, 2012.

28. This concept is not explicitly outlined in legislation and exists primarily through case law.

29. For a more in-depth discussion of ISP secondary liability, see Emerald Smith, "Lord of the Files: International Secondary Liability for Internet Service Providers," *Washington and Lee Law Review* 68 (2011): 1555.

30. The text of the bill, including the struck paragraphs, is available at www .govtrack.us/congress/bills/111/s3804/text.

31. *2011 U.S. Intellectual Property Enforcement Coordinator Annual Report on Intellectual Property Enforcement,* March 2012, www.whitehouse.gov/sites /default/files/omb/IPEC/ipec_annual_report_mar2012.pdf.

32. The newly elected French government has declared the law a "failure" and plans to de-fund the agency's activities. Cyrus Farivar, "French Anti-P2P Agency Hadopi Likely to Get Shut Down," *Ars Technica* (blog), August 3, 2012, http://arstechnica.com/tech-policy/2012/08/french-anti-p2p-agency-hadopi -likely-to-get-shut-down/.

33. The bill stalled in the Senate in August 2012, after a Republican filibuster.

34. European Observatory on Counterfeiting and Piracy, *Evidence and Right of Information in Intellectual Property Rights,* http://ec.europa.eu/internal_market/iprenforcement/docs/evidence_en.pdf.

35. Somini Sengupta, "U.N. Affirms Internet Freedom as a Basic Right," *Bits* (blog), *New York Times,* July 6, 2012, http://bits.blogs.nytimes.com/2012/07/06/so-the-united-nations-affirms-internet-freedom-as-a-basic-right-now-what/.

36. The original document is no longer available online, but an extensive analysis of its contents is Richard Esguerra, "The Entertainment Industry's Dystopia of the Future," April 14, 2010, https://www.eff.org/deeplinks/2010/04/entertainment-industrys-dystopia-future.

37. Gigi Sohn, "Before SOPA and PIPA: A Decade of Bad Ideas," paper presented at The Digital Broadband Migration: The Challenges of Internet Law and Governance conference, February 12–13, 2012, University of Colorado.

38. Tony Chavira, "ACTA: A Government-Approved International Conspiracy," FourStory.org, "Blog," January 31, 2012, http://fourstory.org/posts/post/acta-a-true-american-conspiracy/.

39. Nate Anderson, "Senator: Web Censorship Bill A 'Bunker-Busting Cluster Bomb'" *Ars Technica* (blog), November 20, 2010, www.wired.com/business/2010/11/senator-web-censorship-bill-a-bunker-busting-cluster-bomb/.

40. Macon Philips, "Administration Responds to We the People Petitions on SOPA and Online Piracy," *The White House Blog,* January 14, 2012, www.whitehouse.gov/blog/2012/01/14/obama-administration-responds-we-people-petitions-sopa-and-online-piracy.

41. HM Government, *The Government Response to the Hargreaves Review of Intellectual Property and Growth,* report by Rt. Hon. George Osborne, MP, Rt. Hon. Vince Cable, MP, and Rt. Hon. Jeremy Hunt, MP, August 2011, www.ipo.gov.uk/ipresponse-full.pdf.

42. Dana Smith, "What Warner's Recklessness Says about SOPA," *Public Knowledge Policy Blog,* November 11, 2011, www.publicknowledge.org/blog/what-warners-recklessness-says-about-sopa.

43. Mike Masnick, "Fox Issues DMCA Takedown to Google over SF Chronicle Article . . . Claiming It Was the Movie 'Chronicle'" *Techdirt,* May 29, 2012, www.techdirt.com/articles/20120525/01520819073/fox-issues-dmca-takedown-to-google-over-sf-chronicle-article-claiming-it-was-movie-chronicle.shtml.

44. Ben Sisario, "How a Music Site Disappeared for a Year," *Media Decoder* (blog), *New York Times,* December 9, 2011, http://mediadecoder.blogs.nytimes.com/2011/12/09/how-a-music-site-disappeared-for-a-year/.

45. Jonathan McIntosh, "Buffy vs Edward Remix Unfairly Removed by Lionsgate," Rebellious Pixels.com, "Blog," January 9, 2013, www.rebelliouspixels.com/2013/buffy-vs-edward-remix-unfairly-removed-by-lionsgate.

46. Office of the United States Trade Representative, "Partners Sign Groundbreaking Anti-counterfeiting Trade Agreement," press release, October 2011, www.ustr.gov/about-us/press-office/press-releases/2011/october/partners-sign-groundbreaking-anti-counterfeiting-t.

47. IFPI, *Digital Music Report 2012*, www.ifpi.org.

48. IFPI, *Recording Industry in Numbers 2010*, www.ifpi.org.

49. Maira Sutton, "Spain's Ley Sinde: New Revelations of U.S. Coercion," *Deeplinks* (blog), Electronic Frontier Foundation, January 9, 2012, https://www.eff.org/deeplinks/2012/01/spains-ley-sinde-new-revelations.

50. enigmax, "US Threatened to Blacklist Spain for Not Implementing Site Blocking Law," January 5, 2012, *TorrentFreak*, http://torrentfreak.com/us-threatened-to-blacklist-spain-for-not-implementing-site-blocking-law-120105/.

51. Rick Falkvinge, "Cable Reveals Extent of Lapdoggery from Swedish Govt on Copyright Monopoly," *Falkvinge & co. on Infopolicy* (blog), September 5, 2011, http://falkvinge.net/2011/09/05/cable-reveals-extent-of-lapdoggery-from-swedish-govt-on-copyright-monopoly/.

52. Michael F. Brown, "Can Culture Be Copyrighted?," *Current Anthropology* 39, no. 2 (1998): 193–222.

53. Peter Drahos and John Braithwaite, *Information Feudalism: Who Owns the Knowledge Economy?* (London: Earthscan Publications, 2002), 179.

54. Joe Karaganis and Sean Flynn, "Networked Governance and the USTR," in *Media Piracy in Emerging Economies*, Report of Social Science Research Council, 2011, http://piracy.ssrc.org.

55. Jagdish N. Bhagwati, *In Defense of Globalization* (New York: Oxford University Press, 2004).

56. Michael Heller, *The Gridlock Economy: How Too Much Ownership Wrecks Markets, Stops Innovation, and Costs Lives* (New York: Basic Books, 2008).

57. Madeleine Bunting, "The Profits That Kill," *Guardian*, February 13, 2001.

58. Jeremy Kirk, "Malware Demands Payment for Alleged Copyright Infringement," PCWorld.com, "News," May 6, 2012, www.pcworld.com/businesscenter/article/255108/malware_demands_payment_for_alleged_copyright_infringement.html.

59. My June 9, 2011, blog post is available at http://aramsinnreich.typepad.com/aram_squalls/2011/06/phishers-use-dmca-takedowns-notices-as-malware-links.html.

60. Ernesto Van Der Sar, "200,000 BitTorrent Users Sued in the United States," *TorrentFreak*, August 8, 2011, http://torrentfreak.com/200000-bittorrent-users-sued-in-the-united-states-110808/.

61. Gerard N. Magliocca, "Blackberries and Barnyards: Patent Trolls and the Perils of Innovation," *Notre Dame Law Review* 82 (2006): 1809.

62. Anna B. Folgers, "The Seventh Circuit's Approach to Deterring the Trademark Troll: Say Goodbye to Your Registration and Pay the Costs of Litigation," *Seventh Circuit Review* 3, no. 1 (2007): 452–90.

63. James Bessen, Michael J. Meurer, and Jennifer Ford, "The Private and Social Costs of Patent Trolls," Boston University School of Law, Law and Economics Research Paper No. 11-45, September 19, 2011, 26.

64. Sarah McBride, "US Patent Lawsuits Now Dominated by 'Trolls'—Study," December 10, 2012, available at www.reuters.com/article/2012/12/10/patents-usa-lawsuits-idUSL1E8NA55M20121210.

65. Peter Bradwell, Gemma Craggs, Alessandra Cappuccini, and Joana Kamenova, *Mobile Internet Censorship: What's Happening and What We Can Do*

About It, online report published by Open Rights Group and LSE Media Policy Project, May 2012, www.openrightsgroup.org/assets/files/pdfs/MobileCensorship -webwl.pdf.

66. James Love, "USPTO Blocks Web Access to 'Political/Activist Groups' Including KEI, ACLU, EFF, Public Citizen, Redstate, DailyKos," *James Love's blog,* Knowledge Ecology International, September 18, 2012, http://keionline .org/node/1548.

67. "How Copyright Law Censors Campaigns," Daniel Nazer, *Stanford Law School Center for Internet and Society Blog,* July 19, 2012, http://cyberlaw.stanford .edu/blog/2012/07/how-copyright-law-censors-campaigns.

68. Ryan Singel, "YouTube Flags Democrats' Convention Video on Copyright Ground," Wired.com, "Threat Level," September 5, 2012, www.wired.com /threatlevel/2012/09/youtube-flags-democrats-convention-video-on-copyright-grounds/.

69. Rebecca Giblin, "How Litigation Only Spurred on P2P File Sharing," iTnews .com.au, "Telco/ISP News & Opinions," November 11, 2011, www.itnews.com.au /News/279763,how-litigation-only-spurred-on-p2p-file-sharing.aspx.

70. Paul Resnikoff, "Report: The MegaUpload Shutdown Hasn't Reduced File-Trading at All . . . ," *Digital Music News,* February 10, 2012, www .digitalmusicnews.com/permalink/2012/021012postmegaupload.

71. Nic Healy, "Pirates Who Pay: Do Illegal Downloads Actually Help the Box Office?," CNET Australia, "Home Cinema: News," November 26, 2012, www.cnet.com.au/pirates-who-pay-do-illegal-downloads-actually-help-the -box-office-339342557.htm.

72. Olivia Solon, "French Culture Minister Thinks Hadopi Is a Waste of Money," Wired.co.uk, "News," August 8, 2012, www.wired.co.uk/news /archive/2012-08/08/hadopi-funding.

73. Raphael Satter and Venessa Gera, "US Sites Hacked as Objections Grow to Piracy Deal," *NBC News.com,* February 17, 2012, www.msnbc.msn.com/id /46427642/ns/technology_and_science-security.

74. Matt Warman, "European Parliament Rejects ACTA Piracy Treaty," *The Telegraph,* July 4, 2012, www.telegraph.co.uk/technology/news/9375822 /European-Parliament-rejects-ACTA-piracy-treaty.html.

9. Is Democracy Piracy?

1. The wedding video is available on YouTube at www.youtube.com/watch?v =yYAiZ-L4gXg.

2. "Kopimist Constitution," Kopimistsamfundet.org, www.kopimistsamfundet .org/main/kopimist-constitution.

3. Lawrence Lessig, *Code: And Other Laws of Cyberspace, Version 2.0* (New York: Basic Books, 2006).

4. Det Missionerande Kopimistsamfundet, "Welcome to the Missionary Church of Kopimism," http://kopimistsamfundet.se/english/.

5. The Monastery of Christ in the Desert website, "A Brief History of Scriptoria and the Evolution of the Book," http://christdesert.org/Seeking _God/Scriptoria/index.html.

6. Ibid.

7. There are, of course, strategic risks to sacralizing aspects of communication policy. As William Patry has pointed out, the piracy crusade bears many of the hallmarks of a classic "moral panic," and thus Kopimism runs the risk of reducing the "copyfight" to a moral argument between irreconcilable dogmas rather than maintaining a rational, ends-oriented policy debate.

8. The PPI website is available at www.pp-international.net/.

9. "Can Pirates Shake Up European Politics?," Aljazeera.com, "The Stream," April 9, 2012, http://stream.aljazeera.com/story/can-pirates-shake-european-politics-0022165.

10. Adam Taylor, "German Pirate Party: We're Growing as Fast as the Nazis Did," *Business Insider International,* April 23, 2012, www.businessinsider.com/pirate-party-nazi-martin-delius-spiegel-2012-4.

11. Pirate Party UK, "Greater London Pirate Party Agenda," www.pirateparty.org.uk/forum/viewtopic.php?f=28&p=8699.

12. Jared Moya, "Euro Anti-Piracy Group Calls Pirate Party Message 'Criminal,'" ZeroPaid.com, "News" July 24, 2009, www.zeropaid.com/news/86705/euro-anti-piracy-group-calls-pirate-party-message-criminal/.

13. Jessica Litman, "Real Copyright Reform," *Iowa Law Review* 96, no. 1 (2010): 1–56.

14. Stephen Evans, "Germany's Pirate Party Riding High," *BBC News,* May 11, 2012, www.bbc.co.uk/news/world-europe-18017064.

15 James Madison, "Federalist no. 43," in *The Federalist Papers: Hamilton, Madison, Jay,* ed. Clinton Rossiter (New York: Mentor, 1961), 272.

16. Neil Weinstock Netanel, "Copyright and a Democratic Civil Society," *Yale Law Journal* 106, no. 2 (1996): 386

17. Thomas Jefferson to Isaac McPherson, August 13, 1813, available at http://press-pubs.uchicago.edu/founders/documents/a1_8_8s12.html.

18. U.S. Const. art. I, § 8, cl. 8.

19. *Citizens United v. Federal Election Commission,* 558 U.S. 50 (2010)

20. For a hilarious and instructive meditation on this subject, see Kembrew McLeod, *Freedom of Expression: Overzealous Copyright Bozos and Other Enemies of Creativity* (New York: Doubleday, 2005).

21. Mark Helprin, *Digital Barbarism: A Writer's Manifesto* (New York: HarperCollins, 2009).

22. Cory Doctorow, "Why I Copyfight," *Locus Magazine,* November 2008, www.locusmag.com/Features/2008/11/cory-doctorow-why-i-copyfight.html.

23. Eric S. Raymond, *The Cathedral and the Bazaar: Musings on Linux and Open Source by an Accidental Revolutionary* (Sebastopol, CA: O'Reilly, 1999).

24. Siva Vaidhyanathan, *Copyrights and Copywrongs: The Rise of Intellectual Property and How It Threatens Creativity* (New York: New York University Press, 2001).

25. James Boyle, "The Second Enclosure Movement and the Construction of the Public Domain," *Law and Contemporary Problems* 66, no. 1 (2003): 33–74.

26. Lawrence Lessig, *The Future of Ideas: The Fate of the Commons in a Connected World* (New York: Vintage, 2002).

27. Jessica Litman, "The Public Domain," *Emory Law Journal* 39 (Fall 1990): 965.

28. Tim Wu, "Copyright's Communications Policy," *Michigan Law Review* 103 (November 2004): 278.

29. Tim O'Reilly, "Piracy Is Progressive Taxation, and Other Thoughts on the Evolution of Online Distribution," OpenP2P.com, December 11, 2002, http://openp2p.com/lpt/a/3015.

30. Cory Doctorow, *Content: Selected Essays on Technology, Creativity, Copyright and the Future of the Future* (San Francisco: Tachyon, 2008).

31. *Rip! A Remix Manifesto,* dir. Brett Gaylor, initial release 2008, National Film Board of Canada.

32. *Copyright Criminals,* dir. Benjamin Franzen and Kembrew McLeod, initial release (Canada) 2009, www.copyrightcriminals.com/.

33. *Good Copy Bad Copy,* dir. Andreas Johnsen, Ralf Christensen, and Henrik Moltke, initial release (Denmark) 2007.

34. Aram Sinnreich, Mark Latonero, and Marissa Gluck, "Ethics Reconfigured: How Today's Media Consumers Evaluate the Role of Creative Reappropriation," *Information, Communication & Society* 12, no. 8 (2009): 1242–60.

35. Mark Latonero and Aram Sinnreich, "The Hidden Demography of New Media Ethics," *Information, Communication & Society* (forthcoming 2013).

36. The American Assembly, Columbia University, "Copyright Infringement and Enforcement in the US," research by Joe Karaganis, November 2011, http://piracy.ssrc.org/wp-content/uploads/2011/11/AA-Research-Note-Infringement-and-Enforcement-November-2011.pdf.

37. Ron Grossman, "Where Left Meets Right: Outsiders? They've Always Been In," *Chicago Tribune,* March 7, 2010, http://articles.chicagotribune.com/2010-03-07/news/ct-perspec-0307-movements-20100307_1_tea-party-huey-long-fdr.

38. Hayley Tsukayama, "SOPA (Stop Online Piracy Act) Lawmaker Opposition Grows as Debate Heats Up," *Post Tech* (blog), *Washington Post,* November 17, 2011, www.washingtonpost.com/blogs/post-tech/post/lawmaker-opposition-to-sopa-grows/2011/11/17/gIQAeCEMVN_blog.html.

39. According to publicly available campaign finance data searchable at http://influenceexplorer.com/.

40. For more information, see Tim Jordan and Paul Taylor, *Hacktivism and Cyberwars: Rebels with a Cause?* (London: Routledge, 2004).

41. Ramona Emerson, "SOPA: Anonymous to Protest Anti-piracy Bill on January 18," *Huffington Post,* January 12, 2012, www.huffingtonpost.com/2012/01/12/sopa-anonymous-january-18_n_1201397.html.

42. Ernesto Van Der Sar, "Artists and Hacktivists Sabotage Spanish Anti-piracy Law," *TorrentFreak,* March 1, 2012, http://torrentfreak.com/arists-and-hacktivists-sabotage-spanish-anti-piracy-law-120301/.

43. "'Hacktivist' Group Anonymous Lead Anti-piracy Protests after Claiming New Agreement Will 'Violate Consumer Rights and Censor the Internet,'" *Mail Online,* updated January 27, 2012, www.dailymail.co.uk/news/article-2092990/Hacktivist-group-Anonymous-lead-anti-piracy-protests-claiming-new-agreement-violate-consumer-rights-censor-internet.html.

44. For an in-depth examination of the political role of Anonymous, see E. Gabriella Coleman, "Anonymous: From the Lulz to Collective Action," *The*

New Everyday: A Media Commons Project, April 6, 2011, http://mediacommons
.futureofthebook.org/tne/pieces/anonymous-lulz-collective-action.

45. Among other places, this motto can be found on the AnonymousPress
Twitter profile: https://twitter.com/AnonymousPress.

46. Todd Gitlin, *The Whole World Is Watching: Mass Media in the Making and
Unmaking of the New Left* (Berkeley: University of California Press, 2003).

47. "Hackers Hit Polish Government Websites," Marcin Sobczyk, *Wall Street
Journal, Emerging Europe Blog,* last modified January 23, 2012, http://blogs.wsj
.com/emergingeurope/2012/01/23/hackers-hit-polish-government-websites/.

48. "Polish Lawmakers Don Guy Fawkes Masks to Protest ACTA," Rik
Myslewski, *The Register,* accessed February 6, 2013, www.theregister.co.uk
/2012/01/27/acta_protests_in_poland/.

49. As I discussed in the first chapter, this is hardly a "given"; one could
just as easily interpret the reduction of creative work to the category of labor
as the commodification of the human spirit, and the naturalization of capitalist
ideology. However, for the present purposes, let us assume that this is a goal
legitimately sought by a great many creative individuals.

50. Jennifer Peltz, "Beastie Boys Rapper's Will Bars Ad Use of His Work,"
Seattle Times, August 10, 2012, http://seattletimes.nwsource.com/html
/entertainment/2018890994_apuspeopleadamyauch.html.

51. Raymond, *The Cathedral and the Bazaar.*

52. Information about the terms of the GPL can be found at www.gnu.org
/licenses/gpl.html.

53. Sam Williams, *Free as in Freedom (2.0): Richard Stallman and the Free Software
Revolution* (Boston: Free Software Foundation, 2010).

54. Lawrence Lessig, *The Future of Ideas: The Fate of the Commons in a Connected
World* (New York: Vintage, 2002).

55. Information about the terms of CC licenses can be found at http://
creativecommons.org/licenses/.

56. *The Piracy Crusade* has been published under a Creative Commons 3.0
Attribution-NonCommercial-ShareAlike license, which means that anyone
can access, edit, and/or redistribute it, as long as they (a) give me credit as the
author, (b) don't make any money from their use of it, and (c) make it available
to third parties according to these same terms.

57. Marieke van Schijndel and Joost Smiers, "Imagining a World without
Copyright: The Market and Temporary Protection, a Better Alternative for
Artists and the Public Domain," in *Copyright and Other Fairy Tales: Hans Christian
Andersen and the Commodification of Creativity,* ed. Helle Porsdam (Northampton,
MA: Edward Elgar Publishing, 2006), 147–64.

58. Brad Hall, US Pirate Party, "Questions Concerning Copyright," in *No Safe
Harbor: Essays about Pirate Politics,* http://nosafeharbor.com.

59. James Downie, "What Is the Pirate Party—And Why Is It Helping
Wikileaks?," *Avast Network* (blog), *New Republic,* January 24, 2011, www.tnr
.com/article/world/81963/pirate-party-wikileaks.

60. Congressman Issa has published the Digital Citizen's Bill of Rights and
the text of the OPEN Act at http://keepthewebopen.com. At the time of writing, OPEN has been referred to committee in both the House and the Senate.

61. "The Final Debate" (editorial), *New York Times,* October 23, 2012.

62. Timothy Lee, "Influential GOP Group Releases, Pulls Shockingly Sensible Copyright Memo," *Ars Technica* (blog), November 18, 2012, http://arstechnica.com/tech-policy/2012/11/influential-gop-group-releases-shockingly-sensible-copyright-memo/.

63. Texts of both the brief and the memo are archived on the *American Conservative* website at www.theamericanconservative.com/an-anti-ip-turn-for-the-gop/.

64. Timothy Lee, "Republican Staffer Fired for Copyright Memo Talks to Ars," *Ars Technica* (blog), January 7, 2013, http://arstechnica.com/tech-policy/2013/01/republican-staffer-fired-for-copyright-memo-talks-to-ars/.

65. Data are publicly available and searchable with tools created by the Sunlight Foundation at http://influenceexplorer.com.

66. Richard Hooper, CBE, UK Intellectual Property Office, *Rights and Wrongs,* The First Report of the Digital Copyright Exchange Feasibility Study, March 2012, www.ipo.gov.uk/dce-report-phase1.pdf; Richard Hooper, CBE, and Dr. Ros Lynch, *Copyright Works,* independent report for Intellectual Property Office, July 2012, www.ipo.gov.uk/dce-report-phase2.pdf.

67. Andreas Udo de Haes, "BREIN Dreigt TPB-proxy Met Strafrechtelijke Aangifte," *Web Wereld,* June 28, 2012, http://webwereld.nl/nieuws/110976/brein-dreigt-tpb-proxy-met-strafrechtelijke-aangifte.html.

68. Mark Hachman, "Piracy Pays for Itself, Swiss Government Says," *PC Magazine,* December 2, 2011, www.pcmag.com/article2/0,2817,2397173,00.asp.

69. Pedro Nicoletti Mizukami, Ronaldo Lemos, Bruno Magrani, Pereira de Souza, and Carlos Affonso, "Exceptions and Limitations to Copyright in Brazil: A Call for Reform." *Access to Knowledge in Brazil: New Research on Intellectual Property, Innovation, and Development* (2010): 41–78.

70. Pedro Paranaguá, "Brazil's Copyright Reform: Schizophrenia?," *Intellectual Property Watch,* February 8, 2011, www.ip-watch.org/2011/02/08/inside-views-brazils-copyright-reform-schizophrenia.

71. Michael Geist, "Brazil's Approach on Anti-circumvention: Penalties for Hindering Fair Dealing," *Michael Geist's Blog,* July 9, 2010, www.michaelgeist.ca/content/view/5180/125/.

72. Marcel Leonardi, "Brazil's Proposed Internet Regulation—An Update (That's Actually Good News) (Guest Blog Post)," *Eric Goldman Technology & Marketing Law Blog,* May 6, 2010, http://blog.ericgoldman.org/archives/2010/05/brazils_propose.htm.

73. "Everything Is Connected: Can Internet Activism Turn into a Real Political Movement?," *Economist,* January 5, 2013.

74. "Q&A: Patents in India and the Novartis Case," Doctors Without Borders.org, "Briefing Documents, February 14, 2012, www.doctorswithoutborders.org/publications/article.cfm?id=5769.

75. "Copyright Law of the United States of America," www.copyright.gov/title17/92chap1.html.

76. I make this argument fully cognizant of Benjamin Kaplan's admonition of over forty years ago that "it is almost obligatory for a speaker to begin by invoking the 'communications revolution' of our time, then to pronounce upon

the inadequacies of the present copyright act." Benjamin Kaplan, *An Unhurried View of Copyright* (New York: Columbia University Press, 1967).

77. Aram Sinnreich and Marissa Gluck, "Music and Fashion: The Balancing Act between Creativity and Control," paper presented at "Ready to Share: Fashion and the Ownership of Creativity" conference, USC Annenberg Norman Lear Centertainment, January 5, 2005, 47–69; Kal Raustiala and Christopher Springman, *The Knockoff Economy: How Imitation Sparks Innovation* (New York: Oxford University Press, 2012).

78. Andrew W. Torrance, "DNA Copyright," *Valparaiso University Law Review* 46, no. 1 (2011): 1–41.

79. Adam Liptak, "Supreme Court to Look at a Gene Issue," *New York Times,* December 1, 2012.

80. Nicholas Negroponte, *Being Digital* (New York: Knopf, 1995).

81. Prior to the Copyright Act of 1976, works had to be registered before they were protected. As Lessig and others have observed, this shift effectively privatized the vast majority of the public sphere, which had hitherto belonged to the public domain.

82. John Tehranian, "Infringement Nation: Copyright Reform and the Law/ Norm Gap," *Utah Law Review* (2007): 537.

83. Ray Kurzweil, *The Singularity Is Near: When Humans Transcend Biology* (New York: Penguin, 2005).

INDEX

record and music industries: (*continued*)
by, 12, 120–28, 130, 133–34; marketing
and promotion by, 72, 82–83, 102–3, 119;
during "perfect bubble," 11, 96, 99–105,
117; during "perfect storm," 66, 96,
105–13, 117; and piracy concept, 31–33,
35; piracy loss estimates by, 11–12, 76–77,
94–96, 113–17, 160; producers in, 103–4;
and professionalism, 50, 125; public image
of, 119–22, 125, 128, 130–33; and radio,
44–49; relations with customers by, 61–62,
67, 125–30; retail sector in, 66, 100–101,
109–11; revenue of, 58, 67, 77, 79–82,
86–87, 98–100, 104, 108–9, 111, 138, 191;
structure of, 26–28, 46; and technology,
17, 26–27, 37, 49–50, 54–57, 93, 138–39;
unfair and exploitative labor practices by,
122–23. *See also* anti-piracy agenda; anti-
piracy narrative; piracy crusade
recording formats, 10, 39–45, 100, 107
Recording Industry Association of America
(RIAA), 35, 91–92, 104, 132, 145, 170–71;
lawsuits by, 5, 60–62, 127–31; lobbying
and campaign contributions by, 117, 161;
market data of, 67, 96–98; piracy narrative
of, 78, 94; poor public image of, 120, 133
"recoupment" clauses, 91–92, 124
Republican Study Committee (RSC),
192–93
retail sector, 66, 100–101, 109–11
Reznor, Trent, 85–86, 208n35
Rhapsody, 112
Rhoads, B. Eric, 48
Rietveldt, Melchior, 132–33
Rihanna, 53
Robertson, Michael, 149–51, 158
Rodger, Will, 131
Rogers, Kenny, 122, 123
Romney, Mitt, 176
Root, The, 91
Rosen, Hilary, 56–57, 60–61
Ross, Steve, 28
royalties, 91–92, 98, 112, 122; advances on,
102; hardware, 81; performance, 80, 98;
synch rights, 80, 98
Russinovich, Mark, 131

Sachs, Joel, 21
Sacks, Oliver, 19
Sam Goody stores, 100, 110
sample-based drum machines, 52

Sanchez, Julian, 115–16
San Francisco Chronicle, 131, 172
Satellite Home Viewer Improvement Act, 92
Saturday Night Fever, 48
Scantlebury, Larry, 128
Schmidt, Andreas, 148
Schmidt, Eric, 163
Schon, Neal, 89
Schrade, Matthias, 182
Schwartz, Rae J., 129
scores, musical, 22, 24–25, 123–24; copy-
righting of, 25, 204n26
secondary liability, 167–68
secrecy, 163, 171, 184
security, computer, 132, 174–75
Sgt. Pepper's Lonely Hearts Club Band (Beatles),
108
Shakira, 82–83, 85
Sherman, Cary, 59, 72, 94, 115, 130
shuffle mode, 107–8
Sigismund, 3
Silver, Jeremy, 140–42, 156, 157, 207n11
Simon & Garfunkel, 103
Sinatra, Frank, 50
Sinde Law (Spain), 173, 187
singularity movement, 199
Slotten, Hugh, 47–48
Small, Christopher, 22
Smiers, Joost, 191
Smith, Harry, 84–85
Smith, Max, 152
software industry, 114–15, 160, 162, 184;
innovation in, 71–72
Sohn, Gigi, 170
Solomont, Alan D., 173
Sony, 37, 44, 131–32, 153
Sony BMG v. Tenenbaum, 95
Spain, 173, 187
Spears, Britney, 104, 107
SpiralFrog, 67, 209n37
Spitzer, Eliot, 109–10
sponsorship, 81
Spotify, 67–68, 112, 118, 138
Springsteen, Bruce, 102
Stallman, Richard, 189–90
Stargate SG-1, 62
Steely Dan, 52
Stevens, Sufjan, 87
Stigwood, Robert, 48
Stop Online Piracy Act (SOPA), 116, 163–65,
169–70, 187